THE MOST DANGEROUS BRANCH

The Most Dangerous Branch

How the Supreme Court of Canada Has Undermined Our Law and Our Democracy

ROBERT IVAN MARTIN

McGill-Queen's University Press
Montreal & Kingston · London · Ithaca

© McGill-Queen's University Press 2003
ISBN 0-7735-2614-5

Legal deposit fourth quarter 2003
Bibliothèque nationale du Québec

Printed in Canada on acid-free paper that is 100% ancient forest free
(100% post-consumer recycled), processed chlorine free.

This book has been published with the help of a grant from the
Canadian Federation for the Humanities and Social Sciences, through
the Aid to Scholarly Publications Programme, using funds provided by
the Social Sciences and Humanities Research Council of Canada.

McGill-Queen's University Press acknowledges the support of the
Canada Council for the Arts for our publishing program. We also
acknowledge the financial support of the Government of Canada
through the Book Publishing Industry Development Program (BPIDP)
for our publishing activities.

**National Library of Canada Cataloguing
in Publication Data**

Martin, Robert, 1939–
 The most dangerous branch : how the Supreme Court of Canada has
 undermined our law and our democracy / Robert Ivan Martin.
 Includes bibliographical references and index.
 ISBN 0-7735-2614-5
 1. Canada. Supreme Court. 2. Political questions and judicial power –
 Canada. 3. Judicial review – Canada. I. Title.
 KE8244.M3 2003   347.71'035   C2003-903711-8
 KF8764.ZA2M3 2003

Typeset in Palatino 10.5/13
by Caractéra inc., Quebec City

To my sons – Ivan Martin and Dawson Cabral Martin

Contents

Foreword

I am honoured that Professor Robert Martin has invited me to write this foreword to his book. The proper relationship between the courts, the Parliament, and the cabinet is a subject that greatly interests me. As a public woman, a senator, and member of Parliament, I swore the oath of allegiance to uphold the Constitution and the constitutional order that is the Queen in Parliament, with the Queen in Council acting in ministerial responsible government. A necessary characteristic of this order is constitutional comity between the constituent parts of the Constitution, that is, between the executive as the cabinet, and Parliament, and the courts. This comity is the constitutional equipoise and balance between the constituent parts in their exercise of power. This comity permits the system to operate and provides limits to the natural human tendency to excess of power. This comity provides boundaries to what Saint Augustine called the *libido dominandi*, the lust for power in humans. Constitutions are about governance and the exercise of power by human beings. In our governance, the high and legal sovereign is Her Majesty the Queen. The political sovereign is the electorate. Representative government is based on the principle that political power is derived from the consent of the governed. For many reasons, this equipoise in our Constitution has been greatly disturbed. The courts and the honourable justices have forayed into the arena of determining and deciding public policy, an arena which is unquestionably political and decidedly not judicial. It is well settled that the determination and decisions of public policy are political questions and not judicial ones, and that, further, such decisions belong rightfully with elected representative assemblies and Parliaments chosen by the electorate, and not with the courts and the judges appointed by the royal prerogative.

In 1792, when Lieutenant-Governor John Graves Simcoe summoned Upper Canada's first legislature and delivered its first throne speech, the Speaker was Chief Justice William Osgoode. He in effect was the manager of government business in the legislature's upper chamber, then called the Legislative Council. In the early years of government in Upper and Lower Canada, the justices held seats in both the Legislative Council and in the Executive Council, cabinet. Chief Justice Osgoode sat in the Legislative Council and the Executive Council of Upper Canada from 1792 to 1794. In 1794 he was appointed the chief justice of Lower Canada. Again he was appointed a member of both the Legislative and Executive Councils, and was also the Speaker of the former. This full participation of the judges in politics and their proximity to the executive caused much anxiety, agitation, annoyance, and civil strife in those early years. Upper Canada's reformers, including William Baldwin, Robert Baldwin, and William Lyon Mackenzie, endeavoured to separate the justices from politics, legislatures, and cabinets. The Family Compact, which held both the political and the judicial positions, used its judicial power politically and its political power judicially to fight the reformers, legally and politically.

William Lyon Mackenzie was an elected member of the House of Assembly of Upper Canada for York County, and a former mayor of Toronto. His famous petition and address to King William IV of July 16, 1831, described the grievances of the day. Published in Margaret Fairley's *The Selected Writings of William Lyon Mackenzie, 1824–1837*, it stated: "But we would humbly yet earnestly represent to Your Majesty … for there is not now, neither has there ever been in this province, any real constitutional check upon the natural disposition of men in the possession of power, to promote their own partial views and interests at the expense of the interests of the great body of the people."[1] Mackenzie's address recommended many remedial measures. Measure 9 recommended "That none of Your Majesty's Judges … be enabled to hold seats either in the executive or legislative councils, or in any way to interfere and concern themselves in the executive or legislative business of the province."[2]

The reformers found support in the person of Lord Durham and in British Whigs, antecedent Liberals. The Baldwins personally met with Lord Durham in Canada. Lord Durham's 1839 *Report on the Affairs of British North America* recommended that "The independence of the Judges should be secured, by giving them the same tenure of office and security of income as exist in England."[3] This notion, enacted in the act of settlement 1701, but initially considered for the act of settlement 1689, was legally realized in our Act of Union, 1840, and was carried forward into the British North America Act, 1867. Historically, therefore, the extraction of the judiciary from active politics, active party, legislative, and cabinet politics, and the attainment of responsible government in the Canadas were closely intertwined. It was a significant and unique element of Canadian history.

Later in Canada's development, thoughtful persons again endeavoured to drive yet another set of justices out of politics. These were the judges, the law lords, the most honourable and learned men, the gentlemen of the House of Lords in the Judicial Committee of the Privy Council (JCPC). These eminent and erudite jurists in the JCPC reshaped, nay rewrote Canada's Constitution, the British North America Act, 1867. Specifically, Lord Watson, with the JCPC from 1880 to 1899, and in later years Lord Haldane, with the JCPC from 1911 to 1928, both brilliant men, reshaped the BNA Act, 1867. In a collection of clever JCPC rulings on the question of the distribution of powers between the Dominion and the provinces, the JCPC, Lord Watson, and Lord Haldane decided the cases in favour of the provinces. They purposely tilted the BNA Act toward the provinces. They, in fact, created provincial autonomy. In 1899, Richard Haldane, before his elevation to the House of Lords, published his essay "Lord Watson" in the UK's *Juridical Review.* Of Lord Watson he said: "He completely altered the tendency of the decisions of the Supreme Court, and established in the first place the sovereignty ... of the legislatures of Ontario, Quebec and the other Provinces. He then worked out as a principle the direct relation, in point of exercise of the prerogative, of the Lieutenant-Governors to the Crown. In a series of masterly judgments he expounded and established the real constitution of Canada."[4] Lord Haldane, in a 1921 speech about Lord Watson published in the *Cambridge Law Journal* in 1922, spoke of Lord Watson's political acumen: "Moreover, as he had had large political experience, he became invaluable just for the very qualities that were required in the Judicial Committee of the Privy Council. ... there arose a great fight; and as the result of a long series of decisions Lord Watson put clothing upon the bones of the Constitution, and so covered them over with living flesh that the Constitution of Canada took a new form."[5] Further, in the proceedings of the 1925 case *Toronto Electric Commissioners* v. *Snider et al.*, Lord Haldane spoke about Canada's constitutional struggles commenting that "The real contest was between Sir John Macdonald and Lord Watson."[6]

This recasting, this remodelling of Canada's constitution act, the BNA Act, vexed Canadian jurists and scholars who viewed it as imperialism, and Lord Watson and Lord Haldane as imperialist judges. The movement to end the Judicial Committee of the Privy Council's jurisdiction in Canada was powerful and successful. It included scholars like Frank Scott and William P.M. Kennedy, and even Bora Laskin. Privy Council jurisdiction in Canada was wholly ended in 1949. *En passant*, Mr Haldane, before he was Lord Haldane and a member of the Judicial Committee, acted as attorney and legal counsel for provincial premiers – including Ontario premier Sir Oliver Mowat – against Prime Minister Macdonald in the cases before the Judicial Committee and Lord Watson. Mr Haldane was on retainer for the province of Ontario.[7]

Half a century later, in 1982, the United Kingdom's Parliament passed the Constitution Acts, 1867 and 1982, which included the Charter of Rights – what many believed was finally Canada's full legislative and constitutional autonomy. This change, however, became the foundation for the most unabashed aggressive and blatantly political judicial foray into every aspect of Canadian politics and public policy. This result and the interpretation of the Charter of Rights have astonished many of the provincial premiers, even the former prime minister who brought it about, Pierre Elliott Trudeau. Of interest is the fact that this judicial and curial public policy activism has scant regard for the financial cost of this judicial activism to the taxpayer and the treasury. The courts simply disregard the constitutional notion of Parliament's control of the public purse and Parliament's control of public policies. The progenitor of the Charter of Rights was the late Pierre Elliott Trudeau. The Constitution was repatriated on his watch. In 1991, an aging former prime minister spoke about the Supreme

Court of Canada at the opening of the Bora Laskin Library in Toronto, named for Canada's late chief justice. Mr Trudeau spoke candidly, introspectively, and reflectively about the courts' treatment of the 1980 Repatriation Reference. He also spoke sternly. About the Supreme Court of Canada's role in this opinion decision, he said: "it is not a role to which a court of law striving to remain above the day-to-day currents of political life should aspire."[8] About the Supreme Court's conclusion, he said: "they blatantly manipulated the evidence before them so as to arrive at the desired result. They then wrote a judgment which tried to lend a fig-leaf of legality to their preconceived conclusion."[9] About the Court's manifest political role, he said: "Courts had often in the past refused to answer questions deemed unsuitable for judicial determination. ... In choosing to answer the question there is little doubt that the Supreme Court allowed itself – in Professor P.W. Hogg's words –'to be manipulated into a purely political role,' going beyond the lawmaking functions that modern jurisprudence agrees the Court must necessarily exercise."[10] Mr Trudeau's speech on the Supreme Court's opinion, its politics, and its legal, constitutional, and political consequences for Canada is must reading for all those interested in Canada, limited government, and constitutional balance. Those of us who knew Pierre Elliott Trudeau are aware of much that will never be recorded.

The Canadian courts' foray into politics on the ground and justification of Charter rights and Charter values is currently termed judicial activism. Some have called it kritarchy, that is, government by the judges. The scholarship and literature about the phenomenon of judicial activism is bountiful and multiplying. Many muse about the legality of this activism. This current activism, which sharply differs from Canada's earlier history, is unprecedented. In its redistribution of powers between the Dominion and the provinces, the JCPC did not negative the power itself, as one or the other level retained the power to legislate. In the current context, the courts and the judiciary are defeating the power itself by defeating Parliament's powers. They are defeating the sovereignty of Parliament and the sovereignty of the people.

This remoulding of the country is accompanied and compounded by a very recent feature. This is the judges' newly found role as publicists, propagandists, and proselytizers. Daily, the judges are seen and heard publicly pronouncing on issues in the media and other public platforms. They are aggressively attempting to form, shape, and lead public opinion. In essence they are attempting to lead public opinion to favour their positions. Such publicist, such propagandizing activity by the judges is unknown to our Constitution and to our sense of the proper judicial role. Some judges claim that the Charter of Rights commanded them to usurp Parliament's role. The Charter did no such thing, for the Charter intended constitutional balance. It is also clear that the Charter gave the judges no duty of publicist, no duty of propaganda, and no duty of proselytism. Judicial spin doctors call their activity communications and public information. Proselytism and propaganda are partial, selective, and subjective phenomena. They are not proper judicial functions.

The balance of our Constitution is greatly disturbed. This equipoise and the principles of parliamentary governance, with the attendant maxim, the attendant political maxim called judicial independence, and its corollary, that the continuation of a judge's appointment be subject to "good behaviour,"[11] have always maintained that justices' participation in political and public controversy is undesirable and forbidden. The seeking of public attention, recognition, and acclaim by the judges is distasteful. Public posturing of any kind on any issue by justices is objectionable and odious to the constitutional order. The United Kingdom's Lord Chancellor Kilmuir expressed a learned opinion on the subject of the proper role of the judges in the business of propaganda, both broadcasting and media propaganda. In a 1955 letter to Sir Ian Jacob, the BBC's director-general, regarding the judges, media, and broadcasting (the content of which is now known as the Kilmuir Rules), Lord Chancellor Kilmuir wrote:

the overriding consideration ... is the importance of keeping the Judiciary in this country insulated from the controversies of the day. So long as a Judge keeps silent his reputation for wisdom and impartiality remains unassailable: but every utterance which he makes in public, except in the course of the actual performance of his judicial duties, must necessarily bring him within the focus of criticism. It would, moreover, be inappropriate for the Judiciary to be associated with any series of talks or anything which could be fairly interpreted as entertainment: and in no circumstances, of course, should a Judge take a fee in connection with a broadcast.

My colleagues and I, therefore, are agreed that as a general rule it is undesirable for members of the Judiciary to broadcast on the wireless or to appear on television.[12]

Lord Kilmuir articulated the proper relationship between the judges and the business of propaganda, a business that is subjective, partial, and interest laden. The proper role of the judges is a protected and privileged role. It is not to be tarnished, impaired, or imperilled by any other publicly assumed role. Justices do not have public roles in the same way as do ministers of the Crown and members of Parliament.

Daily, in the print and broadcast media, we hear judges' pronouncements on many questions, questions not properly the subject of judges' public commentary. In fact, certain justices have so habituated Canadians to their publicist role that some, unfortunately, can no longer perceive it for what it is, the quest for political support and political approval for an adopted position or posture. Meanwhile, Canadians' brooding uneasiness about the politicization of the judiciary is growing. The justices' proselytizing roles, the state of the administration of justice itself, the soaring costs of lawyers' fees and resultant unaffordability of justice to Canadians, the growing uncertainty of results in courts, and the elusiveness of justice itself are all causing deep concern. These gargantuan constitutional problems are compounded by a phenomenon now gripping the practice of law. Currently, the practice of law has assumed the form of commerce, a commercial industry, another money-making enterprise. Further, the profit margins are such that the prices paid by consumers for legal services are not balanced by consumer protection rights. Lawyers' fees are now expensive specialty items that few can afford. This commands examination and investigation. Legal costs to the public are an obstacle, nay a barrier, to justice. Canadians know – whether it is in divorce law with its judicially created fatherlessness and subjugation of children's interests, or in criminal law, with its proliferation of wrongful convictions and wrongful accusations – that the state of national justice is wanting and is in dire need of investigation and correction.

In conclusion, I assert that the determination of public policy properly belongs to the elected representatives of the people, to the Queen in Parliament, and not to the courts and the judges.

This mode of governance, its buttressing principles and constitutional balance have been articulated by many great jurists, including the UK's Lord Justice Fletcher Moulton. The guiding principle in the exercise of power is restraint. About a particular need for curial restraint and judicial self-restraint, Lord Shawcross, in his 1959 report *Contempt of Court*, quoted Lord Justice Fletcher Moulton in the Court of Appeal's 1912 *Scott* v. *Scott* judgment saying that "The courts are the guardians of the liberties of the public and should be the bulwark against all encroachments on those liberties from whatsoever side they may come. It is their duty therefore to be vigilant. But they must be doubly vigilant against encroachment by the courts themselves. In that case it is their own actions which they must bring into judgment and it is against themselves that they must protect the public.'"[13] In the paragraph preceding that one quoted by Shawcross, Moulton had also said: "We claim and obtain obedience and respect for our office because we are nothing other than the appointed agents for enforcing upon each individual the performance of his obligations. That obedience and that respect must cease if, disregarding the difference between legislative and judicial functions, we attempt ourselves to create obligations and impose them on individuals who refuse to accept them and who have done nothing to render those obligations binding upon them against their will."[14]

Balance and comity, with their self-restraint, are key characteristics of the Constitution. Comity restrains the excess of power which is the natural human tendency of those who hold power. The judges' proper constitutional role is judicial. Their singular and exclusive function is judicial. This was even enacted in the Judges Act. It instructs them to limit their activities to this prescribed constitutional role, as did the maxim, a political maxim, we termed judicial independence, the term ascribed to the proper relationship between the executive and the judiciary. It was to this end that Parliament "fixed and provided" the justices with excellent salaries and pensions.[15] It was to keep the justices out of politics, political activities, and the inherent temptation and corrupting dangers.

The High Court of Parliament is empowered constitutionally with the power and duty of superintending the administration of justice itself. The Act of Settlement, 1701 had settled many difficult questions of England's revolutions. It settled particularly the relationship between the judiciary and the Crown, or executive, because of the risks of the judiciary seeking the pleasure of the executive. The royal favour and the royal pleasure are a great temptation. The most extreme case of this was Judge George Jeffreys whose ascent to Lord Chancellor is a moral and political lesson in the royal pleasure. This notion of Parliament's superintendence of the judiciary was replicated in the BNA Act, 1867, judicature sections 96 to 101. This superintendence is a protection of the judiciary from the royal pleasure, the executive pleasure, and the displeasure, either royal or executive. Many great UK parliamentarians, like Lord Brougham, William Gladstone, and Sir Robert Peel, have written about this role, as did Canadians Edward Blake and Richard B. Bennett. On March 15, 1843, in the UK's House of Commons, Prime Minister Sir Robert Peel declared in this regard that "the constitution places us as a controlling power over the courts of law. The functions which, in this respect, we may have to discharge, and have a right to discharge, must naturally attract the jealousy of the courts of law."[16] Constitutional jealousy and constitutional greed are serious social and political ills.

I close by quoting Edmund Burke on the superintendence of the judiciary by Parliament, a superintendence of the state and condition of justice itself. As published in James Burke's *The Speeches of the Right Hon. Edmund Burke*, in the UK's House of Commons on March 7, 1771, Edmund Burke said: "I have always understood that a superintendence over the doctrines, as well as the proceedings, of the courts of justice, was a principal object of the constitution of this house; that you were to watch at once over the lawyer and the law; ... I have always looked with a degree of reverence and admiration on this mode of superintendence. ... we come to something, perhaps, the better qualified, and certainly much the better disposed to assert the genuine principle of the laws; in which we can, as a body, have no other than an enlarged and a public interest."[17] Understanding the ills that naturally follow and afflict the exercise of power, and understanding the peculiar crystallized interests that can coalesce and grow amidst judges and lawyers, and understanding the vulnerability of ordinary citizens to those who exercise power, Burke continued: "We have no common cause of a professional attachment or professional emulation to bias our minds; ... so that with our own minds perfectly disengaged from the exercise, we may superintend the execution of the national justice."[18] The state and condition of national justice is a matter of great concern.

Parliamentary governance has evolved with a peculiar division between the legislatures and the judiciary in both their functions and their personnel. An understanding of this history is essential to assess the terrible damage inflicted by the judiciary on these hard fought principles as ably set out by Professor Robert Martin in his excellent analysis of the problem. He documents instance after instance where the judiciary has disturbed the equipoise and balance of the Constitution. Sadly, the most important moral, political, and cultural principles and precepts that affect our lives are persistently being eroded by the judiciary and the courts as they remove them from representative democratic control.

We are deeply grateful to Professor Martin, therefore, for his intelligent analysis and commentary on these manifold constitutional violations that are currently taking place in Canada. The judiciary is profoundly undermining representative parliamentary democracy. In effect, the judiciary is turning Canada into an oligarchy, even into a kritarchy – some call it jurocracy.

Canadians, parliamentarians, lawyers, and laymen must come together to curtail this vandalism of our democratic constitutional system. To do so, however, we must be well informed and well instructed on the issue. In this respect, Professor Martin has provided us with sound guidance with his careful examination of the problem, and of the wanton disregard by the judiciary of its proper constitutional role in representative parliamentary democracy. In recent times, Canadians have not had a strong tradition of criticism of the judiciary, but Professor Martin's book has revealed with fresh clarity that for the sake of our representative democracy we must now develop a renewed tradition so that the excesses of judicial activism can be restrained and excised. For the sake of justice, and for the sake of representative institutions, Canadians have no recourse but to resist these judicial incursions into politics and public policy formation.

Senator Anne C. Cools
Ottawa, Ontario
August 2003

NOTES

1 Mackenzie, William Lyon, in Margaret Fairley's *Selected Writings of William Lyon Mackenzie: 1824–1837* (Toronto: Oxford University Press, 1960), 242.

2 Ibid., 243.

3 Lord Durham, *Lord Durham's Report on the Affairs of British North America, vol. 2, Text of the Report*, ed. C.P. Lucas (Oxford: Clarendon Press, 1912), 327.

4 Lord Haldane, "Lord Watson," (1899) 11 *Juridical Review: A Journal of Legal and Political Science* 280.

5 Lord Haldane, "Work for the Empire of the Judicial Committee of the Privy Council," (1922) 1 *Cambridge Law Journal* 150.

6 Viscount Haldane, *Judicial Proceedings Respecting Constitutional Validity of the Industrial Disputes Investigation Act, 1907* (Ottawa: Department of Labour Canada, 1925), 190. For the case of *Toronto Electric Commissioners* v. *Snider et al.*

7 Evans, Margaret A., *Sir Oliver Mowat* (Toronto: University of Toronto Press, 1992), 175.

8 Trudeau, Pierre Elliott, *Against the Current, Selected Writings 1939–1996* (Toronto: McClelland & Stewart, 1996), 258.

9 Ibid., 256.

10 Ibid., "Patriation and the Supreme Court," in *Against the Current: Selected Writings 1939–1996*, 252.

11 *Constitution Act, 1867*, s. 99.

12 Lord Chancellor Kilmuir, letter to Sir Ian Jacob, 12 December 1955, in *Public Law, 1986*, ed. A.W. Bradley and Graham Zellick (London: Stevens & Sons, 1986), 385.

13 Lord Shawcross, "Substantive Law: Criticism of Judges," in *A Report by Justice – Contempt of Court*, chaired by Lord Shawcross (London: Stevens & Sons, 1959), 14, 15. Lord Shawcross citing Lord Justice Fletcher, *Scott* v. *Scott*, [1912] at 274.

14 *Scott* v. *Scott*, [1912] 107 L.T.R. 211 (Supreme Court Jud. CT. of App.), at 221. Lord Justice Fletcher Moulton speaking in dissent beginning at 218.

15 *Constitution Act, 1867*, s. 100.

16 UK, H.C., Parliamentary Debates, 3rd ser., vol. 67, at col. 1006 (15 March 1843) (Sir Robert Peel).

17 Burke, Edmund, quoted by James Burke, *Speeches of the Right Hon. Edmund Burke* (Dublin: James Duffy, 1860), 361.

18 Ibid., 361.

Preface

An enjoyable aspect of writing a book is being given the opportunity to thank all the people who have assisted in its preparation.

The first person I wish to thank is Frances Andrews. The entire book was written in longhand. She patiently, diligently, skilfully and cheerfully turned my scribbling into a plausible manuscript. I also wish to thank Amy Jacob and Janette Henry for many kindnesses.

As always, Barbara Martin was a source of encouragement and invaluable advice. The book is dedicated to my sons Ivan and Dawson. Their unstinting love and support were essential.

In the Faculty of Law at The University of Western Ontario I am grateful to Albert Oosterhoff and Ian Holloway. The both did a great deal to assist me to come through a difficult period with success.

I must also thank my fellow Benchers of the Law Society of Upper Canada for their warm friendship and constant good wishes.

A substantial part of the book is taken up with criticism of the stultifying orthodoxy which rules Canada. So powerful and pervasive has this orthodoxy become, that a kind of *samizdat* of counter-orthodoxy has developed. Members of this *samizdat* have assisted me with information and intellectual comfort. I specially thank Senator Anne Cools, Alastair Dow, Gwen Landolt, and Harold Merskey. Ted McNabb showed great skill at extracting information from Ottawa judocrats.

Zubin Mancherjee assisted with research. It was always a pleasure to work with him. Laurie Arnott (Western Law Class of 2002)
provided skilled and diligent research assistance.

Anne Gehman, Albert Oosterhoff, R. Kostal, and Jeff Miller all
read the entire manuscript and made many valuable suggestions.
Very special thanks go to Lelia Costantini.

Marianne Welch was helpful on several occasions. She also
prepared the bibliography, index, and table of cases.

I am particularly grateful to Eric Blair, who has inspired me for
decades. I have long sought to emulate his rigourous honesty and
his supremely clear prose.

Sending this manuscript to McGill-Queen's University Press
was one of the smarter things I have ever done. I feel tremendous
admiration for MQUP's integrity and its willingness to publish
counter-orthodox writing. It was a pleasure working with everyone at MQUP, especially John Zucchi. MQUP sent the manuscript
to David Schwinghamer to be edited. David did his work metic-
ulously and with great skill and energy. His contribution to this
book has been magnificent.

Robert Ivan Martin
London, Ontario
April 2003

THE MOST DANGEROUS BRANCH

Introduction

It often seems to me that Canada today is best understood as a kind of theocracy[1] – a country totally in the grip of a secular state religion. I call this phenomenon a secular state religion for three reasons:

1 It is a set of ideological beliefs, largely taken on faith, which appears to underlie and motivate the actions of the Canadian state.
2 It is enforced and imposed, as we shall see, by the state.
3 It is secular, because it aggressively denies the existence of a god.

I describe this secular state religion as "the orthodoxy" and in this introduction set out its central elements and note its many flaws. I also introduce a number of themes which run throughout the book. First, it is suggested that the orthodoxy is the ideology of a small and unrepresentative clique which dominates Canada today. Second, and as a result, it is argued that the orthodoxy is inherently anti-democratic. Third, I argue that the orthodoxy derives from an epistemology which has both disturbing and unpleasant elements. Fourth, the significant feminist content of the orthodoxy is noted.[2] Fifth, and this is one of the central theses of the book, I argue that in deciding cases the judges of the Supreme Court are guided more by the orthodoxy than by the law and the Constitution. From this perspective, the book can be seen as a case study of the ways the orthodoxy has seeped into, and corrupted, our national institutions. A final theme addresses the extent to which university law teachers in Canada, amongst others, have contributed to the triumph of the orthodoxy and thereby compromised their basic intellectual responsibilities.

Before taking a closer look at each of these themes, it is important to set the stage by first examining judicial review, the very practice through which the Supreme Court judges impose this orthodoxy. In the discussion which follows, I express some theoretical concerns about judicial review and then set out the criteria to be used in assessing whether judicial review, as practised by a particular court, is legitimate.

JUDICIAL REVIEW

The title of this book is derived, with a few liberties having been taken, from *The Least Dangerous Branch*[3] by the American scholar Alexander M. Bickel, a long-time professor at the Yale University Law School. Bickel's book was written as a defence of judicial review and in the wake of what he called the *School Desegregation Decisions*[4] of the U.S. Supreme Court. These decisions given in the 1950s were controversial and engendered widespread debate about the legitimacy of judicial review. Bickel is alive to the central problem of judicial review in a constitutional democracy. When unelected, unaccountable judges seek to substitute their views for those of elected, accountable legislators, this can give rise to what Bickel described as the "counter-majoritarian difficulty." He noted that judicial review may "have a tendency over time seriously to weaken the democratic process."[5] Recognizing these concerns, Bickel believed that judicial review was acceptable if it was based upon certain practices and the avoidance of others.

In writing this section I have adopted a substantial part of Bickel's analysis as it addresses many of the same issues this book canvasses. Bickel was attempting to find a justification for judicial review in a democracy. His analysis, in my view, is both thoughtful and compelling and can be applied usefully to the way judicial review is practised in Canada.

Judicial review, Bickel asserted, must involve the making of decisions which are rooted in "reason" and "principle."[6] By "reason," I understand an organized system of thought and analysis which seeks to constrain intellectual processes and to avoid both passion and prejudice in applying the human mind. "Principle"

I take to mean, as Bickel defines it, "a rule of action that will be authoritatively enforced without adjustment or concession and without let-up."[7] Principle, as applied to judges, means a rule which judges are obliged to follow and to enforce, quite apart from their whims and personal references. A principle is, thus, an objective and established standard which exists prior to, and separate from, the subjective inclinations of a judge. Bickel made a useful contrast between "principle" and "expediency."[9] Principles are to be given general and universal application, as opposed to ad hoc expedients.

Bickel cautioned, however, that when judicial review is based on "personal preference" and "personal power," the authority of judges over us is "totally intolerable and totally irreconcilable with the theory and practice of political democracy." In other words, Bickel asserted, a final appellate court "is not a synod of bishops, nor a collective poet laureate."[9]

If we apply Bickel's criteria to today's Supreme Court of Canada, we see that the Court fails to meet his standards and that, therefore, its practice of judicial review must be deemed unacceptable in our political democracy. What we will see in this book is a process of judicial review seriously lacking in principle and reason and characterized to an unacceptable degree by personal preference and personal power. Bickel noted that in the U.S. the "Constitution does not limit the power of the legislature alone. It limits that of the courts as well, and it may be equally absurd (as absurd as leaving it to the legislature to set the limits on its own power), therefore, to allow courts to set the limits."[10] Since, as we shall see, the Supreme Court of Canada has been reluctant to accept limits on its own power, we have a situation in Canada which can be justly described, in Bickel's terms, as absurd. McGill University political scientist Christopher Manfredi made a similar observation in 2000: "The paradox of modern liberal constitutionalism lies in this: if judicial review evolves such that political power in its judicial guise is limited only by a constitution whose meaning courts alone define, then judicial power is no longer constrained by constitutional limits."[11]

Bickel spent much of the opening portions of his book attempting to discover the source in the U.S. Constitution of the power to engage in judicial review. In Canada this is simply not an issue, as the authority of the courts to engage in judicial review is set out in the constitutional text. Section 52(1) of the Constitution Act, 1982 states: "The Constitution of Canada is the supreme law of Canada, and any law that is inconsistent with the provisions of the Constitution is, to the extent of the inconsistency, of no force or effect." Now, it must be recognized that this provision does not, in so many words, directly authorize judicial review. A law which is inconsistent with the Constitution cannot, nor will not, automatically become of no force or effect. Some human agency must declare it to be so. That agency, inevitably, is the courts. The only possible interpretation of section 52(1) is that it authorizes judicial review; and the Supreme Court of Canada has had great difficulty with the question of whether only superior courts should be able to exercise constitutional review powers or whether inferior courts, administrative tribunals, and even labour arbitrators might also do so.[12]

Canada's system of government is, then, premised on constitutional supremacy. The problem, however, is that a system of constitutional supremacy may easily be transformed into one of judicial supremacy. As Christopher Manfredi has observed, "Judicial supremacy ... is overtaking constitutional supremacy," and "the paradox ... is the emergence of judicial supremacy out of the process of enforcing constitutional supremacy."[13]

Conceding that judicial review is authorized by our Constitution, it becomes necessary to ask whether, as practised by the Supreme Court of Canada, such review is legitimate. The title of this book has been chosen to suggest that Canada's judiciary, led by the Supreme Court, is a serious threat to our system of constitutional democracy. It is only a minority of states in today's world which are constitutional democracies,[14] and it is not divinely ordained that Canada shall always be a constitutional democracy. Canadians should recognize this and, at the same time, accept that constitutional democracy can be threatened. The Supreme Court has been subverting constitutional democracy for years and continues to act in a fashion which demonstrates a disregard for the essential elements of constitutional democracy. The meaning and substance of democracy are discussed in detail in chapter 2. Essentially, a democracy is constitutional to the extent that the power of the people is exercised in a way that is consistent with procedural and substantive principles which are set out in a constitutional text and which the courts expound and apply in a reasoned and principled fashion.[15]

I take "constitution" to mean a collection of established rules and principles designed to prescribe the way the state apparatus is to operate. The primary source of these rules and, therefore, the starting-point in attempting to give meaning to a constitution, is the constitutional text itself.[16] A simple reply can be made to those who are inclined to doubt the significance of a constitutional text. Beginning in the 1960s, Canada experienced a lengthy national obsession with constitutional reform. Throughout this dismal period the country's attention was focused on the question of the words which should go into the constitutional text.[17] A group of Canadian scholars attempted this definition: "constitutional law is an open-ended set of rules and principles which represent efforts to identify, define and reconcile competing rights, responsibilities and functions of governments, communities and individuals."[18]

The most essential of these rules and principles is the rule of law. The rule of law demands that all organs of the state, including the Supreme Court, operate within established legal constraints; which is to say, that all state institutions are obliged to obey the law. Every police constable is expected to act within the law and so are judges of the Supreme Court of Canada. In practice, however, the judges behave as if they possess unlimited power and are not subject to any legal constraints. They amend the Constitution at will, rewriting it or inventing new principles, as if the Constitution were their private possession or plaything.[19] The judges have also seriously undermined Canadian democracy. They often reach conclusions based not on law, but on personal preferences. It becomes increasingly difficult to accept that Canada has a legal system, so much has the Court abandoned or subverted fundamental notions of law. This book will seek to demonstrate that, if we are committed to the maintenance of democracy and the rule of law, the Supreme Court of Canada is indeed the most dangerous branch. The only way, in my opinion, in which Supreme Court decisions can be consistently explained is to recognize that the Court often chooses, as will be shown, the approach which will increase both the power and the discretion of the judges. There is no other thread which runs consistently through the Court's decisions.

Constitutional democracy is a matter of structure and process. It depends on the maintenance of a special institutional structure and the observance of certain processes. The Supreme Court has

acted so as to undermine the essential structure and subvert the
processes of Canadian constitutional democracy. My criticism of
the Supreme Court does not concern itself with the results of
particular decisions, but with the ways in which its decision-
making has compromised the structure and processes upon which
our constitutional democracy depends. The critique is principled
rather than political. My critique is strong, largely because, as
someone who is committed to the maintenance of constitutional
democracy, I am deeply offended by the behaviour of our
Supreme Court – I cannot avoid seeing the Court as a collection
of arrogant and unprincipled poseurs, largely out of control.

I will attempt to elaborate the distinction between "political"
and "principled." In 1999 the Montreal-based Institute for
Research on Public Policy began a project to deal with "the Courts
and Legislatures." The project aimed to "stimulate public debate
on questions of importance to Canadian public policy and society
in general [and to focus] on the hotly-contested issue of the judiciary's role in shaping public policy in today's Canada."[20] The
project resulted in three lengthy papers which were published in
the Institute's journal, *Choices*.[21]

These papers suggest that the extent to which Canadians support what the Court has been doing in recent years depends very
much on whether they agree with the results the Court has
reached in its decisions. A survey revealed that 73 per cent of
Canadians who, presumably, only hear about Supreme Court
decisions indirectly, agreed with the following statement: "the
Supreme Court can usually be trusted to make decisions that are
right for the country as a whole."[22] Canadians' support for the
Court is rooted in their tendency to agree with the results reached
by the Court in certain highly-publicized cases.[23] For example,
there is popular support for the *Vriend*[24] decision because Canadians believe that homosexuals should receive protection under
our Constitution.[25] Fletcher and Howe assert of *Vriend* that "the
Court's ruling, far from being counter-majoritarian, seems to
reflect well the view of most Canadians."[26]

The Institute's work provides a context for the important task
of distinguishing between political criticism and principled criticism. A political critique of Supreme Court decisions would be
one which took issue with the results reached in *Vriend* and other
decisions. A principled critique would focus more on the way the

decisions were reached by the court than on the results themselves. Likewise, it appears from the survey discussed by Fletcher
and Howe[27] that Canadian support for the Court is more political
than principled, since the question of whether a particular person
supports what the Court has been doing is primarily a function
of whether he or she agrees with the results reached by the Court
in its decisions. As Bickel has suggested, however, judicial review
can only be justified if it is based in principle. The basis for my
critique is this: If Supreme court decisions have one common
characteristic, it is that they are unprincipled.

THE ORTHODOXY

North America today is gripped by a pervasive and stultifying
orthodoxy. I believe that any sentient Canadian old enough to
reason should be conscious that an orthodoxy exists.[28] The orthodoxy has come to define our public discourse. It has achieved
intellectual dominance in many sectors, effectively controlling the
way in which people in the mass media – especially, in my opinion, in the *Toronto Star*[29] – in the universities, and in the judiciary
think. The pervasiveness of the orthodoxy is such that Canada
gives every appearance of being a de facto one-party state. All
political parties in Canada today promote a politics which combines social radicalism and a return to nineteenth century eco-
nomics. Indeed, what we now have in Canada might best be
described as one party with ostensibly different and competing
wings. When, a number of years ago, I suggested the creation of
a political alternative, I was viciously excoriated for deviating
from the orthodoxy.[30]

The Supreme Court of Canada appears to be guided in its
decision-making neither by principle, nor by law, but by the
orthodoxy. There now exists in Ottawa something called the
National Judicial Institute. This body offers training courses to
federally-appointed judges, and included in these courses is so-
called "Social Context Education." I made a determined effort to
get a copy of the syllabus for Social Context Education, but T.
Brettel Dawson, a professor in the Department of Law at Carleton
University and the senior advisor for Social Context Education at
the National Judicial Institute, refused to let me see it.[31] Fortunately, it has been possible to piece together a sense of what Social

Context Education is about from a variety of sources[32] – material from these sources is reproduced in the appendix. Unfortunately, this material is written in the kind of sanctimonious prose which is favoured by devotees of the orthodoxy.[33]

A disturbing notion is the principle that the National Judicial Institute wishes to have both "community involvement" and "community consultations" in future Social Context Education.[34] The point of this "Education," as I see it, is to make sure that judges are thoroughly indoctrinated in the orthodoxy. In 1996 Chief Justice Antonio Lamer suggested that such education might threaten judicial independence.[35]

The annual cost of the National Judicial Institute is $537,000, of which $268,000 comes from Parliament.[36]

It is difficult to define the content of the orthodoxy, both because it is of recent origin and because there are no generally accepted, canonical statements of it.[37] This is not to say that no one has attempted formal statements of the orthodoxy. A recent book about Justice Bertha Wilson is a kind of primer of post-modernist ideology and with or without intending to – there's no way of knowing – in fact provides a candid look at the orthodoxy.[38] However, this book would, I believe, be better described as hagiography.[39]

The statement of the orthodoxy which soon follows has been pieced together from various sources:[40] I have relied heavily for statements about the orthodoxy on material written by its critics.[41] In my view, the most compelling critique of the governing orthodoxy is Allan Bloom's *The Closing of the American Mind*. The work of Christopher Lasch, the late and distinguished American historian, is key. His *The Revolt of the Elites and the Betrayal of Democracy* has been especially helpful, particularly as it addresses many of the issues which this book attempts to explore. I am encouraged by the fact that, in the United States, some of the most prominent critics of the orthodoxy have been women: Gertrude Himmelfarb, Jean Bethke Elshtain, Christina Hoff Sommers, and Elizabeth Fox-Genovese. While female academics in Canada have been slow to criticize the orthodoxy, one should note the work of three independent-minded Toronto journalists: Christie Blatchford, Donna La Framboise,[42] and Margaret Wente.

There are several key elements in the orthodoxy.

The largely religious nature of the orthodoxy was brought out in a series of four columns written by Dave Brown in December 2001 in the *Ottawa Citizen*. Brown's analysis of our obsession with domestic violence suggested that the way this violence is looked at by both the media and governments is best described as theological. Brown was critical of what he described as the "religion" of domestic violence.[43]

But the real starting point in understanding our orthodoxy is its commitment to relativism – intellectual, cultural, and moral.[44] A paradox is immediately apparent. How can one have an orthodoxy based on relativism? There are two answers. First, I am only trying to set out the elements of the orthodoxy, not defend it: it is shot through with inconsistencies and contradictions. Second, it is essential to understand that the practitioners of the orthodoxy apply it to all ideas except their own. The soundness of relativism is assumed; relativism itself is not subjected to relativistic analysis.

Intellectual relativism, the manifestation most relevant for present purposes, contains a number of sub-elements. First, relativistic thought rejects any notion of absolutes. Most important, it denies the existence or even the possibility of objective truth. A fundamental element of the orthodoxy is a belief in the "social construction of reality."[45] This element of the orthodoxy denies the existence of objective reality. The orthodoxy also seeks to promote the emotional over the intellectual. If there is no objective reality and emotions are more important than thoughts, then the emphasis on feelings becomes understandable. In orthodox "scholarship" and judging, there is little need for proof of anything. If I *feel* that something is true, then it is. The very notion of truth is chimerical; to purport to seek it is to obscure other and probably sinister motives. Since the study of the actual world and the concrete experiences of real human beings in it could lead to brushes with something that might look like objective truth, devotees of the orthodoxy tend to be attracted to the abstract.[46] And since there is no truth, all ideas, hypotheses, and assertions are, by definition, equal. Discriminating amongst ideas is seen to be as invidious as discriminating amongst human beings.[47]

As we shall see, the denial of the possibility of objective truth carries with it some disturbing implications. Two are especially important. While non-relativists generally understood that achieving or expressing the truth was difficult, they did grasp that the distinction between truth telling and lying was salutary. While we might never have been able to agree on the truth, we did understand what lying was about. But once we jettison the notion of truth, we also abandon the corollary notion of lies. To the relativist, the distinction between seeking the truth and telling lies is meaningless.[48] Furthermore, I think it was generally understood that no human being was capable of thinking in a completely unbiased fashion. But the methodological imperatives of both judging and scholarly writing demanded that each individual strive to recognize and overcome his or her own biases. Relativism makes that striving unnecessary.[49] Indeed the distinction between seeking the truth and telling lies has largely been abandoned in the advocacy research which masquerades as legal scholarship in Canada today.

While we might never be able to agree on objective truth, practitioners of orthodoxy embrace subjectivity. What comes to matter in intellectual enquiry, then, is not objective facts, but subjective feelings. If you *feel* something, it must be so. And one person's feelings are as good as anyone else's.

I must affirm that there is both an objective physical world and concrete social reality and that both exist regardless of the vagaries of human subjectivity.[50] To take a well-known example, this planet is spherical. Individual subjectivity cannot alter that fact. No matter how many human beings feel the earth is flat and no matter how passionately they may cling to that belief, neither can change the planet's shape.[51]

Indeed, the orthodox view is that all assertions, whatever their content or character, are simply manifestations of subjectivity. Thus, no matter how long and how thoroughly I may have studied a subject, no matter how rigorous has been my attempt to understand it, anything I say about it is merely an expression of my subjective feelings.[52] And my subjective feelings deserve no more nor less weight than those of anyone else. Since any person's opinion deserves the same weight as anyone else's, the orthodoxy brands criticism of itself or its practitioners as "elitism." Any effort to rise above mediocrity or banality is quickly dismissed as "elitist."[53]

This is a curious epistemology. At its logical extreme it denies the possibility of knowledge, or, if that is overstating the matter, it places knowledge and ignorance on an equal footing. And there is a further problem for the scholar. Expressions of subjectivity are, by definition, unverifiable. Subjectivity therefore demands the rejection of established tests for accuracy.

The orthodoxy also addresses the roots of subjectivity. The primary constituents of an individual's subjectivity are seen to be that person's sex, skin colour, and sexual orientation. Men think differently from women, blacks from whites, and homosexuals from heterosexuals. To be concrete, the orthodoxy would hold that the reason I think the way I do is that I am a white male.

When we combine the three elements of this fascination with subjectivity, we get a clearer sense of where the orthodoxy is taking us. There is no such thing as truth; there is only subjectivity; and subjectivity is simply a manifestation of a particular combination of ascriptive criteria.[54] Thus, no assertion that I make requires either analysis or refutation on its own terms. It is simply me giving vent to my subjectivity. And since my subjectivity is nothing but a reflection of my sex and my colour and my sexual orientation, anything I assert can be accepted or rejected according to how one happens to feel about my sex, race, or sexual orientation. This is not only profoundly anti-intellectual; it is deeply disturbing in its political implications. Both meaningful discourse and the notion of equal citizenship in a political community are denied. The orthodoxy is rooted in an epistemology that is disturbingly reminiscent of both Nazi Germany and apartheid South Africa.[55] As I will show, an apartheid-based view of the world has been endorsed by Canadian judges in some recent decisions.

A view of the world and of society which is reminiscent of apartheid is commonplace in Canada today. Much of the ideology of apartheid came from a 1954 report prepared by Professor F.R. Tomlinson.[56] Tomlinson sought to justify the separation of the various races in South Africa on grounds which were primarily cultural. He argued that Africans should live in a society, and be subject to institutions, all of which were expressions of African culture and traditions. Likewise, Europeans should have a European society with European institutions. The logic of apartheid denied the possibility of common institutions and common citizenship for all South Africans. The arguments made in the *Report* of the Royal Commission on Aboriginal Peoples[57] in favour of aboriginal self-government are uncomfortably reminiscent of the Tomlinson Report. It is not my intention to suggest that the Royal Commission was advocating the establishment of the brutal system of oppression which existed in the Republic of South Africa until the 1990s; my purpose is to draw attention to similarities between the thinking of the Royal Commission and that found in the Tomlinson Report. The Royal Commission grounded its enthusiasm for self-government in its belief that aboriginal peoples should have a system of government consistent with their culture, their basic way of life, and their spiritual traditions.[58]

The orthodoxy appears to be impelling us in the direction of multiple layers of apartheid based on race, sex, and sexual orientation. The courts in Canada have been prepared to accept this tendency. In *R. v. Parks* the accused was black and had been convicted of manslaughter in the killing of someone white. The judgment in the Ontario Court of Appeal had to do with challenges for cause to individual jurors. Specifically, as I understand the decision, the Court of Appeal was suggesting that persons of one race should not be members of a jury which hears the trial of someone of another race. The Supreme Court refused leave to appeal, which suggests that it agreed with the Court of Appeal.

V. (K.) v. E. (T.) (B.C.C.A.) was an even more striking manifestation of apartheid thinking. In this case a white woman and a black man were involved in a custody dispute over their child. The B.C. Court of Appeal awarded custody of the child to the father, holding that since the child was black, he should be in the custody of his black father. The decision was appealed to the Supreme Court, which, after hearing the appeal, released its decision on 28 September 2001.[59] While the Court did overturn the decision of the B.C. Court of Appeal and award custody of the child to his mother, it did not expressly reject the analysis of the Court of Appeal.[60] The Court did accept that race could be considered as a factor in custody matters and talked of something it called "affirming racial identity," a notion common, of course, in Nazi Germany.[61]

Practitioners of the orthodoxy claim to be profoundly concerned about the plight of victims. Victims, as a result, loom large in orthodox expression. The key to social and intellectual legitimacy is to be a victim, or, if one has little or no personal experience of being a victim, to be a member of a recognized victim group. The list of such groups is extensive.

Much of the orthodoxy is fraudulent, however, for while practitioners of the orthodoxy claim to be deeply concerned with the plight of oppressed persons – women, minorities, and so on – this concern is largely non-existent. It is rooted in a profound conde-scension. To turn people into victims is to deprive them of their humanity and their citizenship. Practitioners of the orthodoxy see those for whom they claim to feel sympathy as utterly helpless, incapable of doing anything for themselves, and dependent for their salvation on the well-meaning assistance of condescending lawyers and law professors.[62] There is, today, a lot of money to be made in victimology. (Many lucrative careers have been built on the claim of being a champion of victims.)

Perhaps the most important implication of victimology for the way the orthodoxy operates is that it obviates any need for the concrete analysis of real social conditions. While there have clearly been concrete historical examples of oppression and discrimination, the orthodoxy avoids them, preferring to be guided by ideology. All able-bodied white male heterosexuals are, by definition, wealthy and powerful. All other human beings are oppressed and exploited.[63] Difficult and troublesome questions implied by social class do not arise. Lasch explains why the "thinking [sic] classes" have become so captivated by abstractions: "The thinking classes are fatally removed from the physical side of life. They live in a world of abstractions and images. In their drive to insulate them-selves against risk and contingency – against the unpredictable haz-ards that affect human life – the thinking classes have seceded not just from the common world around them but from reality itself."[64]

The obsession with abstraction is such that devotees of the orthodoxy often write and act as if they believe that history and politics take place entirely inside the minds of human beings.[65] For the orthodox mind, bad things happen because some people think bad thoughts. University of Ottawa law professor Con-stance Backhouse has written an entire book which appears to me to be based on the premise that the major reason for the subjuga-tion of women in the nineteenth century was the thinking of bad thoughts.[66] The social and legal status of women began to improve when people stopped thinking bad thoughts and began thinking better thoughts.

Given their belief that all social ills result from bad thoughts, it does follow logically that devotees of the orthodoxy would be com-mitted to thought control. In such an obsessively abstract world, it makes some sense that converts to the orthodoxy would believe that the worst thing that can happen to a human being is to have his or her feelings hurt or to be made to feel bad. In my opinion, this belief is the basis of the orthodoxy's commitment to relativism. If anyone were ever to state that one thing was better than anything else, somebody's feelings might get hurt. The Supreme Court has adopted this perspective in a number of cases.[67] In its major decision on hate speech, *R. v. Keegstra* (1990), the Supreme Court appeared to believe that the main problem with hate propaganda was that it hurt the feelings of those it was directed at. Mari Matsuda is a law professor in the U.S. and an outspoken critic of racist oppression. She has written that the primary harms caused by racist expression are done to the dignity, self-respect, and sensibilities of members of target groups. Hate expression, for her, is a "psychic tax" imposed upon its objects.[68] Heather Mallick of the *Globe and Mail* took victimology to new heights in January 2002. While she noted that "it's hideous to be a victim of racist speech," she created a whole new category of victims – those who hear or witness racist behaviour.[69] The most reprehensible social sins in Canada today are defined by the orthodoxy as the thinking of bad thoughts. These are, in alphabetical order, homophobia, racism, and sexism. Most ridiculous of these isms is "classism," which reduces class struggle to pure abstraction. Under the orthodoxy, aesthetics and morality subsume politics.

A superb illustration of these tendencies occurred in April 2001. A meeting called the "Summit of the Americas" was organized in Quebec City. The ostensible purpose of this meeting was to prepare the way for the creation of a free-trade area which would cover all of North and South America and the Caribbean. A coalition of victim groups organized a counter-meeting which it called, modestly, the "peoples' summit." A horde of self-absorbed adolescents and their adult hangers-on descended on Quebec City to spend two days frolicking in its streets in what were called demonstrations. This was political activity without politics. The organizers of the counter-meeting regularly expressed their moral outrage at the official summit and issued periodic moral condemnations of it. Every sanctimonious poseur in Canada spoke out against the Americas summit and in favour of the demonstrators. Amilcar Cabral, the great West African revolutionary, denounced this sort of non-politics: "We are not going to eliminate imperialism by shouting insults against it."[70]

It does follow from this discussion of the abstractness of the orthodoxy that a York University political scientist, Ian Greene, could argue that democracy is fundamentally a matter of "the ability of average citizens to think carefully about civil rights issues."[71] For the orthodox the first step in addressing any social issue is to "raise awareness" of it, as if the most efficacious way of overcoming any social problem were simply to think about it. The fact that some Canadian law schools have abandoned the teaching of law in favour of indoctrinating students in the orthodoxy does make a certain sense.[72] The orthodoxy would suggest that, for young lawyers, thinking good thoughts is more important than knowing any law.[73] The Toronto District School Board appears to be moving in a similar direction, abandoning real education in favour of "equity education," which centres on indoctrination.[74]

Here I must thank Veronica Wylie, a student at the Osgoode Hall Law School. She wrote a letter to the editor of the *Toronto Star* which the paper published on 20 April 2001. This letter tends to confirm my hypothesis that the law schools have abandoned teaching law – or anything else for that matter that qualifies as teaching – to their students and now devote themselves to indoctrinating students in the orthodoxy. Veronica Wylie was addressing a controversy which had erupted over a policy of the student legal aid society (Community and Legal Aid Services Programme) at Osgoode Hall Law School. The policy was not to provide representation for men accused of domestic abuse; parts of the letter follow:

I am appalled that the Osgoode legal clinic would even contemplate doing away with the policy to not represent alleged batterers while acting for their victims. I ... believe ... every alleged offender deserves ... vigorous defence, especially since the current neo–liberal, law–and–order agenda uses the criminal justice system in a very heavy–handed manner against the poor. I also believe that a community, student–run legal clinic is not the proper forum to discuss the issue.

...

The legal representation of the poor is not merely a legal issue but an overtly political one. Our politicians have made a conscious choice to underfund the legal aid system and delist many services. Many of the services the clinic provides to women are just not available anywhere else and they are not covered by legal aid.

In order to provide a comprehensive legal educational experience, the legal clinic should not merely concentrate on traditional legal services. Legal jobs involve more than just going to court, they also involve learning how to deal with people in all capacities and the services the clinic provides do just that.

... I believe that providing a service particular to women is necessary to help address the socio–economic marginalization women face in society and at the hands of the justice system. This is particularly true for women of colour and immigrants who, because of racism in the justice system, are hesitant about accessing state resources.

Three observations may be made about this letter.

First, one would assume, and hope, that lawyers are able to construct cogent and compelling arguments. The letter is pathetically ungrammatical and largely written in code. It is, as a result, utterly unconvincing.

Second, it is evident that the letter writer does not understand the nature of criminal prosecutions.[75] Criminal prosecutions are a matter between the state and an alleged offender, yet she appears to believe that such prosecutions are between a victim and an aggressor. In this misinformed view, to represent the accused is to take the side of the aggressor against the victim.

Third, the letter writer has no understanding of either what lawyers do or what the ethics of the profession are about. Her understanding of legal proceedings and the role of the lawyer politicizes both.

The letter concluded:

Democracy should be about substantive equal participation in our society, which women, especially poor women, do not have. Doing away with the policy would be a mistake.

Further then, there is no need for anyone to verify a claim to victim status. If you belong to a recognized victim group, you are a victim; if you don't, you're not. The need for evidence of anything is neatly dispensed with.

As the orthodoxy exempts all members of recognized victim groups from critical analysis, it follows that asking questions about the behaviour, beliefs, or arguments of anyone who belongs to a victim group is called "blaming the victim."[76] The orthodoxy defines such behaviour as unacceptable.

It is equally unacceptable for someone who is not a member of a victim group to write about or discuss the experiences or beliefs of someone who is. This is called "appropriation of voice."[77] In its more extreme forms, this attachment of the orthodoxy to solipsistic ways of thinking further denies the possibility of social thought or analysis. Men cannot understand, and therefore cannot write or think about women; white women cannot understand "women of colour"; heterosexual "women of colour" cannot understand lesbian "women of colour" and on and on.[78] This, of course, is yet another manifestation of apartheid thinking.

The final apartheid-based *reductio* of this obsessive solipsism is that the only person about whom I may legitimately say anything is me. Art, literature, philosophy, and history all become impossible. A particularly foolish debate along these lines broke out in the pages of the *Ottawa Citizen* in February 1997. The suggestion was made that books written by black authors should only be reviewed by black reviewers and so on. It is difficult to imagine a more extreme manifestation of apartheid thinking.[79]

The fourth element in the orthodoxy is the politicization of everything. Work, literature, social intercourse, and personal and family relations are all defined as inherently political. And this is an exceedingly polarized politics. Much of our intelligentsia, especially its members who belong to recognized victim groups, seem to feel constrained to behave as if they are permanently at war. Anger is the preferred mood. The rhetoric is that of implacable struggle and hostility. Rational discourse is not promoted in an atmosphere in which people define anyone who disagrees with them as the enemy and where everyone is at pains to establish the intensity of his or her own passion and commitment.[80]

A common way of stating this element of the orthodoxy is the aphorism "The personal is political." Elizabeth Fox-Genovese offered some telling background for this phrase: "the finest, most internally consistent theory of 'the personal is political' – and vice versa – emerged from the work of Giovanni Gentile, the premier philosopher of Italian fascism, who had the wit to know that he was proclaiming a totalitarian doctrine."[81]

More observations about different aspects of the orthodoxy follow. Each points out a particular deficiency.

It is difficult, being surrounded by the orthodoxy, to avoid reflecting on Yeats's poem "Second Coming." In Canada today, it is unmistakable that the best lack all conviction, while the worst have a passionate intensity which is palpable.

I should also stress again that the various elements of the orthodoxy are by no means consistent with each other. It is, to take an obvious example, logically impossible to be both a highly politicized champion of victims and a relativist. This does not seem to bother anyone.

Another important aspect of the orthodoxy is a belief in the redemptive wondrousness and universality of human rights. This is, perhaps, the genesis of the obsession with human rights discussed in chapter 9.

A further fraudulent element of the orthodoxy is the commitment of its practitioners to "diversity." Diversity is taken to mean that all organizations or institutions must contain a multiplicity of ethnic groups and persons of differing sexual orientations. But diversity, in this usage, is a lie. While diversity purports to embrace a wide variety of human beings who are ostensibly different from each other, it aggressively demands that they all think alike. Diversity of points of view is unacceptable. As Lasch put it, "In practice, diversity turns out to legitimize a new dogmatism in which rival minorities take shelter behind a set of beliefs impervious to rational discussion."[82]

Running through the orthodoxy is a deep, almost reflexive, cynicism. Indeed, cynicism is the inevitable result of embracing the other elements of the orthodoxy. Principles, institutions, and beliefs are taken to be nothing but smokescreens, fashioned for no reason other than to obscure the oppression of victims.[83] The major purveyors of cynicism are the mass media. Knavery and skull-duggery are seen to be endemic. But this cynicism has no goal, no obvious end, and no critical purpose. It is empty and barren, cynicism for its own sake. It has become very popular amongst university lecturers.

The orthodoxy has been embraced by the ruling clique and seems to be the only mode in which journalists, lawyers, academics, and judges are capable of thinking. The ruling clique is coterminous with those whom Christopher Lasch described as the "enlightened elite."[84] It is difficult to understand how an elite which is as lacking in learning and culture as ours can be described as "enlightened." From this perspective it often seems that the Supreme Court behaves more like, as quoted earlier in Bickel's words, a synod of bishops than a court. In the Supreme Court nothing is allowed to contradict the orthodoxy, neither the Constitution, nor the law. Since the judges have largely become passionate devotees of the orthodoxy, it makes sense to characterize their decision-making as primarily based upon personal preference.

It would be an error to leave this discussion of the orthodoxy without saying something about Critical Legal Studies (CLS), which began in the United States in the 1960s. It was an attempt to apply Critical Theory, as developed by the so-called Frankfurt School – Adorno, Habermas, Horkheimer, and Marcuse – to the analysis of law. Many have seen critical theory as an outgrowth of Marxist thought, when, in fact, critical theory was a perversion of Marxism which diminished it to a mere cultural critique and, at the same time, jettisoned an essential element of it, i.e., class struggle. It also abandoned the notion of praxis, the unity of theory and practice that is fundamental to Marxist thought.[85] Without praxis, i.e., class struggle, there is no Marxism. Adherents of CLS liked to describe it as a "movement," though it gained no currency outside the walls of university law schools. One critic described its proponents as "a mandarin class of elite academic radicals."[86] CLS was founded on paranoia and adopted an obsessively reductionist methodology. For the "Crits," law was simply an elaborate smokescreen, cleverly constructed to obfuscate and justify oppressive and inhuman social relations. In the 1990s CLS metastasized into Critical Race Theory, which, borrowing much of the paranoia and reductionism of its progenitor, sees law as existing solely in order to maintain racial oppression.[87]

Finally, if the orthodoxy is, indeed, a secular state religion, the Charter of Rights and Freedoms is its scriptural text. Devotees of the orthodoxy claim a commitment to something they call "social justice." As social justice, like other elements of the orthodoxy, is highly abstract and tends to be thought of primarily in terms of legal rights, it follows that the preferred means of achieving social justice is Charter litigation. Specifically, the Charter's equality guarantee, section 15, is what seekers after social justice rely on. Note that this litigation in no way challenges the oligarchy. In fact, this preference for section 15 has resonated with the judges of the Supreme Court and, as a result, the section gives every sign of eclipsing the rest of the Charter: the other guarantees in the Charter have, in case after case, been superseded by the equality guarantee.

Marx and Engels were scathingly critical of the fatuity of "social justice." They observed that, "this equal right is … a right of inequality in its content, like *every* right."[88] Devotees of the orthodoxy deceive themselves that a nineteenth century Canadian decision, *Union Colliery* v. *Bryden*, was an early affirmation of "equality." An aggressively left-wing periodical in Britain was recently critical of this focus on "equality," deriding the notion that "making sure a few more women, homosexuals and non-whites get cosy, well-paid jobs 'at the top' is a major contribution to producing a more equitable society. It isn't."[89] *Union Colliery* involved a constitutional challenge to a section of an 1890 British Columbia statute called the Coal Mines Regulation Act. The section in question prohibited the employment of Chinese workers below ground in a coal mine. Union Colliery was a part of the vast Dunsmuir family holdings in B.C., and Bryden, who initiated the suit, was both a member by marriage of the Dunsmuir family and a shareholder in Union Colliery. His suit was against Union Colliery for contravening the act by employing Chinese workers in its coal mines; however, it seems likely that Bryden began the litigation hoping that he would lose. It was definitely in the economic interests of the Union Colliery to be able to employ Chinese miners, and it must have been pleased when the Judicial Committee struck the anti-Chinese section down rather than uphold Bryden's claim. Union Colliery's response to the decision was to impose a surtax on the pay of the Chinese miners it was now allowed to employ, in order to pay for the costs of the litigation.[90] Some commentators have contrived to see the decision of the Judicial Committee as a victory for "equality."[91] The only equality which *Union Colliery* recognized was equality of exploitation.

Returning briefly to the abstract shallowness of "social justice," it is worth remembering that one of its earliest proponents was Friedrich Hayek, a fanatical supporter of unconstrained capitalism. He believed that capitalism was a significant means of achieving "social justice."[92] The search for social equality seldom includes a demand for economic equality, since the latter might threaten the wealth and privilege of the oligarchy.

The basis for my principled critique is a deep commitment to constitutional democracy as well as the belief that, by having surrendered their minds to the orthodoxy, the judges are subverting our system of constitutional democracy.[93]

My analysis focuses on the period since the Canadian Charter of Rights and Freedoms became part of our Constitution. The Charter has led to a transformation both of Canadian institutions and of the way Canadians think, and the Supreme Court has been in the vanguard of these transformations. In one of its first Charter decisions, the Court conferred upon itself the distinction "guardian of the constitution."[94] (This phrase points up another unfortunate predilection of Supreme Court judges: using phrases or ideas without acknowledging their source. The source of "guardian of the constitution" is Alexander Hamilton, James Madison, and John Jay, *The Federalist*, 489.) Subsequent decisions suggest that the judges of the Court have difficulty grasping the distinction between "guardian" and "owner." The judges had a better understanding of the true nature of our Constitution fifty years ago when Chief Justice Rinfret stated, "The constitution of Canada does not belong either to Parliament or to the legislatures; it belongs to the country."[95] In a 1985 decision the Court also described itself as "protector and preserver" of the Constitution.[96] Given the theological nature of our orthodoxy, I am surprised that the Court has not yet called itself "defender of the faith."

In reality, the judges of the Court are certainly not the protectors and preservers of our Constitution. Indeed, they are the main threat to it. At the end of the day, I believe that a useful and practical means of protecting our constitutional democracy would be to abolish the Supreme Court. Fortunately, our Supreme Court was not created by our Constitution, but by an ordinary act of Parliament.[97] A simple remedy, therefore, would be the repeal of this act. However, the suggestion is too extreme: Canada, as a federation, does require a final national court of appeal. The remedy, then, would be for Parliament to make far-reaching reforms to its creature. I discuss these reforms in chapter 11.

CRITICIZING THE ORTHODOXY

This book is written from a point of view which is unashamedly and unequivocally counter-orthodox. The high priests and priestesses of the orthodoxy will undoubtedly denounce me as "right-wing," this being the standard epithet applied to anyone who deviates from the orthodoxy,[98] and, in the parlance of the orthodox, right-wing is synonymous with wicked. If language has any meaning, those who use "right-wing" as an epithet must regard themselves as "not-right." Interestingly, it appears that in order to qualify as not-right one must be wealthy and privileged: living in a $1-million-plus home in Rosedale is not essential, but it certainly seems to help. *Not-right* once meant "left." When political terminology still had some meaning, *right* denoted persons who were enthusiastic about capitalism, while *left* referred to those who were not. From this perspective, there has not been a left in Canada for decades, criticism of capitalism being something which never issues from the mouths of those who purport to be not-right. Finally, there was a time when a universal part of the intellectual equipment of everyone who considered himself or herself to be "left" was a skepticism about and hostility toward judges and judicial activism.[99] This resulted from U.S. Supreme Court decisions to slaughter socially progressive legislation[100] and to justify racial segregation.[101]

The general social and political perspective from which this book is written is Red Tory. Red Toryism is the only authentically Canadian political and social perspective to have ever developed.[102] Red Tories tend to be Canadian nationalists and to believe in the value of our traditions and our institutions. The orthodox despise our traditions and our institutions. The orthodoxy, like so many intellectual and social fashions which have done damage to Canada, originated almost entirely in the U.S. The practitioners of orthodoxy are Canadians who have been culturally and intellectually colonized by the U.S. As a Canadian nationalist, I am hostile toward American colonialism.

The bulk of the book is taken up with the development of the various themes which have been introduced. Chapter 1 analyses the ways in which Supreme Court judges have acted so as to subvert our legal system. Chapter 2 investigates the anti-democratic tendencies of Supreme Court decision-making. With Supreme Court judges given to making public pronouncements on almost any subject, chapter 3 analyses the effect this predilection has had on the judges' performance of their proper role. Chapter 4 looks at the judges themselves. Chapter 5 looks at the ways in which the judges have relentlessly expanded their own authority. Chapter 6 looks further at the ways the judges have turned the law into their own personal possession. Chapter 7 investigates in more detail the results of the feminist domination of the legal and political processes in Canada. Chapter 8 looks at the extent to which the judges have transformed the Supreme Court into something other than a court. Chapter 9 discusses at length the role which legal academics have played in the processes described in the book. Chapter 10 further analyses the fact that the Supreme Court has become the dominant policy-making institution in Canada. Last, the final chapter attempts to make practical suggestions for overcoming the problems which the rest of the book has identified.

1

The Attack on Law

Despite the fact that, every year, judgments of the Supreme Court take up thousands of pages in the law reports, it is difficult to continue describing the court's annual production as "law." I would not be so presumptuous or foolish as to attempt a comprehensive definition of "law," even assuming such a thing were possible. Recognizing this, it is still possible to assert that law has certain fundamental characteristics. Law must involve the articulation of established principles, as well as their application in a coherent and consistent fashion to new situations which arise. I am not attempting to suggest that law is a collection of hard and fast rules which can easily be ascertained and applied. But law is neither whimsical nor arbitrary. The main area of law which this book addresses is Constitutional Law. More specifically, the book deals with decisions by the Supreme Court on issues involving the Constitution and, especially, the Charter.[1] It is in its constitutional decisions that one can see most clearly the Supreme Court's abandonment of principle. The Supreme Court, as I understand its decisions, prefers, instead, to talk of values. The notion of principles implies that the law exists prior to the judge and is something more than a function of the subjectivity of the individual judge. In contrast, values are utterly amorphous and subjective, and more appropriate to the thinking of adolescents than to the thought of senior members of what still chooses to call itself a learned profession. "Values" are routinely manipulated by judges in order to achieve results which accord with their personal social preferences.[2]

There once existed in Canada something called the law of torts, but this body of principles has largely been discarded by the

Supreme Court. Tort law in Canada today can be summed up simply in the phrase "Plaintiffs win." In a tort action, one person, the plaintiff, is claiming that he or she suffered a loss as the result of the unlawful act or omission of another person, the defendant. The plaintiff thus looks a lot like a victim and the fact that plaintiffs win can be explained. The Court has regularly abandoned established principles,[3] disregarded statutes,[4] and invented new doctrines[5] to ensure that a plaintiff wins. One commentator stated that the Supreme Court has created "the most aggressively pro-plaintiff doctrinal position on duty of care in the Commonwealth." This same commentator spoke of "conceptual confusion," "fundamental misunderstanding," and "wooliness" in the Court's tort decisions.[6]

Having provided this explanation for recent pro-plaintiff tort decisions rendered by the Supreme Court, it will be helpful to discuss two tort decisions in which the Court did not, strangely enough, find in favour of the plaintiff. The two are *Cooper* v. *Hobart* and *Dobson (Litigation Guardian of)* v. *Dobson*.

In *Cooper* v. *Hobart* an investor was suing the Registrar of Mortgage Brokers (the Registrar) for the Province of British Columbia. A company called Eron was a registered mortgage broker in British Columbia, and the plaintiff was an investor who had advanced money to Eron. The Registrar suspended Eron's licence and placed a freeze on its assets. Subsequently, Eron went out of business and various investors, including the plaintiff, suffered substantial losses. The plaintiff argued that the Registrar should have suspended or cancelled Eron's licence earlier and that, had this happened, the losses would not have occurred. As the Court saw it, the doctrinal question presented by the appeal was whether a legal duty of care existed between the Registrar and members of the investing public. The Court did not believe that such a duty existed and asked itself whether a new one should be recognized. The judges also believed that the primary authority for the resolution of this question should be the statute under which the Registrar operated. The judges were not prepared to create a new duty of care, concluding that to do so would be to "create an insurance scheme for investors at great cost to the taxpaying public."[7]

The decision in *Dobson* is difficult to understand primarily because the text of the decision is largely obfuscation. The judges did not address what the decision was really about. In this case, the defendant, Cynthia Dobson, was the mother of the infant plaintiff, Ryan Dobson. When she was twenty-seven weeks pregnant, Cynthia Dobson was driving a car and, because of her negligent driving, an accident occurred. This accident resulted in injuries to Ryan who was, at the time, still *in his mother*. A caesarean section was performed, Ryan was born with permanent mental and physical injuries, and he subsequently sued his mother, Cynthia, in negligence.

The issue before the Supreme Court was whether a child could sue his mother in respect of injuries caused to him while he was *in utero*. On its face, the case appears to be about tort law, but it is not. The Court's decision has to be deconstructed to determine what the case actually ended up being about. Only then does it become apparent that the case was really about abortion, which is made evident by the fact that the Canadian Abortion Rights Action League (CARAL) intervened before the Supreme Court.[8] Hints as to the true character of the litigation are given in the judgments of Justice Cory and the joint judgment of Justices McLachlin and L'Heureux-Dubé. Cory spoke of "the extensive intrusion into the privacy and autonomy rights of women that would be required by the imposition of tort liability on mothers for tort negligence."[9] McLachlin noted for herself and L'Heureux-Dubé that "the common law must reflect the values enshrined in the *Charter*. Liability for foetal injury by pregnant women would run contrary to two of the most fundamental of these values – liberty and equality."[10] What *R. v. Morgentaler* (1988) really gave Canadian women was an unfettered ability to have abortions. Holding Cynthia Dobson liable, which is to say, recognizing that a foetus might have certain legal rights enforceable against its mother, could have been seen as limiting that unconstrained freedom to abort a foetus, and this was unacceptable to the judges.

If *Dobson* is to be understood fully, it must be read alongside *Winnipeg Child and Family Services (Northwest Area) v. G. (D.F.)*, a decision which the judges referred to in *Dobson*. In the *G. (D.F.)* case a young woman was pregnant with her fourth child. She was also addicted to alcohol and glue-sniffing. Her three previous children had been born with disabilities resulting from her addictions, and, apparently in order to prevent injury to her fourth child, a judicial order had been issued to place her in the custody of the CFS to undergo treatment until the birth of her child. Basing herself on the "fundamental liberties of a pregnant woman," Justice McLachlin held that there was no legal basis for the original judicial order.[11] Both CARAL and the Women's Legal Education and Action Fund (LEAF) intervened before the Supreme Court. The essence of both *Dobson* and *G. (D.F.)*, as I see it, is this: If a woman is to have an unfettered legal right to kill a foetus which she may be carrying, she must, *a fortiori*, have a right to negligently or intentionally injure it.

Turning to the field of income tax law, the Supreme Court's record is no more impressive. Brian Arnold is a leading commentator on Canadian tax law. In a recent article he was critical of the Supreme Court's approach to the question of tax avoidance.[12] Arnold criticized the Court for being too attached to a literalist approach to statutory interpretation and, as a result, failing to give effect to Parliament's purpose in making various amendments to the Income Tax Act. Arnold was also critical of the Court's reliance on a 1936 decision of the House of Lords.[13] Arnold called the Court's reasoning "inconsistent, occasionally contradictory and usually conclusory" and added that its statements were "confused and confusing."[14] This tax decision can be seen as a further manifestation of the Court's unwillingness to allow Parliament to set public policy.

It will now be helpful to again devote some space to an investigation of the meaning of "law." Two scholars who have written about the essence or meaning of law are H.L.A. Hart and Lon Fuller.[15] For many years, Hart was professor of jurisprudence at Oxford, while Fuller taught at the Yale University Law School. Neither is exactly contemporary, but the views of both on the nature of law still deserve respect. While Hart and Fuller certainly did not think alike, and would likely have resented being lumped together in this fashion, each used similar language in seeking to understand law. They both suggested that law, properly so-called, is general, consistent, coherent, and predictable. Fuller argued that "law" cannot be "sporadic" and "patternless." He asserted further that there must be a "relatively stable reciprocity of expectations between lawyer and subject" and that "like cases should be given like treatment."[16] If one applies these conceptions to the recent behaviour of the Supreme Court, it becomes difficult to describe what the Court produces as "law." What we have been getting from the Court in recent years is capricious, arbitrary, unpredictable, and largely ad hoc. The judgment of Lord Halsbury in *Sharp* v. *Wakefield* gives some direction in determining what should be involved in legal decision-making; it should be done "according to rules of reason and justice, not according to private opinion, according to law and not humour. It is to be not arbitrary, vague, fanciful, but legal and regular."[17] The Supreme Court itself has a mission statement which asserts that "the Court assures uniformity, consistency and correctness in the articulation, development and interpretation of legal principles throughout the Canadian judicial system."[18] American legal scholar William B. Harvey argued that the Rule of Law demands that judicial decisions be "reasoned, rationally justified, in terms that take due account both of the demands of general principle and the demands of the particular situation."[19] Contrary to the standards suggested, it often seems to me that the most accurate way of describing Supreme Court of Canada decision-making is "applied subjectivity." Early in its Charter decisions, the Court abandoned the pretence of treating like cases alike and now seems to decide cases largely, if not entirely, on the basis of the personal ideological prejudices of the judges. No rational person would claim to be able to predict the outcome of appeals before the court. I personally believe that a rational and sensible prediction one might attempt would be "If LEAF intervenes, LEAF is likely to end up on the winning side."[20]

If we apply any reasonable and coherent standard, I find it difficult to believe that we still have a legal system in Canada. The judges are guided not by law, in any intelligible meaning of that term, but by the demands of the prevailing orthodoxy. The standard that law should be general has been abandoned by the Court, with "general" in this sense meaning that Canadian law must apply equally throughout the territory of the Canadian state. The "contextual approach" of the Supreme Court denies this notion. The contextual approach was invented by Justice Wilson in her judgment in *Edmonton Journal* v. *Alberta (A.G.)*. As she noted in that decision, "a particular right or freedom may have a different value depending on the context."[21] She rejected what she described as an "abstract approach" to the definition of the various guarantees in the Charter. As she put it, "the contextual approach acknowledges the legal framework of the Charter, it emphasizes the context in which the dispute before the Court has arisen, rather than the text itself."[22]

As I understand the abstract or principled approach to freedom of expression, it begins with the actual text of the Charter. It thus starts from the statement in section 2(b) of the Charter that "everyone" has freedom of expression. That means to me that everyone, regardless of whom it may be, is free to express himself or herself regardless of what is being expressed. In contrast, the contextual approach appears to focus on who is doing the expressing and what it is that he or she is expressing. Thus, the contextual approach discards principle in favour of the personal preferences of the judge.

By appearing to decide that Canadian law does not apply to Aboriginal persons, the Supreme Court has largely negated the principle that the law should be general.[23] For several years, the Court has in fact been the dominant institution in the making of public policy toward aboriginal persons. So much so that, in December 2001, Prime Minister Chrétien announced that his government would be following a new policy direction with respect to aboriginal peoples. The announcement suggested that the prime minister had come to understand that litigation was not a desirable means of making public policy.[24]

A final court of appeal's decisions should be generalizable, which is to say, capable of application to all litigants in all parts of the territory of the state. But Supreme Court of Canada decisions are not, largely because they are often unintelligible and ad hoc.

It was once thought that law provided a mechanism through which citizens could be protected against arbitrary and oppressive behaviour on the part of state officials. In Canada today, citizens no longer have any protection against such behaviour from Supreme Court of Canada judges. The judges have largely forgotten that there are certain fundamental principles which underlie Canadian law. For example, in November 2000 in *Winnipeg Child and Family Services* v. *K.L.W.*, the Court upheld the validity of the action of the Winnipeg Child and Family Services Agency in removing a one-day old infant from its mother while the infant and mother were both under treatment in a hospital, and without the agency having first obtained a judicial authorization to do so. The Court held that the agency could constitutionally act in such a fashion even when there was no emergency. Justice L'Heureux-Dubé wrote a chilling majority judgment. She concluded that where the agency had reasonable and probable grounds for believing that a child was at risk of harm, it could legitimately seize the child. What follows is my interpretation of L'Heureux-Dubé's decision.

Her judgment appeared to say that protecting children from abuse or harm was highly desirable and that any action the state might take with the ostensible purpose of protecting children was just fine. She believed that requiring the state to seek a prior judicial authorization might place a child at an additional risk of harm. L'Heureux-Dubé's judgment was exceedingly difficult to follow. She adopted the so-called "contextual" approach. This, as I explained above, is code for saying that the question of whether a litigant may claim a Charter right will depend largely on a judge's purely subjective view of the litigant and of the litigant's situation. L'Heureux-Dubé expressed herself in double-talk. According to her, courts should be "reluctant to import procedural protections developed in the criminal context into the child protection context."[25] This is yet another example of a judge treating the Constitution as if it were her personal possession. L'Heureux-Dubé saw this litigation as a contest between parental rights and the interests of the state in the protection of children. Although there was no discussion in her judgment of the liberty or equality interests of children, in one other judgment L'Heureux-Dubé did write at length of the need to respect the equality rights of children.[26] Because adults in Canada may not be arbitrarily seized and detained by the state, a concern with the equality rights of children would demand that a similar right be afforded to children. Yet L'Heureux-Dubé seemed to think that an "emergency situation" was different from an "emergency" and that "proactive" was a word.[27] The essence of L'Heureux-Dubé's judgment in *K.L.W.*, as I understand it, was that if the state claims to be seeking *good* objectives any action it may take in ostensible pursuit of those objectives is fine.

Fortunately, the chief justice and Justice Arbour retained some commitment to the basic principles of our legal system. Chief Justice McLachlin's dissent should be regarded one day as one of the monuments of our legal system. She recognized that children have an interest in staying with their parents and that harm might come to a child from "precipitous and misguided state interference."[28]

She concluded that the seizing of a child by the state should be regarded a last resort, and that when there is no emergency the state must first obtain a warrant from a court authorizing such action.

L'Heureux-Dubé's judgment is a classic justification for arbitrary and oppressive action on the part of the state.[29] When our most senior judges are no longer prepared to protect citizens against high-handed and arbitrary behaviour by state agencies and would rather construct incoherent justifications for such behaviour, I can no longer believe that Canada is a country governed by law.

A full understanding of *K.L.W.* requires that it be read alongside the Supreme Court's decision in *Winnipeg Child and Family Services (Northwest Area)* v. *G. (D.F.)*, the previously mentioned case of a young woman addicted to alcohol and glue-sniffing who was pregnant with her fourth child. Apparently K.L.W. was not an ideal mother either. The child whose apprehension led to these proceedings was her third, and her two other children had been apprehended because K.L.W. was drunk, neglecting them, or in contact with men who had abused her. Remarkably, L'Heureux-Dubé did cite the *G. (D.F.)* decision in her judgment in *K.L.W.*[30] The obvious question is this: Why was the Court so concerned about preventing harm to K.L.W.'s third child when it did not appear to care about what happened to G. (D.F.)'s fourth child? This decision manifests the judges' fundamental misunderstanding of the nature and purpose of a Constitutional guarantee of rights like the Charter. The point of such documents is to protect the citizen against the state, not to create a pretext for allowing the judges to impose their personal policy preferences on society.

Much of the practice of judicial review in Canada today makes clear that this perspective is no longer sound. Charter-based claims which go before the Court today seldom involve an attempt by an individual to use the Charter to protect himself or herself against the state. When interest groups litigate today, we regularly see a contest between what is often a state-created and state-financed organization, on the one hand, and the state itself on the other. Charter litigation, thus, turns out to be a series of struggles amongst different fragments or fractions of the state.[31] Much of this litigation, of course, is financed by the state through the Court Challenges Programme.

At this point, it will be useful to make the distinction between negative judicial review and positive judicial review. Negative judicial review involves enforcing limits on the power of the state, such as those found in the Charter. The Charter text, not that it seems to matter, is largely a statement of things which the state may not do to individuals. Negative judicial review means striking down state acts which infringe the limits established by a constitution. Positive judicial review involves enforcing obligations which a constitution casts upon the state. Since much Charter litigation seems to be inspired by the desire to extract benefits from the state, this distinction may no longer be helpful.[32] Section 52(1) of the Constitution Act, 1982, which says that any state act which is inconsistent with the Constitution is to be of "no force or effect," strongly suggests that only *negative* judicial review is contemplated under Canada's Constitution. The sole provision in the Charter that casts obligations upon the state is section 23, which under certain circumstances obliges the state to provide minority language education.[33] With only this limited textual authorization, the Supreme Court has nonetheless regularly engaged in positive judicial review.[34]

I wish now to return to Justice L'Heureux-Dubé's approach to judging. As I interpret many of L'Heureux-Dubé's judgments and speeches, it appears that she eschewed her basic responsibilities as a judge and declined to address the issues actually raised before her. Instead, she preferred, particularly in cases involving sexual assault,[35] to deliver a well-worn sermon on the need to overcome what she usually described as "myths" and "stereotypes." When she actually was prepared to give a judgment on the issues raised in the appeal before her, L'Heureux-Dubé often contented herself with setting out her own myths and stereotypes. In *K.L.W.* she appeared to believe that all parents were inherently hostile toward and dangerous to their children. She also appeared to believe that children would be better off out of the clutches of their parents and in the custody of the state. Many of L'Heureux-Dubé's judgments avoid discussing law and are questionable exercises in amateur sociology.[36]

In 1994 L'Heureux-Dubé took to the pages of the *Ottawa Law Review* in an attempt to justify her reliance on social science research rather than evidence – or, at least, evidence as evidence has traditionally been viewed. She dismissed the notion of judges deciding cases on the basis of established legal principles, stating that "underlying questions of social policy are obfuscated by a mask of legal principles."[37]

She was prepared to give herself wide latitude to conduct independent social research and to then rely on that research in her decision-making. She did, however, concede that there might be a risk in such an approach: "This risk, in turn, can constitute legitimate grounds for caution, and for requesting the parties to make submissions on social science evidence of which the judge proposes to take notice."[38] Throughout this paper L'Heureux-Dubé relied heavily on the writing of feminist academics, including Lenore Walker, the creator of both the battered woman syndrome and the Super Bowl Sunday hoax.[39] L'Heureux-Dubé concluded her essay with this disturbing comment which revealed the extent to which she had abandoned the pretense of even trying to act like a judge applying the law:[40] "By recognizing that exclusive reliance on the adversarial framework, and all of its accompanying legal baggage, may not be the best means by which to address family law concerns, we open the door for more innovative and co-operative solutions that should ultimately improve both the interpretation and application of family law in Canada."[41] In other words, judges should be free to do as they please.

One other judge did express some criticism of L'Heureux-Dubé's ideas. This judge, R.J. Williams of the Nova Scotia Family Court, believed that L'Heureux-Dubé's approach would both make judges less accountable and expand their discretion.[42] He noted further that much social science "evidence" is of questionable reliability and that such information should be closely scrutinized by judges.[43] Williams also noted that even Lenore Walker had expressed certain caveats about social science evidence and that L'Heureux-Dubé had disregarded these caveats.[44]

The judges of the Supreme Court are the highest-paid public officials in Canada. The chief justice earns $254,500 per year and the other judges receive $235,700 each.[45] Canadians could be getting better value for their money.

My primary reason for believing that what the Supreme Court produces can no longer be dignified by the term *law* is the way in which the judges have politicized their role. The dominant orthodoxy has become the primary factor that determines the outcome of litigation before the Court. Canadians used to believe that the existence of courts which were ideologically and intellectually independent of the officials who exercised political power afforded Canadians substantial protection against the oppressive and arbitrary misuse of political power. This is no longer the case. The Supreme Court has taken the lead in transforming the courts into eager instruments for the application of the dominant ideology. Canadians recoiled in horror at the sight of Nazi judges raving at the persons accused of taking part in the July 1944 plot to assassinate Hitler. The Stalinist show trials of the 1930s evoked a similar revulsion. While drawing parallels between Canada and Nazi Germany or Stalinist Russia may seem ludicrous, by actively obliterating the barriers between law and politics and between law and the dominant ideology, the judges have moved us closer to these historical situations. All Canadians can be pleased that in *Winnipeg Family Services* v. *K.L.W.* our chief justice, McLachlin, retained some commitment to the basic notions which have been the foundation of our legal system.

Two notions which are inextricably linked are the state and law. Law does not and cannot exist in the abstract, in the air. Law can only be the law of a particular state. There is something called Canadian law because there is a Canadian state. By appearing, in several cases, to contemplate the dismemberment of the Canadian state, the Supreme Court has contributed further to the abolition of Canadian law. In 1998 the Court was prepared to contemplate the secession of a province – though there is nothing in Canada's Constitution about secession – and, as if that were not enough, invented detailed rules to govern how secession might actually be accomplished.[46] But the Court has not stopped there. The Court has been prepared to accept that the Canadian state has little or no jurisdiction over aboriginal peoples,[47] thereby promoting the dismemberment of the Canadian state by seeming to accept that there can be areas of Canadian territory not subject to the jurisdiction of the Canadian state.

I will now set out a probably idealized version of how the legal process should operate. My purpose is to create a standard against which to assess the work of the Supreme Court and, thereby, to demonstrate the extent to which the court has abandoned basic notions of law. Legal proceedings involve a concrete dispute between two parties. A court which is seised of a dispute is expected to listen, in an impartial fashion, to the way the parties present their dispute. The court is required to rely entirely and exclusively on the parties to define and elucidate their dispute, and the court is to confine itself to the information and arguments presented by the parties. Once the parties have completed their presentation of the case, the court is required to make a decision. Assumed to be a fully qualified and experienced lawyer, the judge decides a case by assessing the information and arguments presented by the parties in light of the applicable legal principles. Having done that, the judge, favouring neither party and treating both equally, reaches a decision. The judge is then obliged to justify his or her decision by demonstrating that it conforms to the legal principles which govern the case. The decision should be reasoned and consistent.

The way in which the Supreme Court of Canada operates bears little resemblance to this model. First, because the Court allows just about any outsider who is not a party to the dispute to intervene if he, she, or it wants to, the hearings resemble legislative-committee meetings far more than judicial proceedings. In this context, intervention means the Supreme Court permits a person or organization that is not a party to a particular appeal before the Court to take part in the appeal by presenting both written and oral arguments to the Court. Second, the Court no longer relies solely on the arguments formally presented to it. Each judge has three judicial law clerks and these clerks do independent research for their judges. Much of this research involves questionable social science. One hallmark of judicial, as opposed to Supreme Court of Canada, proceedings, however, is that the opposing party is entitled to question and attempt to rebut arguments introduced by the other party. When a clerk presents the results of his or her research to the judge, this principle is negated. Third, when it comes to actually making a decision, there is reason to believe that the judges of the Supreme Court may not always make their own decisions, and that they often allow their clerks to draft their judgments for them. Finally, the decisions which emerge often appear to be far more "political" than "legal."[48]

What is the central distinction between a legal decision and a political decision? The defining characteristic of a "legal" decision is that it is principled. A "political" decision can be, and often is, unprincipled and ad hoc. On what bases are political decisions reached? What follows are common justifications for political decisions:

a This is what the people whom I represent wanted.
b This is the result dictated by my party's policy.
c This is the right thing to do.
d This was what I had to do to get re-elected.

But Supreme Court of Canada decisions have become systematically unprincipled. This is the result of two tendencies. First, some of the judges tend to see themselves as delegates or representatives of a particular section of the community and have therefore largely abandoned the effort to be impartial.[49] Second, and even more important, has been the tendency to adopt the so-called contextual approach, created by Justice Wilson and eagerly embraced by Justice L'Heureux-Dubé. A judge following this approach asks, first, whether she likes a party before the court and, second, whether she approves of what that party is doing. If the answer to both questions is "Yes," the judge decides in favour of that party. In sum, Supreme Court judgments are no longer reasoned attempts to apply legal principles to a particular dispute. On the contrary, they reveal themselves as exercises in justifying a decision already reached for other, which is to say, political, reasons. The Court has so politicized itself and its decision-making that it often seems reminiscent of the courts in apartheid South Africa. The South African courts, like the Supreme Court of Canada, systematically disregarded the law in order to render decisions that were consistent with the official ideology.[50] The South African judges, like the judges of our Supreme Court, utterly compromised their own independence. The approach taken by Supreme Court judges is often the opposite of what one would expect in a process which is properly to be described as legal. If one accepts that the essence of legal decision-making lies in the unbiased and reasoned application of established principles, one has no choice but to conclude that what occurs in the Supreme Court of Canada is not a legal process.

The degree to which the Court has politicized itself and its work is apparent in newspaper articles written about it, as journalists write about the Supreme Court judges in the same way they write about politicians. A lengthy newspaper article written in January 2001 spoke of combinations and coalitions of forces on the court. Judges were portrayed as deciding cases based far more on their personal ideological predilections than on the law. A judge's past decisions were described as his or her "voting record," as if there were little difference between being a judge and being an MP.[51]

2

The Attack on Democracy

Canada is, and has been for many years, a democracy. However, Canada did not become fully democratic until 1960. It was only in that year that Canadians having the legal status "Indian" became entitled to vote.[1] During the Second World War the extraordinary mobilization of the entire nation for the struggle against fascism made overwhelmingly clear both the extent and the depth of Canadians' commitment to democracy. *Democracy*, to go back to the word's Greek roots, means rule by the people. There are many different types of democratic political system.[2] Many years ago, Canada adopted representative democracy. This form of democracy requires that at regular intervals the people elect representatives who make the laws, set the country's social, economic, and political agendas, and oversee the operation of the state machinery. The primary institutions through which representative democracy has manifested itself have been, nationally, Parliament, and at a more local level, the provincial legislatures.

It must be recognized that in recent years notions about the meaning and essential elements of democracy have changed. A recent book about the Supreme Court has argued: "But democracy is not just about majoritarianism; it is also about individual and minority rights, about limits to what even a large and determined majority can do. Therefore, there is a sense in which a strong and independent judiciary *is* democratic – not because the Courts are overtly democratic in their organization or their selection or their process (they are not), but because they are the mechanism that serves this 'other face' of democracy."[3] This formulation neatly conflates liberalism, which is about individualism, and democracy, which is about power to the people.

Now representative parliamentary democracy, like all human systems, is not without its flaws. Money can come to play a dominant role in elections, if not a subversive one. In addition, rather than the legislature controlling the executive government, the reverse can become the norm. Representative parliamentary democracy in Canada has its drawbacks and its failings.[4] To say this, however, is not to argue that it is failing as a system; it is simply to note that it is not perfect. Electoral democracy does not necessarily give a voice to every group, nor to every point of view, only to those strong enough to receive significant electoral support.

Whatever flaws may exist in Canada's system of representative parliamentary democracy, however, none is so serious as to justify replacing it with rule by the judges. For decades, Canadian electoral democracy has been founded on universal suffrage, which is to say, the principle that every adult citizen is entitled to vote and that one citizen's vote is the equal of every other citizen's vote. Electoral democracy also requires that elected representatives face periodic re-election.

THE SUPREME COURT AND DEMOCRACY

Judges in Canada are not elected; they are appointed through a process which a former chief justice once described as "mysterious."[5] Once appointed to the Supreme Court, a judge may stay in office until age seventy-five.[6] In order to be appointed a judge, a person must be a lawyer and have been one for at least ten years. The principle of the independence of the judiciary requires that judges not be accountable or answerable to anyone for their decisions. It is difficult to remove a judge from office.

It might be thought that in a constitutional democracy unelected, unaccountable judges should not do certain things. Included amongst these would be setting the social agenda, amending legislation, amending the constitution, and publicly attacking democracy and democratic institutions. The judges of the Supreme Court have, in recent years, done all these things. They have not hesitated to address and purport to resolve highly contentious and divisive issues, such as abortion, assisted suicide, the legitimacy of homosexuality, and Quebec secession.[7] Using a technique which it invented, and to which it gave the name "reading in," the Court has been prepared to amend legislation.[8] The Court has even gone to the point of altering the text of the Constitution.[9] Some judges have also delivered public speeches pointing out imagined deficiencies in democracy.

In one decision, Chief Justice Lamer was forthright enough to recognize that judicial review could be problematic in a democracy: "In a democracy like Canada [judicial review] is inherently controversial because it confers on unelected officials the power to question decisions which are arrived at through the democratic process."[10] He was apparently not prepared to accept that either administrative tribunals or courts might exercise judicial review powers.

The Supreme Court's attack on democracy began at the same time as the adoption of the Canadian Charter of Rights and Freedoms in 1982. Conrad Black recently observed that the effect of the Charter was "to unleash on this country swarms of mad judicial tinkerers, social worker judges ignoring the law and carrying out what they took to be the moral imperative of remaking society along faddish and idiosyncratic lines."[11] It must be remembered that the adoption of the Charter coincided with the Reagan/Thatcher counter-revolution. There is a reason for this "coincidence." A major result of that dismal interlude was a profound loss of legitimacy for politics and government, and the idea that the state could and should play a central role in social and economic affairs was discredited.[12] Apparently as a result of Reaganism/Thatcherism, capitalism achieved its greatest political and ideological triumph, with the virtue and universal desirability of capitalism now seemingly beyond question. The ideology of individual rights is an inevitable concomitant to this triumph of capitalism. This ideology justifies an essential credo of our dominant orthodoxy – that the state may not and should not interfere with the ability of individual capitalists to maximize their profits.[13] At the same time, Canadians began to abandon the notion that social betterment would occur through collective political action, which is to say that Canadians appeared to abandon their longstanding commitment to "peace, order and good government."[14] Over many decades and as a result of collective political action, Canadians had constructed a governmental system which sought to uphold the collective interests of the Canadian people. This system constrained the worst excesses of capitalism, provided a range of social services, and entrusted the performance of certain essential economic functions to the state.

THE OBSESSION WITH RIGHTS AND THE FLIGHT FROM POLITICS

Around the time of the adoption of the Charter, the dominant class in Canada turned its back on the collective good and became attracted to the idea of unlimited individual freedom. Individual rights, as enshrined in the Charter, took precedence in the minds of Canadians over the collective good. Here we see an illustration of Marx and Engels's dictum that "the ideas of the ruling class are, in every epoch, the ruling ideas."[15] Similarly, Christopher Lasch has observed that the whole notion of individual rights has come to mean, insofar as the elite, or more accurately, the chattering classes are concerned, the "right to do as they please."[16] Since the central postulate of Reaganism/Thatcherism was the right of capitalists to do as they please, we have seen in Canada, contemporaneously with the rise of the Charter, the dismantling of the governmental edifice which sought to uphold the public good. This has been accomplished through the individualistic trinity of privatization, cutbacks, and deregulation. At the same time as this was happening Canadians became captivated by rights. Rights were seen as swell things and the more rights, the better – it should be added that the whole notion of rights is highly individualistic. This increasing obsession with rights was initially caused by the growing disenchantment with politics, but the obsession then fuelled the disenchantment.

One result of the adoption of the Charter has been the publication of a great many bad books. The worst of these, in my opinion, is *The Charter of Rights* by Ian Greene, who teaches political science at York University. To demonstrate more fully the shortcomings of Greene's book, I will quote at length from a review I wrote in 1992.[17] Since Greene's book manifests many of the deficiencies and anti-democratic tendencies of orthodox academic writing, I propose to discuss it at length. As I noted in my review of *The Charter of Rights*:

The judges and the lawyers have used the Canadian Charter of Rights and Freedoms to transform our law and our politics. Some have applauded the transformation. Others have not.

It behooves Canadians who are not lawyers to attempt to understand the Charter – where it came from, what it says, how it has been applied. And teachers have a special responsibility of informing themselves about the Charter, for it now looms large in a number of subjects – history, social studies, and, of course, law.

But the task is not easy. There has, to be sure, been an enormous amount of writing about the Charter. Unfortunately, the bulk of this consists of books and articles written by lawyers for lawyers. As a result, most of the available material is badly written and consciously obfuscating and neither attractive nor useful to persons other than lawyers.

All of which is to say there was a clear need for a general book about the Charter aimed at ordinary Canadians. Greene has tried to achieve this admirable objective. He has, I regret to say, failed.

In the first place, Greene's approach to the task of scholarly writing is breathtaking. In two introductory chapters he attempts to explain how the Charter came to be part of our constitution. These chapters are so riddled with errors that they raise questions about whether Greene can be taken seriously as a scholar.

The problem is a most fundamental one: factual accuracy. Basic errors abound. Greene's grasp of historical fact is, to put it kindly, tenuous. The errors are so numerous that it is possible to provide only a brief sampling of them.

Greene devotes a great deal of space to discussing the 1938 decision of the Supreme Court of Canada in a case called *Re Alberta Statutes* [*Reference re Alberta Legislation*]. He states the following on page 19:

> The package of legislation referred to the Court included the Accurate News and Information Act, better known as the "Alberta Press bill." This legislation gave a government agency, the Social Credit Board, the power to prohibit the publication of a newspaper, force a newspaper to print corrections of articles that the board considered inaccurate, and prohibit newspapers from publishing articles written by blacklisted persons.

The statute was in fact called "An Act to Ensure the Publication of Accurate News and Information." The powers under the Act were to be exercised not by the Social Credit Board as a whole, but by the Chairman of the Social Credit Board (the Premier). The Social Credit Board was not a "government agency," it was, *de facto*, the Government of Alberta. The Chairman could not order newspapers to print corrections of "articles" generally, but only of "statements relating to any policy or activity of the government of the province." There was no reference whatsoever in the legislation to "articles written by blacklisted persons."

The Supreme Court of Canada decided the Press Bill was beyond the competence of a provincial legislature, in part because of the restrictions the law placed on what Chief Justice Duff called the "free public discussion of public affairs." Duff did not reach this decision because, as Greene suggests, "the preamble to the *B.N.A. Act* has the effect of implanting in Canada the civil liberties principles of the U.K." This was the approach taken by another judge in another case nearly 20 years later.

The suggestion in the Alberta Press Bill decision, that basic liberties could not be infringed under provincial legislation, was taken up by other judges in other cases. This approach came to be called "The Implied Bill of Rights" – *implied* because it was not expressly stated in the *B.N.A. Act* and *Bill of Rights* because it did offer some constitutional protection for rights. Greene says, "This reasoning became known as 'The Duff Doctrine'." As far as I know, none of the people who have written about the Implied Bill of Rights has ever called it "The Duff Doctrine."

Speaking of the aftermath of Igor Gouzenko's 1945 revelations about an alleged Soviet spy ring in Canada, Greene stated on page 21:

> ...twenty-six persons were arrested and held incommunicado. The usual procedural rights were suspended under the authority of the War Measures Act and secret trials were held in 1945.

This is not what happened.

A number of persons were, indeed, arrested pursuant to an Order-in-Council made under the *War Measures Act* and held incommunicado. But they were then brought before a Royal Commission, chaired jointly by Mr. Justice Kellock and Mr. Justice Taschereau of the Supreme Court of Canada. The purpose of the Royal Commission was to enquire into Soviet espionage in Canada. Persons were forced to testify before the Royal commission without legal representation. *Public* trials were held after the Royal Commission finished its work. Most of the accused, including one M.P., Fred Rose, were charged with conspiracy to violate the *Official Secrets Act*. The Royal Commission sat in 1946 and all the trials were held in 1946. I agree completely with Greene that the whole business was shameful. The point is, however, that, as in so many other places in the book, Greene has his facts wrong.

Greene refers to *Roncarelli* v. *Duplessis*, one of our most significant constitutional decisions. In one short paragraph he made two basic factual errors. He talks of "harassment of Jehovah's Witnesses by Quebec authorities in the 1950's." There was certainly harassment of the Witnesses, but it happened in the 1940s. The act which led to the litigation, the cancellation of Roncarelli's licence to sell liquor in his restaurant, occurred in 1946. Greene states that Roncarelli was ultimately successful in his action against Quebec Premier Maurice Duplessis and "regained his licence." Again, Greene is wrong. Roncarelli did not get his licence back. The reason for this is that by the time the Supreme Court of Canada gave its judgment in 1959, Roncarelli's restaurant had long since closed and he had moved to the U.S. He was, in fact, awarded $33,123.53 in damages.

Since Greene is writing about the Charter one might imagine he could get the events leading to its adoption right. He doesn't.

In discussing "The Road to Charter" Greene begins, sensibly enough, with the Victoria Charter of 1971. He described Alberta Premier Peter Lougheed's hostility to the Victoria Charter in this fashion:

> Lougheed was opposed to the proposed constitutional amending formula in the Victoria Charter because by giving a veto power only to Ontario, Quebec and British Columbia, it made Alberta and the other six provinces "second class." (p. 39)

This statement is not accurate. The Victoria Charter did not give a veto over constitutional amendments to British Columbia. Indeed, it did not expressly give a veto power to any named province. It merely provided, in Article 49, that any constitutional amendment would have to receive the support of the legislative assembly of any province which had "at least twenty-five per cent of the population of Canada." In 1971, as would be the case today, only two provinces – Ontario and Quebec – qualified.

I will not burden the reader with a detailed dissection of Greene's account of the process of constitutional diplomacy which resulted in the proclamation of the *Canada Act 1982* in April of that year. Suffice it to say, it would be exceedingly unwise to rely on Greene's statement of the facts.

Some, no doubt Greene himself, would say I have been nitpicking. I'm not. Scholarship requires attention to detail. One must, of course, excuse the odd error. We are all, we like to tell ourselves, human. But Greene makes more than the odd error.

The problem is compounded by Greene's apparent distaste for footnotes or references. He does make reference to judicial decisions, but none of the other factual assertions he makes is accompanied by any indication as to its source. So the reader, inevitably, is left wondering where Greene got his facts from. Did he overhear them? Did he read them on the back of a corn flakes box? Or did he simply make them up?

In more recent years Greene has continued his attack on basic notions of democracy. His essential postulate appears to be that democracy is not about "power to the people," but rather about "power to the judges and the academics." He has argued that democracy means "government based on the principle of mutual respect." He apparently believes that "more conscious thinking about the nature of mutual respect may lead to more effective refinements of democratic institutions and procedures."[18]

For Greene, as far as I can understand him, democracy is little more than a graduate seminar in political science, one taught, I would guess, by Greene. Naturally enough, Greene argued in favour of judicial review. He asserted that in their decision-making the "personal values of judges count." He noted further: "As long as the judicial process is organised to promote mutual respect, there is no inherent contradiction between the law making role of courts and democracy."[19] Thus, the judges can do whatever they like as long as they get the answers *right*.

Greene neatly redefines democracy in such a way as to exclude the majority of the people from active decision-making. The following is code for Greene's redefinition: "we need to think about improvements [sic] to our political system to promote the highest quality of elected members."[20] At the end of the day, political decision-making should be entrusted exclusively to those who might think correct thoughts. Greene's writing provides a clear illustration of Christopher Lasch's dictum that the reigning orthodoxy is a form of class warfare whereby the "enlightened elite (as it thinks of itself) seeks to impose its values" on the unenlightened and to exclude the unenlightened from active participation in civic affairs.[21] I interpret Greene's notion of "improvements" in the political system to mean ensuring that neither the unenlightened nor persons who might think unenlightened thoughts are ever elected to public office. It is evident that, for Greene, democracy means government of the few, by the few, for the few.[22] The enlightened will get on with the business of government while the rest stay home and "think" about civil rights and mutual respect.

Implicit in this fascination with rights is the notion that the real or imagined rights of the individual can and should take precedence over the collective good. This, of course, is the fundamental ideological postulate of Reaganism/Thatcherism. Thus, at the same time as Canadians became entranced with rights, they were becoming less committed to democratic politics. In its decisions, the Supreme Court has affirmed the desirability of both these tendencies. The Court began to be perceived and to perceive itself as the source of rights, that is, as the source of good things as opposed to the wickedness that comes from politics. Parliament and the provincial legislatures were de-legitimated for being enmeshed in the bad old days of politics,[23] while the Court was seen more and more as the bringer of rights and virtue. Professor Peter Russell has argued that the transfer of the policy-making focus from the legislative to the judicial arena "represents a further flight from politics, a deepening disillusionment with the procedures of representative government and government by discussion as means of resolving fundamental questions of political justice."[24] Indeed, with the flight from politics, Canadians appear to have abandoned their commitment to the resolution of social issues through democratic discussion. Meanwhile, the dominant class in Canada has been converted to the religion of human rights.

The international religion of McHuman Rights is an important element in the homogenization and corporatization of the world. Human rights in no way challenge the oligarchy which rules us in Canada, since the oligarchy has been effectively converted to the religion of human rights. Human rights do not challenge wealth and privilege. Human rights will not resolve the crisis in health care, nor transform our regressive tax system. Human rights are abstractions. This allows the oligarchy to support human rights without in any way compromising its position. Professor Michael Mandel, in commenting on the legalization of politics, noted that "as capitalism becomes increasingly unable to deliver the goods ... it must seek forms of legitimation which are abstract ... A *Charter* is a logical response, which makes litigation a safe alternative to genuine democracy."[25] Speaking of health care, I should note that I became very ill in 1998. I received a great deal of very high quality health care financed by the state. This was completely concrete. A *right* to health care would have been meaningless. Any rational person would prefer *actual* health care to a *right* to health care. The oligarchy would probably prefer to see a right to health care, since such a right would cost it nothing.

Being utterly abstract, the human rights perspective denies the existence of classes and, thereby, reinforces class domination. Popular democracy provides the only mechanism through which ordinary people might challenge the dominant clique.

In 1988 I wrote that the judges of the Supreme Court of Canada contributed to the dominance of their class by maintaining the notion of judicial neutrality.[26] The judges have abandoned the notion of neutrality and now propagate the gospel of rights and equality. This is the Court's contribution to the continued dominance of the oligarchy, although to describe the group which rules Canada today as an oligarchy is to impute to it a degree of representativeness it does not merit. Canada is dominated by a tiny clique, all of its members believers in the orthodoxy.[27]

A belief in the wondrousness of rights is a central element in the orthodoxy. Indeed, Canadians have been persuaded that rights and more of them are the answer to all social ills. As part of its annual income tax package the Canada Customs and Revenue Agency publishes a "Taxpayer Bill of Rights." Hospitals have "Patient Bills of Rights" and airlines have "Passenger Bills of Rights." A recent report argued that most social ills can be traced to the fact that Canadians do not have enough rights.[28] I confidently await the day that some scholar announces to the world the connection between tooth decay and the denial of rights.

It must not be forgotten, however, though it often is, that the things which Canadians value most, like health care and an orderly and humane society, are the result of political action, not of litigation over rights.

As the institution in the forefront of propagating the ideology of rights, the Supreme Court has, of necessity, played an anti-democratic role. This can be seen in one other result of the adoption of the Charter: the "judicialization of politics."[29] This phrase denotes a politics where the central issues which engage a society are resolved in the courtroom, making judges the significant political decision-makers and lawyers the mediators of political activity. Such a politics can hardly be described as democratic. Canada has reached the same point as noted by de Tocqueville in *Democracy in America*, where all social issues eventually become legal issues.[30]

We also appear to have arrived at a point where the social, intellectual, and moral agendas are set by lawyers. This domination of the political process by lawyers and judges necessarily excludes the active participation of citizens. Writing in dissent in *R. v. Morgentaler* (1988) – the decision in which the Supreme Court struck down section 251 of the Criminal Code, which had placed certain restrictions on the availability of abortions – Justice McIntyre was highly critical of the notion that there must be a constitutional remedy for every social ill. McIntyre's dissent is an eloquent statement in favour of judicial modesty and circumspection. Barry L. Strayer, now a judge of the Federal Court of Appeal and the main drafter of the Charter, agreed with McIntyre. "There was no presumption created that every wrong must find a remedy in the *Charter*," Strayer wrote.[31] It would be an exaggeration to suggest that the judges of the Supreme Court *caused* the judicialization of politics. They have simply done little to resist the process.

CLASS POLITICS AND TRIBAL POLITICS

The Supreme Court's most obviously anti-democratic behaviour has arisen out of its embracing of both interest group and identity politics. Both these tendencies have fundamentally anti-democratic implications. McCormick, who generally supports the Court, argued in favour of these tendencies, asserting that "In recent decades, democratic politics have been transformed by what we often call the politics of identity as distinct from the more 'old-fashioned' politics of interest."[32] Thus, class-based politics in which ordinary people might seek to challenge the dominant clique can be dismissed as "old-fashioned."

Interest group politics is based on an organized group of individuals championing one goal or cause to the exclusion of all others. Persons who seek a particular objective organize themselves around the effort to achieve that objective, and anyone who does not subscribe to the goal is necessarily excluded from the organization and, indeed, often perceived as the enemy. Identity politics is organized around sex, ethnic background, or sexual preference. It, too, is highly exclusivist, eliminating everyone who is not a believer or does not share the requisite identity.[33] Democratic politics is based on the citizen, the undifferentiated individual who is the political equal of all other citizens. This "citizen" does not actually exist. Citizenship, so defined, is largely a theoretical construct. As there is no society in which all persons are socially and economically equal, the political equality of citizens is primarily theoretical and a matter of definition. An essential element of democratic politics should be the fungibility of citizens. The Supreme Court, however, has tended to take the approach that this formal notion of equality masks inequality.[34] To take the approach, as the Supreme Court has, that some citizens are more equal than others is to subvert one of the essential foundations of democratic politics and the basis of political democracy in Canada – the equality of citizens. Interest group politics and identity politics are, by their very natures, anti-democratic. It should be evident that organizations based on the exclusivity essential to such politics and identity politics are unlikely to achieve significant electoral support. Consequently, the individuals involved have turned to litigation, hoping to win victories from the courts which they could not have achieved through the ballot box.[35] We must remember that the organization which was, historically, the best-known vehicle for identity politics was entitled the National Socialist German Workers' Party.

Because it has relaxed, if not abandoned, any restrictions on interventions in cases before it,[36] the Supreme Court has turned itself into the forum of choice for interest group and identity politics. At the same time, the Court has largely discarded earlier rules about "standing."[37] Standing denotes the ability of an individual to bring an issue before the courts. It used to be that a person could not institute a legal challenge to a state act simply because he or she did not like that act. It now appears that mere dislike of a state act is sufficient to give an individual the necessary standing to challenge it.

It also appears that a litigant may bring a matter before the court on the basis of an alleged violation of someone else's rights, not necessarily of his or her own. An example is *R. v. Morgentaler* (1988), where Morgentaler based his challenge on the denial of women's rights. Morgentaler was, of course, also seeking to defend himself against a criminal charge. Being granted standing may actually depend upon whether or not one's claim is consistent with the orthodoxy. Joe Borowski sought to attack Canada's open approach to abortion from a pro-life perspective. He was denied standing on the basis that he was neither "a pregnant woman nor a foetus."[38] Henry Morgentaler, neither a pregnant woman nor a foetus, was nonetheless allowed to attack the existing abortion law from a pro-choice perspective. Since he was charged with committing an offence contrary to section 451 of the Criminal Code, Morgentaler did have the standing to challenge the constitutionality of this section. Nonetheless, the substance of Morgentaler's Charter challenge to section 451 was based on a claim that someone else's (i.e., women's) rights were being violated. The fundamental distinction between the Morgentaler and Borowski cases lies in the fact that Morgentaler's Charter claim arose in the concrete circumstances of his attempting to defend himself against a criminal charge, whereas Borowski's was purely abstract.[39]

The message of the Supreme Court to interest groups and the practitioners of identity politics has been, "Forget about the democratic process, you can disregard it and come to us and, as part of our commitment to rights, we will give you what you want." Two prominent critics of the Supreme Court – F.L. Morton and Rainer Knopff – have described this constellation of litigants as the "Court Party" and suggested that the Court Party has been successful in "hijacking" the Court.[40] In a 1999 article, James B. Kelly made a distinction between early and more recent Charter litigation. In its early Charter decisions, the Court "placed itself in a confrontational relationship with democratic actors for control of the policy process in Canada."[41] Kelly argued further that in recent years this relationship has become less confrontational and that judicial support for the Court Party has declined. The clear message from the Court has been that the democratic process really does not matter, primarily because it does not deliver the goods, i.e., rights.

The very process of turning political and social issues into legal battles over rights is by its nature anti-democratic. This process inhibits the kind of discourse essential to democracy. In the discourse of rights talk,[42] a dispute between A and B can only go like this: A asserts, "I have a right to such and such." If B does not agree, her only reply can be, "No, you don't." A is forced to respond, "Yes, I do." What results is a schoolyard fight, not the discourse among citizens which should exist in a democracy. The fact that abortion remains such a divisive and intractable social issue in Canada is probably a result of the attempt by the judiciary to resolve it. If politics really is the "art of the possible," notions of negotiation and give-and-take must inhere in any political process. But there is no negotiation, no give-and-take in the endless public shouting-match over abortion. Litigation is a winner-take-all process which precludes negotiation and give-and-take, and abortion has thus been confined to the straitjacket of adversarial litigation, thereby guaranteeing that it will remain bitterly divisive.

It is important to remember that courts are simply incapable of finally resolving social issues like abortion. If *A* sues *B* in a dispute over the ownership of a piece of property, this litigation raises precisely the kind of issue a court is capable of resolving. At the end of the day a court can make an enforceable order which will resolve the dispute. In contrast, the dispute which broke out in New Brunswick in 2000 over Aboriginal fishing is a striking example of rights discourse. At the beginning of this dispute, I watched an Aboriginal spokesperson being interviewed on television. In order to underline the crucial importance of the Aboriginal claims, he asserted, "We're fighting for our rights." The intractability of the resulting dispute has been enhanced by the rhetoric of rights; in other words, the Aboriginals' claim that they are fighting for their rights has effectively precluded compromise and negotiation.

I suspect the main reason capital punishment is not a social issue in Canada today is that it was resolved by Parliament, not the courts. Abortion reveals the futility of looking to the courts to provide answers to social issues.

The essential democratic discourse is further subverted by another common practice of interest group and identity politics. Citizens in a democracy must be able and prepared to disagree with each other. It should be possible for me to say to someone who does not agree with me, "I believe you are mistaken." But interest group and identity politics define anyone who does not agree with me as my enemy. Disagreeing with the practitioners of interest group and identity politics typically results in the critic being publicly denounced as "racist," "sexist," or "homophobic" (the etymology of this questionable word literally means exactly the opposite of what those who use it imagine it to mean). The extravagant use of such phrases has had a deeply destructive effect on democratic discourse: as Christopher Lasch observed, when identity politics are involved "democratic debate ... degenerates all too easily into a shouting match."[43]

FREE EXPRESSION AND CITIZENSHIP

Free Expression

There are two conditions which are essential to the existence of democratic politics. Without both, democratic politics is either unlikely or impossible. They are free expression and citizenship; and the Supreme Court's actions have undermined both.

While freedom of expression is protected in section 2(b) of the Charter, the Court has shown little enthusiasm for it. In cases involving freedom of expression, the Court has consistently upheld the restriction on expression which was being challenged. As long ago as 1938, the Supreme Court of Canada understood the connection between free expression and democracy.[44] As Chief Justice Duff put it, "The free public discussion of public affairs is the breath of life for parliamentary institutions."[45] Today's judges do not seem to have a clear idea about why free expression does or should matter, contenting themselves with sanctimonious twaddle such as noting that free expression contributes to "individual self-fulfilment" and "human flourishing."[46] Assuming that either of these phrases has any meaning, the connection of either with democracy is not apparent. Two interpretive predilections of the Supreme Court suggest, in fact, a certain hostility toward free expression. First, the Court's lack of enthusiasm for free expression had become so apparent by December 2000 that a journalist could write, "The thing to remember about any Supreme Court ruling upholding freedom of speech is that the Supreme Court does not actually believe in freedom of speech."[47] The fact that an informed journalist could make such an observation is not proof that the observation itself is correct, but does suggest that there must be some basis for it.

A significant exception to Supreme Court decisions on freedom of expression is Chief Justice McLachlin's judgment in *R. v. Sharpe*, the "kiddie porn" decision of 2001. In this judgment McLachlin provided some direction on why free expression does and should matter. She noted that freedom of expression "makes possible our liberty, our creativity and our democracy." She continued, "While some types of expression, like political expression, lie closer to the core of the guarantee than others, all are vital to a free and democratic society." She also added that "the guarantee of free expression extends even to offensive speech."[48]

Second, in *R. v. Keegstra* (1990), the Court adopted two ideological devices in its approach to free expression which were borrowed from post-modernism. These were "voice" and "silencing."[49] The Court's approach appeared to say that whenever I exercise my freedom of expression, I am thereby "silencing" your "voice." The *Keegstra* case involved a challenge to section 319(2) of the Criminal Code which creates an offence of wilfully promoting hatred against an "identifiable group." The majority decision in *Keegstra* appeared to conclude that the really important thing about the guarantee in section 2(b) of the Charter involved "free expression values," something not even mentioned in the text of the Charter.[50] As I understand the decision, the Court believed that making sure people do not get their feelings hurt is a free expression value. The majority decision stated that suppressing free expression in order to uphold free expression values was acceptable. Thus, the way to protect freedom of expression is to suppress it, and free expression becomes a zero-sum game and a disreputable activity.[51]

In *Edmonton Journal* v. *Alberta (A.G.)*, Justice Wilson invented what she was pleased to call the "contextual approach" to freedom of expression. The judge following this approach looks at the particular expression in order to determine whether he or she agrees with it. The judge then looks at the personal characteristics of the party claiming to rely on freedom of expression in order to determine whether he or she belongs to a social group the judge supports. Thus, if the judge likes me and agrees with what I am saying, my claim based on freedom of expression may succeed; otherwise it will not. The cumulative effect of these decisions is to make freedom of expression a decidedly hollow guarantee.

The invention of the "contextual approach" to freedom of expression is another example of the judicial amendment of our Constitution. Section 2(b) of the Charter states that "everyone" has freedom of expression. The contextual approach amends that simple formulation so that it appears to read, "Anyone a judge likes and who is expressing ideas or analysis the judge agrees with may have freedom of expression." In sum, then, the Court has decided that the central consideration in freedom of expression cases is what it has been pleased to call "free expression values," although the Charter nowhere mentions "values" – which are, of course, totally subjective. The Court also decided that if there is a conflict between freedom of expression itself and "free expression values," freedom of expression must give way to "free expression values." Thus, expression which is consistent with the orthodoxy will be upheld, while expression which contradicts or criticizes it will not. The approach followed in *Keegstra*, that freedom of expression is to be protected by suppressing it, is a classic example of double-think. This illustrates the Court's unprincipled and politicized approach to constitutional litigation and amounts to saying that the judges will uphold freedom of expression only when it suits their fancy to do so. In a recent book, Ellen Anderson wrote of Justice Bertha Wilson's "principled contextuality."[52] "Principled contextuality" sounds an awful lot like an oxymoron to me. It is noteworthy that one of the very few cases in which the Supreme Court struck down a limit on expression involved commercial expression, i.e., advertising.[53]

One of the few cases in which the Court recognized the essential connection between democracy and free expression is *Libman* v. *Québec (A.G.)*. This case was about a provision in the Quebec legislation dealing with referenda which limited the amount of money independent individuals or organizations might spend during a referendum campaign. Here the Court did affirm "the paramount importance for Canadian democracy of freedom of expression in the political realm."[54] Manfredi described this decision as "judicial micro-management of public policy."[55] To be fair to the Court, I should note that it did recognize the connection between freedom of expression and democracy in *R.* v. *Sharpe*.

On 26 January 2001, the Supreme Court of Canada released its judgment in what will probably always be known as the "kiddie porn" case. John Robin Sharpe had been charged with two counts of possessing child pornography, contrary to section 163.1(4) of the Criminal Code,[56] and two counts of possession of child pornography for the purposes of distribution or sale, contrary to section 163.1(3). Sharpe argued that these sections of the code infringed his freedom of expression as guaranteed in section 2(b) of the Canadian Charter of Rights and Freedoms. The trial judge accepted that there was an infringement of freedom of expression, that the infringement could not be justified in a free and democratic society, and ruled, "courageously," as Chief Justice McLachlin subsequently put it, that the Criminal Code section was unconstitutional. Therefore, Sharpe was acquitted. The B.C. Court of Appeal then upheld the acquittal by a two-to-one majority, and the Crown appealed to the Supreme Court of Canada.

The appeal was heard in the atmosphere of public hysteria which has become commonplace in Canada. The appeal was portrayed publicly as a contest between freedom of expression and the protection of children. The idea was promoted that, unless the Supreme Court upheld the Criminal Code prohibitions against child pornography, all Canadian children would be at risk of serious harm. The hysteria became such that an Ottawa father who took photos of his naked four-year-old son to a photo lab to be processed was arrested and the son was apprehended by the Children's Aid Society.[57]

The current prohibition against child pornography was a very long time in the making. In 1977, Bill C-329 to amend the Criminal Code was introduced in Parliament. Clause 2 of the bill would have made it an offence to "photograph, produce, publish, import, export, distribute, sell, advertise or display in a public place anything that depicts a person who is or appears to be under the age of sixteen years performing a sexual act or assuming a sexually suggestive pose while in a state of undress."[58]

Then, on 23 March 1978, the Standing Committee on Justice and Legal Affairs made a report on pornography to the House of Commons. This report recommended the creation of an offence to prohibit the depiction of a person under sixteen engaged in sexual acts or displaying "any portion" of his or her body in a sexually suggestive manner.[59] In 1987, Bill C-54 contained proposed amendments to the Criminal Code which would have prohibited "any visual matter which showed a person who is, or appears to be, under the age of eighteen years engaged in sexual conduct."[60] Finally, in 1993, Parliament amended the Criminal Code by adding the following after section 163:

163.1 (1) In this section, "child pornography" means a photographic, film, video or other visual representation, whether or not it was made by electronic or mechanical means, that shows a person who is or is depicted as being under the age of eighteen years and is engaged in or is depicted as engaged in explicit sexual activity.

(2) Every person who makes, prints, publishes or possesses for the purpose of publication any child pornography is guilty of .

(a) an indictable offence and liable to imprisonment for a term not exceeding ten years; or
(b) an offence punishable on summary conviction.

(3) Every person who distributes or sells any child pornography is guilty of

(a) an indictable offence and liable to imprisonment for a term not exceeding ten years; or
(b) an offence punishable on summary conviction.

(4) Every person who possesses any child pornography is guilty of

(a) an indictable offence and liable to imprisonment for a term not exceeding five years; or
(b) an offence punishable on summary conviction.

(5) It is not a defence to a charge under subsection (2) that the accused believed that a person shown in the representation that is alleged to constitute child pornography was or was depicted as being eighteen years of age or more unless the accused took all reasonable steps to ascertain the age of that person and took all reasonable steps to ensure that, where the person was eighteen years of age or more, the representation did not depict that person as being under the age of eighteen years.

(6) Where the accused is charged with an offence under subsection (2), (3) or (4), the court shall find the accused not guilty if the representation that is alleged to constitute child pornography has artistic merit or an educational, scientific or medical purpose.

(7) Subsection 163(3) to (5) apply, with such modifications as the circumstances require, with respect to an offence under subsection (2), (3) or (4).[61]

As has become inevitable in Supreme Court hearings, a large number of parties intervened in R. v. Sharpe. They included the attorney general of Canada, the attorneys general of six provinces, and a host of organizations, including the Canadian Association of Chiefs of Police. All nine judges heard the appeal, and the majority judgment was delivered by Chief Justice McLachlin.[62] She briefly described the material which led to the charges against Sharpe: two computer disks seized by Canada Customs containing a text entitled *Sam Paloc's Boyabuse – Flogging, Fun and Fortitude: A Collection of Kiddiekink Classics.* Sharpe was charged with illegal possession of this material as well as with possession for the purposes of distribution and sale. Inevitably, Sharpe pleaded the Charter. He argued that the Criminal Code sections infringed his freedom of expression as guaranteed in section 2(b) of the Charter and his right to liberty in section 7. The majority accepted that child pornography was constitutionally protected expression under section 2(b) of the Charter. As has been true of most Supreme Court decisions dealing with freedom of expression, the appeal, which is discussed next, turned on the application of section 1 of the Charter.

The Majority Judgment   Dealing with the first element of the section 1 analysis, the Supreme Court held that Parliament's objective in creating this limit on expression was "pressing and substantial." Parliament, Chief Justice McLachlin said, criminalized the possession of child pornography because such material posed a "reasoned risk" of harm to children. She held, further, that the state was not obliged to adduce proof based on concrete evidence that the possession of child pornography caused harm to children. On the contrary, "a reasoned apprehension of harm" would suffice. What, in the view of the majority, was the connection between child pornography and harm to children? First, "child pornography promotes cognitive distortions." I have no idea what a "cognitive distortion" is, although I suspect it may involve the thinking of bad thoughts. McLachlin did not actually define "cognitive distortion," but did suggest that child porn might cause "attitudinal harm." She further adverted to the fact that there was "limited scientific evidence linking cognitive distortions to increased rates of offending." She did try to explain this link by noting that "possession of child pornography fuels fantasies, making paedophiles more likely to offend." The majority in the Supreme Court provided no further direction, although it did suggest that child pornography might invite offenders to offend. How or how often this might happen were not issues which the Court chose to address. Child pornography was also bad because it could be used for grooming and seducing children, and "children are abused in the production of child pornography." It is disturbing that the majority did not require concrete evidence to support any of these hypotheses. The trial judge was less confident of his own omniscience and demanded proof of the actual harm caused by child pornography. The majority in the Supreme Court, nonetheless, was convinced that the means chosen by Parliament went too far, "regulating expression where it borders on thought."[63] The judges did not wish to strike the Criminal Code provisions down in their entirety; they instead decided to redraft the sections by "reading in" certain exceptions where the actual wording of section 163.1 was "problematic."

McLachlin's judgment was useful as she did provide some guidance about the importance of freedom of expression. This is the case in which she noted that free expression "makes possible our liberty, our creativity and our democracy" and added that freedom of expression also protects "unpopular or even offensive expression."[64] The difficulty, however, with Supreme Court decisions about the guarantee of freedom of expression in section 2(b) of the Charter is that most of them say little about the meaning or significance of expression. This is largely a consequence of the approach the Court took in *Irwin Toy* v. *Québec (A.G.)*. In that case the Court stated that if an activity had expressive content and sought to convey a meaning, then it qualified as constitutionally protected expression. The Court also stated that one activity which would not qualify as expression was an act of physical violence. Thus, pure commercial advertising was expression,[65] as were hate propaganda[66] and pornography.[67]

Since almost any activity qualifies as expression, the first stage in freedom of expression cases – determining whether the state has limited the Charter right in question – is largely a given and the heart of Supreme Court decisions on expression is usually found in the section 1 analysis – determining whether the particular limit on a right which the state has created is one which can be demonstrably justified in a free and democratic society. Because of *Irwin Toy*, Supreme Court decisions on expression generally do not involve much in the way of discussion or analysis of expression and appear to be little more than ad hoc evaluations of the desirability of particular state policies. This would explain why Professor Hogg has described these decisions as "unprincipled and unpredictable."[68] The *Sharpe* decision is no exception to this pattern.

In its decisions on freedom of expression the Supreme Court has accepted that this freedom is valuable and desirable because it is essentially connected to three important social values: seeking truth, democratic government, and self-realization – a notion first set out by Thomas Emerson.[69] The Supreme Court has relied on these values in many of its decisions regarding the Charter's freedom of expression guarantee,[70] and it first enunciated the Emerson approach in its *Irwin Toy* decision. There it opined:

6 seeking and attaining the truth is an inherently good activity;
7 participation in social and political decision-making is to be fostered and encouraged;
8 the diversity in forms of individual self-fulfilment and human flour-ishing ought to be cultivated in an essentially tolerant, indeed welcoming, environment not only for the sake of those who convey a meaning, but also for the sake of those to whom it is conveyed.[71]

Given the central importance of the expression, one might hope that the Supreme Court could have managed a clearer and more precise statement.

Chief Justice McLachlin's opinion in *Sharpe* was also consistent with the approach taken in other Supreme Court decisions in that she talked at length about "harm,"[72] thus adopting the fundamen-tal principle set out in J.S. Mill's *On Liberty*, that the state may only legitimately limit basic freedoms in order to prevent harm.[73]

In her judgment, McLachlin conducted a meticulous and detailed analysis of the scope of the Criminal Code prohibitions. She rigorously analysed the wording of section 163(1), spending considerable time defining and delineating the different defences found in the section. She noted that the section "evinces a clear and unequivocal intention to protect children from the abuse and exploitation associated with child pornography." She added, for-tunately, that the Code provisions would not catch "innocent baby-in-the-bath photos and other scenarios of non-sexual nudity." She concluded that Parliament's purpose was to "pro-hibit possession of child pornography that poses a *reasoned* risk of harm to children."[74] It was only after having satisfied herself as to the precise meaning of section 163(1) that McLachlin moved to an analysis of whether the limit on expression created in the Criminal Code could be justified under section 1 of the Charter. Again she conducted a thorough analysis, this time noting that the law might "also capture the possession of material that we would not normally think of as child pornography and that raises little or no risk of harm to children."[75] She thought the Code prohibition went too far because, as quoted previously, it "regulates expression where it borders on thought." For these reasons, the chief justice decided to "read in" certain new exceptions to the Criminal Code prohibitions.

"Reading-in" is a technique invented by Chief Justice Lamer in *Schachter* v. *Canada* and followed in *Vriend* v. *Alberta* and *M.* v. *H.* This technique allows a court to avoid invalidating a problematic statute by adding words to it which will render it constitutional. Using this technique, McLachlin created two exceptions:

1 Self-created expressive material; i.e., any written material or visual representation created by the accused alone, and held by the accused alone, exclusively for his or her own personal use
2 Private recordings of lawful sexual activity; i.e., any visual recording created by or depicting the accused provided it does not depict unlawful sexual activity and is held by the accused exclusively for private use

Exception 1 addresses the case of the closet paedophile who, say, writes down his fantasies, or creates drawings depicting them and keeps these creations entirely for his own private use. Exception 2 has been called "the horny teenager exception" and might involve two persons under the age of eighteen who videotaped themselves engaging in sexual activity. The videotape would have to be kept private and be for personal use only. In Chief Justice McLachlin's view, these exceptions would avoid what she called "problematic applications" of section 163.1.

The formal disposition of the case was that the appeal was allowed and, with the constitutional issues out of the way, Sharpe was remitted for trial on all the charges.

The Dissenting Judgment   As often happens in Charter litigation, Justice L'Heureux-Dubé dissented.[76] She was joined in her dissent by Justices Gonthier and Bastarache. Once more, as is the case with many of her dissents, L'Heureux-Dubé's judgment was difficult to follow.[77]

To begin with, L'Heureux-Dubé was not sure whether child pornography was constitutionally-protected expression. The established approach to the guarantee of freedom of expression in section 2(b) of the Charter is complicated. The first step in this analysis requires that a court look at the activity in question to determine if it is constitutionally protected expression. If the activity is constitutionally protected expression, a court must then determine whether the state has acted in such a way as to limit expression. If the state has limited expression, the court must then decide whether the particular limit is one which can be justified in a free and democratic society. The dissent rendered this entire analysis more complicated than it had previously been. While the authors of the dissent were not entirely clear whether child pornography was protected expression, they, nonetheless, concluded that section 163.1(4) limited expression.[78]

Next, L'Heureux-Dubé appeared to believe that child pornography was bad because it could "undermine the *Charter* rights of children" and because "all members of society suffer when harmful attitudes are reinforced." The dissenting judges could not find any evidence of actual harm caused by child pornography and observed that it might cause "attitudinal harm." They did not attempt to define what, if anything, that phrase might mean.

The authors of the dissent were also not concerned about the lack of concrete evidence concerning the harm caused by child pornography: they simply concluded that child pornography was "inherently harmful." They were worried about the so-called "attitudinal harm," of which they stated, "the attitudinal harm inherent in child pornography is not empirically measurable, nor susceptible to proof in the traditional manner but can be inferred from degrading or dehumanizing representations or treatment." Some guidance as to the possible meaning of attitudinal harm came when the dissenting judges observed that paedophiles use child pornography to reinforce the opinion that children are appropriate sexual partners, and "paedophiles show child pornography to children in order to lower their inhibitions towards engaging in sexual activity and to persuade them that paedophilic activity is normal." According to the dissenting judges, "the harm of child pornography is inherent because degrading, dehumanizing and objectifying depictions of children, by their very existence, undermine the *Charter* rights of children and other members of society."[79] The judges gave no indication as to how they reached this conclusion, but we must, I assume, accept that they *just knew* all this to be true.

The real problem with child porn, so it appeared, was that its dissemination created a heightened risk of L'Heureux-Dubé's "attitudinal harm." She was not concerned about "the lack of scientific precision" in the social science evidence available to Parliament when it enacted the section. It was enough for her that Parliament had a "reasoned apprehension" that child pornography caused "attitudinal harm." Parliament's action in enacting section 163.1 was okay because it promoted "children's right to equality."[80] Once again, we must assume that Justice L'Heureux-Dubé *just knew*. Finally, the dissenting judges thought that the section in its pristine form was just fine: they would not accept Chief Justice McLachlin's two exceptions.

In sum, following a "contextual" approach, the dissenting judges believed that it would be easier for the state to justify limits on child pornography than to justify limits on other forms of expression.[81] This suggests a hierarchy of forms of expression, something which seems to contradict the approach set out in *Irwin Toy*, where all forms of expression are to be treated equally. The emphasis on equality is a thread which runs through many of L'Heureux-Dubé's decisions.[82]

It is difficult to understand many of the reactions to the *Sharpe* decision without referring to the wave of hysteria about paedophiles which had been convulsing Canadians. Paedophilia was imagined to be endemic and it was believed that paedophiles lurked everywhere, preying on children without number. It was widely believed that the child pornography offence in the Criminal Code, by some magical means, protected Canadian children against paedophiles. Ontario's former attorney general, James Flaherty, contributed to the general hysteria through his incessant public pronouncements in favour of a tough law-and-order agenda.

Much of the reaction to the Supreme Court's decision appeared to be based on an unstated assumption that tens of thousands of paedophiles had been awaiting the decision and that, had the Court struck down section 163.1 of the code, this army of paedophiles would have concluded that it was now free to sally forth and begin ravaging Canada's children. The two preceeding sentences convey some sense of the general irrationality of the response to the *Sharpe* decision.

There were, of course, some very specific reactions to the Supreme Court's decision. Ontario attorney general Flaherty observed that the two exceptions "read in" by the Court would make it "more difficult for law-enforcement agencies and Crown prosecutors to effectively deal with child pornographers."[83] *Toronto Star* columnist Michele Landsberg wrote a column about the *Sharpe* decision. Her opinions were strikingly vitriolic and, in many places, less than accurate. She said that the *Sharpe* decision "opened up a damaging breach in the shield meant to protect children from sexual abuse" and congratulated L'Heureux-Dubé on a "vibrantly written" dissent. Landsberg had scathing words for "civil libertarians," who, she said, attempt to "confuse people" with "high-flying theories about freedom of expression." She exaggerated known facts about child porn and child abuse, referring to the "routine sexual abuse and exploitation" of "tens of thousands" of victims.[84] So much for rational discourse about child pornography. The belief that only section 163.1 stood between Canadian children and a horde of paedophiles was regularly repeated. An op-ed piece in the *Globe and Mail* stated that the *Sharpe* decision had "weakened our protection" and quoted Canada's justice minister, Anne McLellan, describing the decision as an "astounding victory for children."[85] Attorney General Flaherty expressed his intention of meeting with McLellan to discuss the "loopholes" created by the *Sharpe* decision.

Someone must have influenced McLellan because, on 14 March 2001, she introduced a strange bill in the House of Commons.[86] This bill would amend the Criminal Code by extending the ambit of the existing child pornography offence. It would now be an offence even to view child pornography on a computer. The implications of such an offence are chilling. Will hardware manufacturers be required to supply a police officer to watch the way each machine is being used? An offence of "luring" a child using a computer system was created. The bill would also create a series of offences with respect to cruelty to animals.

On 31 March 2001, McLellan wrote a letter to the editor of the *Toronto Star* in which she sought to justify Bill C-15.[87] Her argument was simple: Bill C-15 is designed to protect children;

therefore it is okay. This argument – that if the state claims to be pursuing noble objectives it is justified in taking any steps that might be thought likely to achieve those objectives – is subverting our system of constitutional democracy. In 2000 the Ontario legislature enacted an Act to Better Protect Victims of Domestic Violence. This may well have been the most high-handed and oppressive statute ever enacted in Canada, but it was believed to be just fine because its ostensible purpose was to "protect" women against domestic violence.[88] That same year the Court decided the case of *Winnipeg Child and Family Services* v. *K.L.W.*, where, as mentioned in chapter 1, the agency had seized a one-day old infant without having first obtained a judicial authorization to do so. Justice L'Heureux-Dubé had concluded that, since the agency claimed to be acting so as to "protect" a child, its actions were legally and constitutionally proper.

The Rule of Law will not survive for long when both judges and legislators adopt this good-ends-justify-oppressive-means attitude.

Despite the *Sharpe* decision and Bill C-15, the hysteria about paedophilia did not abate. Nor is it confined to Canada. A man who sat next to two children on a British Airways flight was asked to move to another seat.[89] In March 2001, Toronto police carried out a pre-dawn raid on the house of a Toronto schoolteacher. They seized computers and videotapes and then moved on to raid his office, where other material was seized. The man was charged with making, possessing, and distributing child porn and was remanded in custody. A *Toronto Star* story about the arrest was, itself, hysterical and probably unlawful. The story, complete with a colour photo of the man who was arrested, created an unmistakable impression that the man was guilty.[90] Canadian journalists are usually more scrupulous than this, carefully observing established practices designed to ensure that they do not break the *sub-judice* rule, which limits what may be said about proceedings before courts in order to ensure that the proceedings are not prejudiced through media publicity.[91] Once again, it appears that, when dealing with child porn, the normal rules do not apply.

Another recent Supreme Court decision which was given in the same atmosphere of public hysteria was *R.* v. *Latimer* (2001). Latimer had murdered his twelve-year-old daughter ostensibly to free her from the pain and suffering of cerebral palsy. He was convicted of second degree murder and given the statutory minimum sentence of life imprisonment with no eligibility for parole for ten years. Latimer attempted to attack this sentence, raising an argument of "compassionate homicide" and claiming that the imposition of a ten-year sentence was, in the circumstances of this case, cruel and unusual. Disabled persons and organizations claiming to speak for disabled persons became very interested in the appeal. The argument was raised that if the Supreme Court reduced Latimer's sentence it would be open season on disabled people in Canada. Once again, it appeared to be widely believed that, without the "protection" of the law, disabled persons would be murdered in droves.

As Canadians have lost whatever moral sense they once possessed, the social cement that used to be provided by moral notions has been sought in the law. Law is seen more and more as providing the key to human behaviour. Without the criminal law, or so it appears to be imagined, children would be abused and exploited and disabled people would be murdered. If the criminal law is the only basis for social cohesion and social order, we do not have much of a society left.

It is worth comparing a prosecution launched in 1977 to the *Sharpe* decision. In *R. v. Popert* the accused published a magazine called *The Body Politic* which was aimed at homosexual men. In December 1977, *The Body Politic* ran an article titled "Men Loving Boys Loving Men," which advocated sexual relations between boys and adult men. The accused were charged with using the mails for the purpose of transmitting indecent, immoral, or scurrilous matter contrary to section 164 of the Criminal Code. This case, which went through two trials and two appeals, was viewed as raising a host of civil liberties issues and became something of a *cause célèbre*. Chief Justice McLachlin indirectly adverted to *R. v. Popert*, suggesting in her judgment in *Sharpe* that "materials that advocate or counsel sexual offences with children may qualify [as child pornography]."[92] If a prosecution under section 164 were to be launched today, section 2(b) of the Charter would likely be raised as a defence. If section 164 were found to create a limit on expression, a court might well conclude that the limit was too vague[93] and too broad[94] to be justified. One recent decision suggests that the Supreme Court might take a sympathetic attitude toward homosexual pornography.[95]

Citizenship

The Supreme Court has also acted in other cases so as to under-mine the very notion of citizenship. Section 15(1) of the Charter, the equality guarantee, begins with the words "Every individual is equal." The meaning of those words would seem to be pretty clear. Justice Wilson nonetheless decided that only persons who were members of "historically disadvantaged" groups might claim equality rights.[96] This approach removes much of the con-tent from citizenship and renders the whole notion of common citizenship empty. By deciding that the state may not legitimately make distinctions between citizens and non-citizens[97] and by holding that non-citizens may claim Charter rights,[98] the Court has substantially weakened the significance of citizenship.

To connect the discussions of freedom of expression and of citizenship, imagine two Canadian citizens, X and Y. X is a member of a "historically disadvantaged group"; Y is not. On the Court's approach to both expression and citizenship, for Y to say anything which criticizes or disagrees with X is to "silence" X's "voice" and is, therefore, impermissible. Yet, an important and widely-shared goal of Canadians is the creation of a harmonious, multi-cultural democracy. The Supreme Court's approach to both freedom of expression and citizenship will frustrate the achieve-ment of this goal. To support identity politics is to support tribal politics, a phenomenon which fundamentally contradicts the basic principles of multicultural democracy.

Indeed, Canada is increasingly a country in which individuals are confined to hermetically-sealed categories based on sex, ethnicity, and sexual preference. The Supreme Court did not invent this neo-apartheid, but the Court has consistently given it its blessing. This phenomenon contradicts the notion of common citizenship and probably renders democracy unattainable.[99]

THE CANADIAN STATE AND CANADIAN HISTORY

Canadian democracy is premised on the continued existence of the Canadian state. The Court, however, has made a major con-tribution in recent years to the dismantling of the Canadian state. There are, for example, the cases involving Aboriginal persons where judges have upheld land claims and denied the Canadian state jurisdiction over both Aboriginal people and reserves.[100]

At a deeper level, the most significant anti-democratic force in North America today is a relentless and unconstrained self-absorption. The Supreme Court has allowed itself to be influenced by this adolescent mode of thought, appearing to have accepted that whining expression of the worldview of fifteen-year-olds: "No one has the right to tell me what to do." If no one has a right to tell me what to do, government is impossible. From another perspective, the Court's Charter jurisprudence can be seen as a celebration of the self and of the unconstrained freedom of the individual to do whatever he or she pleases.

In our current culture of rights, individual whims and preferences are quickly characterized as rights. The Court appears to be convinced that the state may not constitutionally limit the freedom of individuals to behave entirely as they please, and in the Court's jurisprudence on these matters, much has been made of the notion of "choice." The freedom of choice here seems analogous to the freedom of the consumer in the marketplace. When the citizen is reduced to the consumer, additional damage is inflicted on democracy. A consumer is not active; a consumer simply makes reactive choices about buying goods which are offered for sale by others. Justice Wilson was prepared to rewrite the Charter in order to further expand the notion of individual autonomy. In *R. v. Morgentaler* (1988), she stated that the Charter "erect(ed) around each individual an invisible fence over which the state will not be allowed to trespass."[101] The Charter text nowhere mentions fences, either visible or invisible. If Wilson is correct, the specific guarantees set out in the Charter text are unnecessary. She has managed here to collapse the entire Charter text into one sentence, thereby manifesting the defining tendency of Supreme Court judges in Charter litigation – treating the document as if it were their personal possession.

When the citizen is reduced to the consumer or the litigant, as has been the effect of Charter litigation, little is likely to remain of democracy.

Canadian democracy has been premised on the existence of a shared history. The longstanding fascination of Canadians with constitutional reform, however, has led to a wholesale rewriting of our history,[102] and likewise, the Charter has led to the abandoning and degrading of our history. First-year law students are unshakably convinced, as it seems are judges of the Supreme Court, that Canadian history began on 17 April 1982, the day the Charter became part of our Constitution. A corollary belief has developed that, prior to the Charter, Canada was a vile and oppressive country in which citizens were absolutely without rights.[103] This abandonment of our past has had a destructive effect on our democracy. There is one case in which a Supreme Court judge spoke out against the jettisoning of our sense of ourselves and of our traditional ways of doing things. Writing in dissent in *Dagenais* v. *Canadian Broadcasting Corp.*, Justice Gonthier stated: "I disagree with those who argue that the *Charter* requires that we emulate American society and discard the unique balance of fundamental values which existed in this country prior to 1982."[104]

THE AMERICANIZATION OF CANADA

The Charter has played an essential role in the ongoing Americanization of Canada. American political scientist Seymour Martin Lipset observed that, "perhaps the most important step that Canada has taken to Americanize itself – far greater in its implications than the signing of the free trade treaty – has been the incorporation into its constitution of a bill of rights, *The Charter of Rights and Freedoms*."[105]

Canadians appear to be unaware that the propagation of American ideas about law and litigation was an important element of U.S. foreign policy during the Cold War. During the 1960s and 1970s the International Legal Center, an arm of the Ford Foundation, played a major role in spreading U.S. approaches to legal education throughout the world. Its publication, *Legal Education in a Changing World*, is both a manifesto extolling the virtues of American legal education and a detailed manual on how to imitate it.[106]

Inspired by the belief that they had created a superior kind of legal system and convinced of their own wondrousness, American lawyers devoted substantial efforts to bringing the benefits of American legal thought to the rest of the world.[107] The underlying motives for this effort were "missionary," prompted by beliefs like "Lawyers are the handmaidens of justice ... the technicians of democracy."[108] Canada has been much affected by this missionary zeal. As Gardner notes was the case with many other Third World countries, prospective teachers for Canadian law schools were often sent to the U.S. for a final, ideological polishing. American teachers, likewise, invaded Canadian law schools. These "legal missionaries" scoffed at antiquated legal thinking and promoted the "American vision of the problem-solving legal engineer."[109]

A classic example of the "legal missionary" is Professor William W. Black. Black served his apprenticeship as a missionary when he was a U.S. Peace Corps volunteer at the Faculty of Law of University College, Dar es Salaam, in the late 1960s. He moved to the Faculty of Law at the University of British Columbia and was, subsequently, director of the Court Challenges Program and of the Human Rights Education Centre at the University of Ottawa.[110] Black has also actively propagated the ideology of rights.[111]

Modern Canadian university legal education began in imitation of U.S. models[112] and is, today, a pathetic parody of American legal education.

A RETURN TO CHRISTOPHER LASCH

To use Christopher Lasch's terminology, the Supreme Court today is the most substantial stronghold of the "enlightened." If the whole point of today's class struggle, as Lasch argued, is to deny a voice in policy-making to the "unenlightened," then the anti-popular and anti-democratic role of the Court becomes clearer. If democracy is about "power to the people," it is nearly impossible to describe contemporary Canada as a democracy. A major purpose underlying much Charter litigation has been the relentless effort of the dominant clique to extend its power and its privilege – a goal which is the very opposite of democratic politics. The clique has had unremitting success in the Supreme Court. The classic illustration of this predilection of the dominant clique for using Charter litigation as a means of expanding its wealth and privilege is *Symes* v. *Canada*. In this case, a wealthy Toronto lawyer, whose litigation was subsidized by the state, attempted to use the Charter as the basis for forcing all Canadian taxpayers to subsidize the salary she paid to her personal domestic servant. Such litigation is both an assault on and an affront to democracy.

The Court has gone to considerable lengths to obfuscate the anti-democratic nature of much of its work. In this regard, the judges have attempted to rewrite history. The process which led to the constitutional reforms of 1982 was systematically undemocratic. Yet according to Justice Iacobucci in *Vriend v. Alberta* – one of the Court's most anti-democratic decisions – the adoption of the Charter and the judicial activism which followed it were "choices of the Canadian people through their elected representatives as part of a redefinition of our democracy."[113] This is not accurate. The "Canadian people" were sedulously excluded from the process which led to the adoption of the Charter.

As a conclusion to his unconvincing justification for judicial review, Iacobucci argued that "judges are not acting undemocratically by intervening when there are indications that a legislative or executive decision was not reached in accordance with ... democratic principles."[114] This argument was borrowed, without acknowledgment, from J.H. Ely's *Democracy and Distrust: A Theory of Judicial Review*. Ely taught at the Harvard Law School, and his book is a justification for judicial review. His thesis was that judicial review is justified because it enables judges to intervene in the political process and so ensure that democratic institutions do in fact work as they were intended to.

In the *Vriend* decision, Iacobucci even asserted that the adoption of the Charter as well as *"the consequential remedial role of the courts* were choices of the Canadian people through their elected representatives as part of a redefinition of our democracy" (italics mine). He referred in the same vein to a "new social contract that was democratically chosen."[115]

This is, at best, a bizarre view of how the Charter came to be part of our Constitution. In the same judgment Iacobucci adopted the strange notion that in interpreting the Charter the courts are taking part in a "dialogue among the branches."[116] A more accurate and less mystical view would be to see the interaction between the courts and the other organs of the state as a monologue.

The judges have attempted to deny that they bear any responsibility for the role they have played in redefining Canada's political system. Their consistent plaint has been, "Don't blame us; blame the Charter." Former chief justice Antonio Lamer actually asserted in one judgment that it was "the elected representatives of the people of Canada ... who extended the scope of constitutional adjudication and entrusted the Courts with this new and onerous responsibility."[117] This is simply not true. The judges have also consistently denied personal responsibility for the decisions they make. In the 1970s there was a comedian named Flip Wilson on American television. Wilson had a character named Geraldine. Whenever Geraldine misbehaved, her plaint was "The Devil made me do it." In like fashion, the judges' plaint is "The Charter made me do it."

There is a further anti-democratic tendency which has been fuelled by the Charter. Canada is a federation. Implicit in the very notion of federalism is the idea that there will be variations in the ways in which the different units of the federation deal with the matters which have been constitutionally entrusted to them. Thus, it is to be expected that the laws of one province will be different from the laws of other provinces. Federally-appointed judges, however, have used the Charter to enforce uniformity on the provinces. In *Vriend* v. *Alberta* and *M.* v. *H.*, the Supreme Court used the Charter to force recognition of gay rights on provinces whose legislatures had declined to do so.[118] It is apparent that even fundamental elements of our history and Constitution, such as federalism, will not be allowed to stand in the way of the realization of the orthodoxy. The message of these decisions is that all Canadians must embrace the orthodoxy and the Supreme Court will force them to do so even if their provincial legislators do not wish them to. In other words, while under the Canadian federal system the primary jurisdiction in social policy-making rests with the provincial legislatures, federally-appointed judges have used the Charter as the basis for imposing their own social policy choices on the provinces.

The idea that the Supreme Court will act as the ultimate guarantor of goodness, virtue, and rights, of its taking on the role of constitutional and political *deus ex machina*, has gone a long way toward persuading Canadians to abandon democratic habits. The idea that the courts will look after everything induces passivity amongst citizens. If Canadians began to rediscover politics, they might be able to regain democratic control over the public agenda.[119]

The saddest manifestation of the flight from politics and the abandonment of democratic habits was the Operation Dismantle matter. With the inauguration of Ronald Reagan as U.S. president in 1981, the Cold War entered a new and dangerous phase. Reagan was an even more fanatical cold warrior than J.F. Kennedy and he quickly began inflaming anti-Soviet hysteria through the use of epithets such as the "Evil Empire." Reagan's defence secretary,

Caspar Weinberger, launched a new arms race. The danger of nuclear war became especially acute and the U.S. Air Force asked the Canadian government for permission to conduct tests of air-launched cruise missiles over Canadian territory. In 1983 the Trudeau government gave its permission for these tests to proceed. Many Canadians were deeply opposed to this decision.

There were two reasons for this opposition. First, Canadians were not enthusiastic about the prospect of nuclear war and, second, the decision appeared to be a major blow to Canadian sovereignty. A significant popular movement in opposition to cruise missile testing developed and was both co-ordinated and co-opted by an umbrella organization called Operation Dismantle. Major demonstrations against cruise missile testing occurred all across Canada. But tiring of political action, Operation Dismantle decided to resort to litigation. Its argument, farfetched in the extreme, went like this:

a If the USAF perfects its air-launched cruise missile, the likelihood of nuclear war will be increased substantially;
b if there is nuclear war, many Canadians will die;
c the death of many Canadians would involve the denial of the right to life as guaranteed in section 7 of the Charter;
d cruise missile testing is, therefore, unconstitutional.

Operation Dismantle took this bizarre argument to the Supreme Court and lost.[120] The loss meant both the end of Operation Dismantle and of opposition to USAF testing of cruise missiles over Canada. A significant popular and democratic movement soon disappeared, but, before doing so entirely, devoted whatever energy it had left to attempting to raise enough money to pay its lawyers.[121] Only people blinded by ideology could have believed that litigation might have prevented nuclear war.

Canadians have been seduced into believing that the Constitution and the courts will, magically, take care of everything. In a democracy, however, citizens take care of everything.

ACCOUNTABILITY

It often seems that we, in Canada today, are ruled by buzzwords. A significant buzzword is *accountability*. The idea is that in a democracy persons who make decisions affecting our society should be "accountable" for those decisions. While elected decision-makers are, indeed, accountable – they must face re-election at periodic intervals – judges, because of the principle of judicial independence, are accountable to no one. The Supreme Court has exploited this non-accountability. In *Singh* v. *Canada (Minister of Employment and Immigration)*, Justice Wilson stated that judges would have no regard for the administrative or financial consequences of their decisions. This rejection of accountability is the antithesis of democracy. In 1990 the Court released its decision in *R.* v. *Askov.* In this case the court dealt for the first time with the provision in section 11(a) of the Charter that "any person charged with an offence" has the right to be tried "within a reasonable time." Justice Cory decided that a "delay in a range of some six to eight months between committal and trial might be deemed to be the outside limit of what is reasonable."[122] In response to this judgment, 43,000 criminal charges in Ontario were stayed or withdrawn. These were serious charges, up to and including murder, manslaughter, and sexual assault. In a speech he gave over a year later, Justice Cory said that the Court had not intended its decision to have this effect and was surprised that it had. He said, "But quite frankly we didn't intend the impact it had. We were not aware of the extent of that impact."[123] This, of course, was the famous "I didn't know the gun was loaded" defence.

Such a denial of responsibility for one's decisions is unacceptable.

Even if one accepts the notion, propagated by Justices Wilson, L'Heureux-Dubé, and others, that female judges are the representatives of Canadian women, the lack of accountability again becomes apparent. Canadian women had no say whatsoever in the appointment of these judges, nor are they in any way answerable to Canadian women.

Another element in accountability is the notion of "transparency." Transparency requires that what happens in the institutions of the state be open and visible to citizens. Not surprisingly, the principle of transparency does not seem to apply to the judiciary. There is a federal statute called the Access to Information Act which purports to give citizens "a right of access to information in records under the control of a government institution."[124] The act makes clear that "a government institution" does not mean *any* government institution; it only means such institutions as are specified in Schedule 1 to the act. If a particular institution is not named in Schedule 1, citizens have no right of access to information about it. Significant institutions *not* found in Schedule 1 include the following:

- The Canadian Judicial Council
- The Court Challenges Program
- The National Judicial Institute
- The Supreme Court of Canada

Why are these institutions not mentioned in Schedule 1? Is there something to hide?

Doing research about these institutions can be difficult.[125] I found it hard to get detailed budgetary information about the Supreme Court and, as mentioned earlier, the National Judicial Institute refused to let me see the syllabus for Social Context Education. This lack of transparency with respect to the judicial system is unacceptable in a modern democracy.

3
Philosopher Kings and Queens

This chapter is highly critical of the judges' predilection for turn-ing themselves into public oracles. The reason is simple. Through this practice judges compromise their appearance of being impar-tial and abuse their judicial offices. I will provide many examples of this abuse.

It used to be thought that judges were under an obligation to refrain from expressing themselves publicly on matters of social or political controversy.[1] This restraint on the part of judges was seen as an element in the independence of the judiciary,[2] and each judge had a role to play in maintaining his or her independence. The judges were obliged to act in a way consistent with the public appearance of their impartiality.[3] If a judge took a public stand on a controversial issue, such action might be seen as an expression of bias or partiality, and the public would have reason to doubt the judge's impartiality. Judges, however, were not expected to have no opinions whatsoever. Rather, they were not to exploit their special position and special status in order to give themselves a public platform.[4] They were to respect the limits and constraints which were inevitable features of their role as judges. They were to give the impression of being above the political fray. Indeed, in 1982 a public statement by Justice Thomas Berger of the Supreme Court of British Columbia led to a complaint to the Canadian Judi-cial Council and, eventually, his resignation from the bench.[5] That was more than twenty years ago. Canadian judges no longer seem to feel constrained to avoid public pronouncements. In 1991 a public debate broke out between judges over the question of whether they should make public pronouncements. Justice John

Sopinka of the Supreme Court said they could and should. Justice Sydney Robins of the Ontario Court of Appeal said that when judges go public it "threatens the impartiality of the judiciary and public confidence in the legal system."[6]

The judges of the Supreme Court have become minor celebrities. This celebrity is both national and international. A recent report to Parliament about the Court's activities noted that "the Court is an increasingly active member of the international community of judges and jurists" and added, "the benefits that derive from the visits of the Supreme Court of Canada judges outside of Canada have been widely acknowledged."[7] They seem to be constantly in motion, criss-crossing the country from conference to conference and from law school to law school. With this celebrity has come a tendency to forego impartiality. Justice Bertha Wilson was an inveterate speech maker who expressly embraced a feminist perspective in her speeches. In one speech she asserted that all judges were inevitably biased by their sex.[8] As noted in chapter 2, in a speech Justice L'Heureux-Dubé gave in 1998, she asserted that equality should be preferred over fundamental freedoms.[9] As a matter of law this assertion is incorrect. In *Dagenais* v. *Canadian Broadcasting Corp.*, Chief Justice Lamer concluded that there was no "hierarchy" of rights in the Charter and that all the guarantees in the Charter should be afforded "equal status." L'Heureux-Dubé's assertion is a straightforward expression of bias.

When looking at public pronouncements by judges, we should specially note a report on gender equality in the legal profession which Bertha Wilson prepared for the Canadian Bar Association in 1993.[10] This report gives rise to legitimate concerns about Justice Wilson's impartiality and about her intellectual integrity. Wilson began her report with these observations:

A *white* view of the world is not neutral.
A *masculine* view of the world is not neutral.[11]
A *heterosexual* view of the world is not neutral.[12]

I do not know what special powers Wilson possessed which allowed her to know that all white people think alike, as do all males and all heterosexuals. Presumably, she possessed other special powers which allowed her to penetrate these monolithic forms of thinking. Reading those words I cannot help thinking of

Josef Goebbels denouncing Einstein for practising what Goebbels called "Jewish physics." The notion "Jewish physics" comes from the same epistemology and makes about as much sense as does the notion "white view of the world." What Wilson was expressing here was the essence of Nazi epistemology. There is no such thing as the individual. Each human being is reduced to a function of the colour of his or her skin and the shape of his or her genitals. Wilson stated in her judgment in *R. v. Morgentaler* (1988) that "it is probably impossible for a man to respond, even imaginatively, to such a dilemma [the one faced by a pregnant woman] ... because he can relate to it only by objectifying it, thereby eliminating the subjective elements of the female psyche which are at the heart of the dilemma."[13] Although not acknowledged in the judgment, this idea, which is a clear expression of a gender-based apartheid world view, is straight out of Carol Gilligan.[14] In her *Morgentaler* decision, Wilson did engage in some facile and laughable speculation about how men and women think. Through her suggestion that a man could not understand the dilemmas confronting a pregnant woman, Wilson appeared to be suggesting that a person of one sex cannot understand the way a person of the other sex thinks.[15] If this be correct, she, as a woman, could not possibly understand how a man would think and her whole argument collapses. This solipsistic view of the world logically denies the possibility of democratic politics. This speculation revealed both Wilson's presumption and, as I interpret it, the banality of her thought.

In the examples quoted above, Wilson was expressing something which is obvious. I would think that most people understand that each individual's experience is bound to affect the way he or she thinks. Even if one accepts that each human being is inherently biased, the task facing judges is evident. Judges must recognize their own subjectivity and their own biases and struggle to put both behind them in the making of their decisions. Justice Wilson evidently rejected this notion and preferred to wallow in her own subjectivity. In so doing she was denying the fundamental intellectual responsibility cast upon judges in a democracy. However, the Supreme Court appears to share her approach.

In *R. v. R.D.S.*, the Supreme Court recently approved the notion that judges might rely on their own subjectivity in approaching cases before them: this was called "contextualized judging."[16] The

Court noted that judges "will undoubtedly approach the task of judging from their varied perspectives." Not only did the Court not state that the judge must attempt to put his or her own personal biases aside, but it was prepared to see the judge being guided by his or her own subjectivity. In another classic statement of judicial double-think, the court decided that judicial subjectivity could be "an important aid to judicial impartiality."[17] The Court appeared, in reaching this conclusion, to accept Wilson's notion of the judge as a delegate or representative of his or her own community. In *R. v. R.D.S.* the Court effectively abandoned the notion that judges should strive to be impartial and to decide cases solely on the basis of their facts and the applicable law. The whole idea of principled decision-making has thus been abandoned.

There has been extensive academic commentary about *R. v. R.D.S.*, much of it tending to support the apartheid perspective on judging expressed by the Supreme Court. The most aggressive statement of this perspective was expressed by Richard Devlin and Dianne Pothier.[18] The authors took issue with the notion that "individual witnesses must be treated by judges on an individualized basis without regard to their group characteristics." In a similar vein they questioned whether it is "possible for a person from one context to come to terms with the position of another." And they continued, "our racialized and gendered experiences make a difference in the way we understand the world." This is a classic statement of an apartheid world view. There are no individuals. Human beings are simply functions of certain ascriptive criteria like skin colour and the shape of their genitals. The authors added, in order to dispel any doubt as to their true position, "all attempts to cross the structural patterns that divide us (whether it be on the basis of race, gender or (dis) ability) are troubling."[19] I do not wish to fall into these two authors' way of thinking, but I would surmise that Devlin's tribal consciousness may well stem from the fact that he grew up and studied in Northern Ireland.[20]

Justice L'Heureux-Dubé has given her blessing to this apartheid view of judging. In an article, she noted the difficulties that arise in judging from the "lack of shared reality between judges and parties."[21]

Justice Wilson's previously mentioned report on gender in the legal profession was shot through with horror stories about the ways in which women, at every level of the profession, were subjected to oppression and discrimination. The report was strikingly short on evidence to support any of her assertions. She stated that female judges were regularly harassed, treated unfairly, and discriminated against by their male colleagues. In response to this, sixteen female judges of the superior courts in British Columbia wrote an open letter to Wilson, in which they denied that any of them had ever been subjected to such behaviour. The B.C. judges noted the complete absence of evidence to support Justice Wilson's sweeping assertions and called upon her to provide some. Justice Mary Southin of the B.C. Court of Appeal wrote a letter to the editor of the *Vancouver Sun* in which she stated, "I have never been the victim of any sort of discrimination and I have not observed, nor had reported to me, any sort of discrimination against the other members of either court [B.C. Supreme Court and Court of Appeal] who happen to be women."[22] Wilson did not respond to this letter.

The methodological deficiencies in the Wilson report are apparent in the sections dealing with legal education.[23] In these sections, as in others, the report relied heavily on responses to questionnaires. Some serious methodological flaws immediately became apparent. The committee mailed questionnaires to all women teaching in Canadian university law schools and to an equal number of men similarly employed. There had been considerable advance publicity surrounding the Wilson committee and its work and Wilson's politics were very well known throughout the legal profession as a result of her judgments and the many speeches she had made. It is inconceivable to me that there was anyone, male or female, teaching in a law faculty in Canada who did not know what the Wilson committee was and, more important, the directions toward which it was predisposed. To put it bluntly, every recipient of the questionnaire must have known what the right answers were. Further, the respondents to the questionnaire were self-selected. Those who received the questionnaire who wished to return it to the committee did so; those who did not, didn't.

The questionnaire (which was not reproduced in the published version of the report) asked respondents to give subjective responses to a series of open-ended questions. They were asked whether they had experienced, observed, or been made aware of unwanted teasing, joking, or comments directed at themselves or female colleagues by professors or students. The responses to questions such as this were then treated as proof of the accuracy of the facts asserted. If female professors felt their opinions were not given "appropriate weight," the mere expression of that feeling was taken as proof that, indeed, their opinions were not receiving appropriate weight. This methodology neatly avoids any questions about the content of these opinions and whether they merited "appropriate weight," whatever that might mean.

The report was littered with unattributed anecdotal comments, the veracity and accuracy of which, since they were purportedly made by women, were assumed to be beyond question, but which certainly could not be tested. Contentious assertions made throughout the report are given the authority of footnote numbers. When the footnote is consulted, it usually turns out to be a reference to an article by a noted feminist. For example, reference is made to an article by Professor Bruce Feldthusen, formerly of the Faculty of Law at the University of Western Ontario, and now dean of the Faculty of Law (Common Law) at the University of Ottawa, called "The Gender Wars: Where the Boys are." The article is pretentious, exaggerated, self-serving, and riddled with errors. He is forthright enough to admit, triumphantly, that he does not observe the norms of scholarly discourse: "Often, I write first and research afterwards," he stated.[24]

Wilson's report abounds with assertions of this quality: "A substantial percentage of women had heard professors make derogatory or sexist comments about feminists, at least occasionally."[25] What is a "substantial percentage"? What were the comments? What does "at least occasionally" mean? The report also makes assertions without offering any evidence at all: "Women, particularly junior faculty, are marginalised through poorly located offices."[26] Again, fundamental methodological questions are simply ignored. What is meant by "marginalised"? According to what criteria was it determined that a particular office was "poorly located"? Was a physical survey conducted of every law faculty building in Canada to determine which offices were "poorly located" and the percentage of those offices occupied by female faculty members?

Where evidence is given to suggest a conclusion adverse to the orthodoxy, the evidence is rejected. The report noted on one page that the proportion of "visible minorities" in law schools was twice the proportion of visible minorities in Canadian society as a whole,[27] but on another page talked about "discrimination" in law school admissions policies, asserting that the Law School Admission Test "adversely affects students from non-Anglo-Saxon backgrounds."[28] No evidence was presented for this assertion, but I suppose everyone knows how difficult it is for persons of Jewish, Irish, or Scottish ancestry to get into law school.

The report also suggested in several places that criticism of or disagreement with feminism or feminist ideas should be regarded as a form of sexual harassment.

Another incident raised further doubts about Wilson's integrity. In late 1974 the United Church established a Commission on Abortion and appointed Bertha Wilson as the commission's chair. Wilson was later appointed to the Ontario Court of Appeal in December 1975 and resigned from the commission.[29] She was, therefore, not a member of the commission when it made its final report. While the commission recommended that the section of the Criminal Code dealing with abortion be removed,[30] its recommendations did not go nearly as far as the position which resulted from Wilson's *R. v. Morgentaler* (1988) decision – the commission stopped short of recommending unrestricted abortion. Even though Justice Wilson was not a member of the United Church commission when it made its report, it is reasonable to assume that she was sympathetic to its generally pro-choice drift. It therefore seems fair to surmise that Wilson's mind was made up before the hearing in the *Morgentaler* appeal began.[31] One commentator stated that her judgment "reads like a manifesto issued by a pro-choice group."[32]

In 1992 Chief Justice Antonio Lamer spoke at the law graduation at the University of Toronto. In his speech he expressed his distaste for democracy – a political system which was deficient because it did not sufficiently guarantee something Lamer was pleased to call "human flourishing." The chief justice suggested that a benevolent absolute monarchy might be preferable to democracy. Once again, the banality of the minds of the judges was revealed. Every first-year political science student understands the nature of the problem with a benevolent absolute monarchy, but Canada's chief justice apparently did not. The simple problem is this: if the monarch is absolute, how can the people ensure that the monarch remains benevolent?

None of the judges' words and actions thus far mentioned in this chapter is likely to promote the idea of an impartial, unbiased judiciary. They all suggest a judiciary unprepared to accept limits on its activities. Justice L'Heureux-Dubé was consistently the worst offender in this regard.

In 1998 the American Bar Association held its annual meeting in Toronto and L'Heureux-Dubé made no fewer than three speeches to the assembled throng of American lawyers. One of the three was entitled "Are We There Yet? Gender Equality in the Law of Canada." In this speech, L'Heureux-Dubé manifested her contempt for the notion that judges should avoid commenting publicly on issues of political controversy. This was a highly political speech. In it L'Heureux-Dubé sounded more like a political activist than a judge, as this extended excerpt will make clear:

I think that these cases[33] especially are significant for their recognition of how a full and proper realization of equality rights may require that they take priority, in certain circumstances, over other fundamental rights. Indeed, the broad scope accorded to equality would ring hollow if it were to be subordinated to every other value a court recognizes as legitimate.

The case of R. v. Lavallee represents another significant development in the area of criminal law and equality rights. It constitutes an express recognition by the Supreme Court of Canada that the law must be reappraised where the principle it has developed reflects norms which may not fit many women's experiences or realities. In Lavallee, the Court was called upon to decide whether the defence of self-defence was available to a women who had killed her husband after he had repeatedly threatened to kill her. At trial, the history of the abusive relationship was presented and expert evidence on battered woman's syndrome was adduced. Wilson J., for the Court, indicated that the criminal law must take into account the differing experiences and perspectives of those affected by the law. By questioning the appropriateness of the traditional "reasonable man" standard to the case at bar, she invoked the language of substantive equality. Thus, even though s. 15 was not formally at issue in this appeal, its goals animated the Court's decision. Lavallee clearly rejects the old view of sexual equality that women have the right to be treated equally to men only to the extent that they are the same as men. It replaces that view with the recognition that sometimes different people must be treated differently in order for substantive equality ultimately to prevail.

I think that *Lavallee* was important for another reason. Namely, I think that it sets perhaps the best example we have to date of the need to re-examine longstanding laws, institutions and assumptions through the relatively new prism of substantive equality. *Lavallee* constituted a recognition by the majority of the Court of an approach that I subsequently took in the minority in *Seaboyer*. Equality, after all, is not self-contained like other rights. In order for it to be properly realized, it must permeate our thinking. In fact, if we truly deem the values of substantive equality to be so fundamental to our society that they merit constitutional entrenchment, then that examination is long-overdue.

Of course, there are still equality rights claims being raised directly to challenge government legislation or action. More straightforward cases like *Benner v. Canada (Secretary of State)* illustrate that, even after over a decade of constitutionally entrenched equality rights, there are still some blatantly discriminatory laws on the books that need to be reformed. The reality of the process of making all of Canadian law "equality" sensitive, is that it will take many more years to work out.

The value of a sensitive, contextual approach to equality has nowhere been more evident than in the area of employment law. Indeed, although not directly applying s. 15, some of the greatest strides in the achievement of gender equality through the application of substantive equality principles can be found in successful discrimination in employment complaints by women under human rights legislation. Two particularly instructive examples come immediately to mind. The first is the case of *Janzen v. Platy Enterprises Ltd.*, where the Court had to consider whether sexual harassment was a form of sex discrimination within the meaning of the *Manitoba Human Rights Act*. The Manitoba Court of Appeal had accepted the employer's argument that sexual harassment was gender-neutral, and not a form of categorical discrimination against women. However, the Supreme Court undertook an examination of the context of sexual harassment, and noted that "those with the power to harass sexually will predominantly be male and those facing the greatest risk of harassment will tend to be female." At the same time the Court ruled that there could be discrimination even if all members of the target group were not treated uniformly. As a result, the Court concluded that sexual harassment constitutes sex discrimination and could be addressed through the remedial mechanisms in human rights legislation.

Similarly, in the second example of *Brooks*, the Court adopted a contextual approach in determining that the exclusion of pregnant women from an employer's accident and sickness plan is a form of sex discrimination. In reaching the conclusion that to impose the costs of pregnancy exclusively on women did, in fact, constitute sexual discrimination, Chief Justice Dickson observed as follows: "That those who bear children and benefit society as a whole thereby should not be economically or socially disadvantaged seems to bespeak the obvious. It is only women who bear children; no man can become pregnant." There is no doubt in my mind that he spoke the language of substantive equality in refusing to impose all the costs of pregnancy upon only half of the population. In reaching these conclusions, the Court overruled its earlier decision on the same issue in *Bliss*. Thus, *Brooks* underscores the need to re-examine existing doctrines in the light of our new, contextually sensitive understanding of equality.

The evolution from *Bliss*, decided under the *Bill of Rights*, to cases such as *Brooks* and *Janzen* is astonishing. In my view, these cases truly represent a high point along the road to equality and provide a sensitive examination of what is required for the attainment of substantive equality.

Finally, I would like to briefly touch on the common law as one of the last great, largely untouched frontiers awaiting cultivation by equality minded jurists. Commentators have pointed out, correctly in my opinion, that the common law as a system essentially presumes inequality, and does not question in any way the correctness of treating people differently from one another on any basis. Efforts to invoke common law principles of contract, tort or property to, for instance, attack racially discriminatory business practices or deeds, have in the past, met almost universally with failure.

Nowhere did this point become more clear than in the contrast between the approaches taken by the Ontario Court of Appeal and Supreme Court in *Bhadauria v. Seneca College*, just prior to the entrenchment of our *Charter* in 1981. The plaintiff alleged that racial discrimination had caused her to be denied an employment offer. Rather than filing a complaint under the *Ontario Human Rights Code*, however, she filed a civil suit against the College premised upon the existence of the tort of discrimination. Madam Justice Wilson concluded for the Court of Appeal that such a common law tort did indeed exist, but she was overruled in this respect by the Supreme Court of Canada. Although Chief Justice Laskin commended her attempt to, in his words, "advance the common law," he concluded that her finding was foreclosed by the legislative initiative of the *Human Rights Code*. By referring to the tort of discrimination as an "advance of the common law," it is clear that this Court was of the opinion that none had ever previously existed.

David Lepofsky, a well-known Canadian human rights specialist, has commented on this fact as well. He makes the valuable observation that while the common law has shown the ability to evolve over time to create other new doctrines that meaningfully responded to changes in society and social values, it has shown an inability to do so where discrimination is concerned. For instance, principles of equity, amongst them fiduciary duties, arose very early out of the recognition that there were situations and relationships in which the assumptions underlying contract and tort – namely that persons act autonomously and in their own best interests – were not always appropriate. Far later, doctrines such as unconscionability and duress evolved to temper the absolute freedom to contract in circumstance where the value of fairness was now seen as outweighing the value of certainty of contract. Why is it, I ask you, that the common law could accommodate changes in our attitudes toward the protection of property and contractual interests but failed so miserably with respect to human rights?

In part, I sense, the common law was slow to change in this respect not because it lacked the *capacity* for change, but rather because it lacked the *motivation* to do so. It may have been assumed by advantaged groups to be to their advantage to perpetuate their position of relative advantage. After all, the direct consequences of discrimination rarely heap upon the discriminator. I submit that it is not until the latter half of this century that we gained greater awareness of our interdependence as a society and of the *indirect* consequences of discrimination. Only then did we become aware of the costs of inequality, and only then did the motivation for true equality begin to set in. Crime, poverty, unemployment, lower quality of life: few will now dispute that all of these problems have at least some of their roots in inequality. Thus, while working to stamp out inequality will not make these problems go away, it is clear that ignoring inequality may very well aggravate them. As Madam Justice Rosalie Silberman Abella has observed, we have no business figuring out the cost of justice until we can figure out the cost of injustice.

Ironically, the common law's snail-like response to inequality was, to some degree, self-perpetuating. Early attempts to remedy inequality through human rights legislation were frustrated by the common law presumption against legislative interference with common law rules. When the Supreme Court eventually held this presumption to be inappropriate in the context of human rights legislation, I would argue that its decision was motivated by the necessity to respond to changing social values and goals. The practice of re-examining entrenched wisdoms and assumptions through the prism of equality rights begins with something as unspectacular as qualifying the presumption against legislative interference with the common law.

Perhaps the greatest hurdle that remains ahead of us in this respect is the challenge that our commitment to substantive equality poses to conceptions of procedural equality entrenched in the rule of law itself. I fear that an over-zealous commitment to procedural equality may sometimes obfuscate the fact that occasionally, as was illustrated in *Lavallee*, differences must be recognised and accommodated in order ultimately to achieve equal treatment by, under and before the law. In a similar vein, Catharine MacKinnon suggests that many of the societal structures put into place to remedy inequality are themselves flawed in that the referent is always male. I think that both of these points merit far more attention than they have thus far received, both from lawmakers and from the legal community generally.

This speech can only give rise to reasonable apprehensions that, in her judging, L'Heureux-Dubé is biased. Justice L'Heureux-Dubé even employed rhetoric which suggested she saw herself as being at war. She adverted to "the task of rooting out inequality and injustice from our society" and referred to "the main battleground of equality rights litigation." Such language does not suggest the sort of sober, reasoned detachment one ought to expect from a judge of our highest court.

Even more disturbing, and further re-enforcing the sense that it was a political activist speaking, was L'Heureux-Dubé's disavowal of any notion that "equality" had a clear meaning. She asserted that "equality is a term that ... means nothing. It has no universally recognized inherent or intrinsic content." This statement is reminiscent of the approach advocated by Diana Majury, a feminist law professor with the Department of Law at Carleton University. Writing in the *Wisconsin Women's Law Journal*, Majury agreed that equality should mean whatever women want it to mean: "I argue that it is in women's interest to refuse to subscribe to or commit themselves to any single meaning of equality. Feminist advocates need to learn to use the equality discourse on behalf of women in as many and as diverse situations as the term can bear. The needs and experiences of women will dictate the meaning of equality in each particular context. It is these needs and experiences which need to be brought into the open and promoted, not some reified idea of equality."[34] In another speech, L'Heureux-Dubé spoke approvingly of Majury's ideas on equality.[35] Majury is famous for having published an article about a judicial decision which, as she noted in the article, she had not read.[36]

Was L'Heureux-Dubé, in her 1998 ABA speech, suggesting that equality, which may well loom large in litigation before her, will mean whatever she decides it is to mean? If she was, this would be a breathtaking expression of judicial arrogance.

L'Heureux-Dubé has regularly embraced a popular, but inaccurate, view of Canadian history. She has suggested that traditionally Canada was a place where persons other than "white, able-bodied men" suffered vast legal disability. In this essentially undergraduate understanding of Canada and its history, for decades this was a truly awful, oppressive place; then, that watershed in Canadian history occurred – the Charter – and we began, thanks to our judges, to be transformed into a decent, respectable country. Canada, in this view, only became interested in the promotion of equality with the coming into force of section 15 of the Charter in April 1985.

Perhaps I am exaggerating when I associate L'Heureux-Dubé's thinking with undergraduate thought. Consider the following:

And as you reflect on these ideas, I ask you to keep this in mind: where equality is concerned each and every one of us has a role to play. Remember that equality is about attitude and note that, social change happens one individual at a time. I invite you to challenge stereotypes and to question your assumptions, and I ask you to help others do the same.

Equality must not only be part of our thinking, it must be part of our living. If we embrace equality as a culture and encourage others to do the same, you will be one step closer to creating a society in which you, your children and your children's children need not fear disempowerment or oppression. That, I call justice for all.[37]

If my thoughts were that banal, I would keep them to myself. I am not here being critical of the notion of equality, but of L'Heureux-Dubé's expression of her political biases. Her 1998 speech was a presumptuous rewriting of Canadian history and an insult to our Canadian forebears who fought for fairness and reform. It was a further insult to the early Canadian judiciary which, though imperfect, made decisions which promoted fairness and equality.

Did Justice L'Heureux-Dubé believe she was the first Canadian judge ever to favour equality?

In her speech, L'Heureux-Dubé congratulated herself on her dissent in *Symes* v. *Canada*, where she decided that all Canadian taxpayers should subsidize the salary a Toronto lawyer paid her nanny. She likewise congratulated herself for her dissent in *R.* v. *Seaboyer*. In that judgment, she was prepared to deny a man charged with sexually assaulting a woman the ability to defend himself against a criminal charge. This approach was based very much on arguments advanced by the American law professor Catharine MacKinnon, whom L'Heureux-Dubé quoted approvingly. MacKinnon has recently proven too extreme even for American feminists and it is strange to observe the degree to which L'Heureux-Dubé identified herself with MacKinnon.[38] Consistent with her judgment in *Seaboyer*, in her speech L'Heureux-Dubé also asserted that "equality rights may ... take priority, in certain circumstances, over fundamental rights." This seems to me to be about as close as a Canadian judge has ever come to a public affirmation of bias. I interpret that statement to mean that if L'Heureux-Dubé were to hear a case where there was an apparent conflict between a male litigant's claim to a fundamental right and a female litigant's claim to equality, she would decide in favour of the female litigant.

Still in her speech, L'Heureux-Dubé reaffirmed her attachment to a simplified view of the world by asserting that "crime, poverty, unemployment have at least some of their roots in inequality." The way to have a better world, she implied, was more litigation under section 15 of the Charter.

In February 1999 L'Heureux-Dubé became involved in a squalid public mudslinging match with a judge of the Alberta Court of Appeal. This unseemly incident can hardly have strengthened the public perception of her impartiality. As a result of her judgment in *R.* v. *Ewanchuk*, a complaint about her was made to the Canadian Judicial Council. The council dismissed the complaint, holding that judges should feel free to express themselves in their judgments and that, while L'Heureux-Dubé's language was "robust," it was not improper.

Ewanchuk was a prosecution for sexual assault. The accused was acquitted at trial and the Crown appealed to the Alberta Court of Appeal, which upheld the acquittal by a two-to-one majority. The

Crown entered a further appeal to the Supreme Court of Canada. The accused had invited the seventeen-year-old female complainant into a trailer, ostensibly to discuss a job, where he initiated sexual contact with her. He attempted to raise what he described as the defence of "implied consent," arguing that the complainant's behaviour amounted to an implied consent to his advances. The Supreme Court was adamant and forthright in concluding that there could be no defence of implied consent in a sexual assault prosecution. The Supreme Court allowed the Crown's appeal and substituted a conviction. In her concurring judgment, L'Heureux-Dubé was critical of one of the judges, Justice McClung of the Alberta Court of Appeal, suggesting that his judgment dismissing the Crown's appeal had been based on "myths" and "stereotypes" and was "discriminatory." The specific elements of McClung's judgment with which L'Heureux-Dubé took issue were as follows: McClung noted that the seventeen-year-old complainant was the mother of a six-month old child and was co-habiting with her boyfriend. He also observed that when the complainant entered the trailer of the accused she did not "present herself ... in a bonnet and crinolines."[39] These remarks triggered L'Heureux-Dubé's intemperate response. She intimated that McClung's "impartiality" might have been "compromised" by "biased assumptions." At the risk of labouring the point, the Court's decision in *Ewanchuk* was simply another expression of its attachment to the reigning orthodoxy. McClung's sin was that he departed from the orthodoxy. It was truly breathtaking for L'Heureux-Dubé to have publicly questioned another judge's impartiality.

L'Heureux-Dubé's judgment in *Ewanchuk* and her subsequent public remarks were the object of criticism. Prominent criminal lawyer Edward L. Greenspan wrote, "Madam Justice L'Heureux-Dubé has shown an astounding insensitivity and an inability to conceive of any concepts outside her own terms of reference and has thereby disgraced the Supreme Court."[40] Alan Gold, president of the Criminal Lawyers' Association, was quoted as saying of her judgment in *Ewanchuk*, "This radical feminist judgment is just extremely disappointing in 1999."[41] An editorial in the *Ottawa Citizen* added that, "She showed how far her desire to entrench extreme feminist ideology in law now guides her reasoning. Her decision reads less like a Supreme Court judgment than a manifesto in feminist legal theory."[42] Speaking in the Senate of Canada on 4 March 1999, Senator Anne Cools stated that Justice L'Heureux-Dubé's judgment and subsequent conduct had the effect of "placing the administration of justice itself in disrepute."[43]

One must enquire about the effect which L'Heureux-Dubé's behaviour throughout this wretched incident had on the public perception of the impartiality of judges of the Supreme Court of Canada. For one judge to make this sort of comment about another judge was unusual. McClung responded by writing a letter to the editor of the *National Post*. In the letter he reiterated his opinion that Ewanchuk was not guilty and added, gratuitously, that because of L'Heureux-Dubé's comments he could understand the growing male suicide rate in Quebec.[44] As it turned out, L'Heureux-Dubé's husband had killed himself twenty years earlier. Mudslinging between the two judges continued in the media for some time thereafter, with McClung eventually apologizing to L'Heureux-Dubé. L'Heureux-Dubé later spoke at a public conference in Ottawa at which she revealed she was active in an organization which sought to "teach judges in developing countries how to interpret international laws against domestic violence and laws upholding equality."[45]

The Canadian Judicial Council is a committee of senior superior court judges which was established under the Judges Act[46] to exercise supervisory jurisdiction over other superior court judges. Complaints were made to the council about both McClung and L'Heureux-Dubé. As mentioned above, the council dismissed the complaint against L'Heureux-Dubé. However, it reprimanded McClung,[47] and did so despite the fact that it has no statutory authority to do anything other than recommend that a judge be removed from office.

In response to the complaint against her to the Canadian Judicial Council, L'Heureux-Dubé wrote a letter to the council on 11 March 1999 in which she stated, "I am not now, nor have I ever been, to the best of my recollection, associated with the International Federation of Women Lawyers." Closer analysis strongly suggests that when Justice L'Heureux-Dubé wrote her letter she was not telling the truth or her memory was beginning to fail her. In 1981, several years before her appointment to the Supreme Court, L'Heureux-Dubé was the Canadian vice-president of the International Federation of Women Lawyers (FIDA). To be fair, L'Heureux-

Dubé did not actively pursue involvement in FIDA, nor was she active in the organization after 1981.

Former chief justice Lamer once held that "judges must develop a state of mind marked by serenity, detachment, levelheadedness and moderation. Without cutting themselves off from human reality and society, they must remain on the sidelines to some extent."[48] Based on her public pronouncements, L'Heureux-Dubé appeared to have abandoned all effort at reaching the standard of "serenity" and "detachment."

If a country is to have a truly independent judiciary, each citizen must feel that the courts would address his or her case fairly and impartially. A Canadian citizen who read some of L'Heureux-Dubé's public pronouncements might reasonably doubt the extent to which she would be prepared to act in a fair and impartial fashion. In August 2000, L'Heureux-Dubé gave a speech to the annual meeting of the Canadian Bar Association. In this speech she attacked critics of the judiciary, who, she claimed, were undermining the "courage" judges required in order to make "controversial decisions" and, thus, threatening the independence of the judiciary.[49] L'Heureux-Dubé apparently believed that Canada still had an independent judiciary and that there might be judges who would have the "courage" to render decisions which went counter to the orthodoxy. I believe there is little evidence to support either proposition. She returned to these issues in a speech she delivered in August 2001 when she admonished critics of the judiciary to, "shut up."[50]

As far as I can determine from reading her decisions and her speeches, L'Heureux-Dubé's approach to judging appeared to be this: Before the hearing began, she would make up her mind as to which party she favoured. The arguments and evidence advanced by the other party, the one she did not favour, would be dismissed as "myths" and "stereotypes." Buttressing herself with heavy doses of academic articles written by feminist authors, L'Heureux-Dubé would, as I interpret her approach, then write a judgment reaching the conclusion she had already decided upon in advance of the hearing.

What I am attempting to suggest here is that L'Heureux-Dubé did not approach her judicial responsibilities in an impartial fashion. In two cases the Supreme Court suggested two questions that should be addressed in determining the presence or absence of impartiality. In the first case it was put this way: "The question is whether a well-informed and reasonable observer would perceive that judicial independence had been compromised."[51] In the other, the question is implied in Chief Justice Lamer's observation that, "The overall objective of guaranteeing judicial independence is to ensure a reasonable perception of impartiality."[52] I find it impossible to maintain the perception that L'Heureux-Dubé might have been impartial. She had so undermined the perception that she was impartial that a Canadian journalist could write, "The authorities and quotes L'Heureux-Dubé chooses to illustrate her judgments and speeches are relentlessly anti-male, illiberal and anti-equality."[53]

Justice L'Heureux-Dubé, as if to confirm her biases, spoke at a "Persons' Day" fundraising breakfast organized by LEAF in Sudbury, Ontario, on 22 October 2000. She, thus, publicly identified herself with an organization which regularly appears before the Court.

"Persons' day" is a further feminist misrepresentation of Canadian history. On 22 October 1929, the Judicial Committee issued its decision in *Edwards* v. *Canada (A.G.)*. The Board decided that the word "persons" in section 24 of the British North America Act included women and that women could, therefore, be appointed to the Senate of Canada. Feminists have attempted to turn 22 October into a feminist festival. The suggestion, which is implicit in "Persons' Day," and which is totally false, is that prior to the Judicial Committee's 1929 decision women were simply not persons in Canada.

In early 2001, Chief Justice McLachlin released a public statement in which she affirmed her commitment to the basic purpose of the Court: "We are not there to respond to this or that particular public pressure at a particular moment. Our mission is simply to try to give the best answers we can to the very difficult questions that Canadian men, women and governments put before us."[54]

In January 2001, Justice Bastarache made some public utterances which were unusual. In an interview[55] he expressed the general reservation that the Supreme Court was too political: "I think that legal principle is different from legal policy and that policy is for Parliament and principle is for the courts." He continued, "I don't think that we have a mandate to sort of define social policy for Canada."

He was critical of the Court's decision in *R. v. Marshall* – the case which raised a question of the extent to which Canadian law applied to Aboriginal persons – stating, "the court was maybe seen as being unduly favourable to the native position in all cases and that it sort of has an agenda."[56]

Justice Bastarache's remarks led to his being subjected to criticism. Bastarache had committed the appalling sin of publicly breaking with the orthodoxy. He was vigorously criticized by a few law professors, those most resolute defenders of orthodoxy. These critics included Allan Hutchinson of the Osgoode Hall Law School[57] and Don Stuart of the Law Faculty at Queen's University.[58] As would be expected from Canadian law professors, neither individual's criticism was particularly articulate. Hutchinson revealed that "it's all politics," while Stuart commented, "I don't think you have another instance that I can remember ever in 30 years that a judge on the Supreme Court has actually not only expressed sort of overall views." Stuart, as is noted in chapter 7, has on occasion expressed counter-orthodox opinions. How dare a mere judge of the Supreme Court depart from the truth as revealed in our law schools?

In April 2001, Chief Justice McLachlin made another sensible public statement. She suggested that the Court should end its "equality" frolic and show some restraint in dealing with claims based on section 15 of the Charter.[59] One could have expected a firestorm of criticism from the academy. Around the same time, former chief justice Lamer made a public utterance which suggested that he had taken leave of his senses. He attacked the Alliance party for "yelping" about the Court and the Charter.[60] He added that the Charter was introduced by Parliament, which, of course, it was not, and noted that he was not the one who "crafted" the Charter, as if anyone had ever suggested that he was.

In March 2002, Justice Arbour gave an interview in which she was highly critical of governments for not providing sufficient funding for legal aid.[61] Reduced legal aid funding is a hot political issue in both Ontario and B.C. Her comments sounded very much like those of a politician running for office.

4

Who Are These People?

The formal qualifications for becoming a judge of the Supreme Court are few. No certificates or examinations are required. The Supreme Court Act[1] stipulates that, in order to be eligible for an appointment, a person must be a lawyer and have been one for at least ten years.[2] Under the act, three of the nine judges must be members of the bar of the province of Quebec.[3] Certain conventions[4] have developed concerning the six other seats on the Court. Three judges are to be from Ontario, two from the West, and one from the Atlantic region; it also appears that, of the two judges from the West, one should be from B.C. While appointments to the Court are, in a formal sense, made by the governor-in-council, the practice is that the decision to appoint a particular person is made by the prime minister. Judges are often chosen from amongst sitting members of provincial courts of appeal and the Federal Court of Appeal, but there is no requirement that a person have had any judicial experience before going to the Supreme Court.[5] The entire Canadian non-system for the selection of judges was once described by former chief justice Brian Dickson as "mysterious."[6] For many years, political patronage was the dominant factor in the making of judicial appointments.[7] Patronage has not been a factor in Supreme Court appointments for decades. Nonetheless, the prime minister has an untrammelled discretion in deciding who to appoint. There is no formal consultation process, nor is the prime minister ever required to justify a particular appointment. No Superior Court judge has been removed from office since Confederation and, therefore, a person appointed to the Supreme Court can expect to stay there until age seventy-five.[8]

To begin to understand something about the people who are appointed to the Court, I will turn to some earlier research which I published in 1988.[9] We begin by looking at the backgrounds of the judges who sat on the Court between 1949 and 1988. The first thing to note about the thirty people who sat on the Court during these years is that twenty-eight of them were men. And even with the first woman to become a member of the Court, the homogeneity that is the overriding characteristic of this group asserted itself. Bertha Wilson, prior to her appointment to the Ontario Court of Appeal in 1975, was a partner, albeit the first female partner, in the prestigious Toronto firm of Osler, Hoskin and Harcourt.

Only four of the judges went to private schools. It was in their higher education that the judges received their most intensive class socialization. Four were Rhodes Scholars. Two more went to Oxford without Rhodes Scholarships. Curiously, none of the judges attended Cambridge. Five attended Harvard Law School. Only one, Locke, received no institutional legal education at all.

Eleven of the judges played an active part in politics. The activity ranged from being a federal minister (Abbott), through being an advisor to the prime minister of Canada (Beetz and La Forest), to holding office as a provincial attorney general (J.W. Estey and Rand), to being elected to a provincial legislature, or being a defeated candidate, and finally to merely being publicly identified with a party. It is noteworthy that no one who had been identified with the CCF or the NDP has been appointed to the Supreme Court of Canada. Indeed, when Hall was a Conservative candidate in the 1948 Saskatchewan election, he suggested that T.C. Douglas was a "National Socialist."

What is striking is the number of judges who were, at one time or another in their careers, involved in teaching law. Sixteen of the judges taught, although only eight were full-time teachers. Bora Laskin was undoubtedly the best known in this group, but several deans of university law schools are also included. Pratte, Beetz, Le Dain, and La Forest were deans before being appointed to the Court; Rand became a dean after his retirement; and Fauteux was a dean while still sitting on the Court.

Nine of the judges served in the military. In most cases, this was real military service. Three of the judges (Cartwright, Locke, and Nolan) were awarded the Military Cross, while Dickson, who also was awarded the MC, was seriously wounded in action in

Normandy in 1944. One judge managed to become a professional athlete. John Sopinka played with the Toronto Argonauts and the Montreal Allouettes.

About a third of the judges could be described as coming from haute-bourgeois backgrounds. A handful (Laskin and Wilson, at least) rose from humble circumstances. The rest appear to have had comfortable, if less than grand, petit-bourgeois origins. But nearly all had noteworthy careers in academe, politics, or with prestigious law firms. The exceptions are Judson, Kellock, and Kerwin, who, so far as I can discern, had unmemorable careers prior to their translations to Ottawa. Most of the judges joined the Rideau Club on coming to Ottawa, although this practice has not been so true in recent years.

Looking at the nine judges who sat on the Court in 2002, it is interesting to note how little has changed. There has been one striking change – three of today's judges are women.[10] Five of the nine judges are francophone. There are no Rhodes Scholars on the Court and two – Ian Binnie and Frank Iacobucci – actually attended Cambridge at some stage in their education. I do not attribute any particular significance to this fact. It is interesting that, of the judges who sat on the Court up to the 1980s, many had attended Oxford, but none Cambridge. It is also interesting, I think, that of the most recent appointments to the Court, two actually went to Cambridge at the same stage in their education. Perhaps the most striking characteristic of the current judges is the number who were, at some period in their careers, full-time law teachers. This group includes Bastarache, Iacobucci, Arbour, and McLachlin. Lebel had a distinguished academic career as a classicist and produced an extraordinary body of writing during his time as an academic. Arbour left law teaching for the bench and a highly visible public career with international war crimes tribunals.[11]

There is probably no one who has a stronger claim to membership in Canada's ruling clique than Louise Arbour. She was a clerk at the Court in 1971–72, then worked for the Law Reform Commission of Canada and moved thence to the Osgoode Hall Law School, Canadian Civil Liberties Association, and Ontario Court of Appeal before returning to the Supreme Court as a judge.[12] Arbour thus became the first former judicial law clerk to be appointed a judge of the Court.

A theme to which this book keeps returning is that of judicial lawlessness. Louise Arbour, in 1996, was involved in a major instance of judicial lawlessness. Section 55 of the Judges Act[13] states: "No judge shall, either directly or indirectly, for himself or others, engage in any occupation or business other than his judicial duties, but every judge shall devote himself exclusively to his judicial duties." In April 1996, Arbour accepted an appointment from the UN Security Council as prosecutor for the International Tribunal for the Prosecution of War Criminals, then sitting in the Hague. She was at the time a judge of the Ontario Court of Appeal. In accepting this appointment, therefore, Arbour was acting in direct contravention of the Judges Act. Senator Anne Cools noted that Arbour's salary in the Hague was to be US$250,000 tax free, as well as various handsome allowances.[14] I do not in any way question Justice Arbour's motives in accepting this international appointment. It is simply worth noting that she was acting in clear contravention of the Judges Act. Parliament took the extraordinary step of amending the Judges Act specifically to accommodate Arbour. Parliament added section 56.1 to the Judges Act.[15] Section 56.1(1) began: "Notwithstanding section 55, Madam Justice Louise Arbour of the Ontario Court of Appeal is authorized to take a leave from her judicial duties to serve as Prosecutor of the International Tribunal for the Prosecution of Persons Responsible for Serious Violations of International Humanitarian Law." This unprecedented statutory amendment referred to Arbour by name no less than five times.[16]

Another example of possibly questionable behaviour can be found in Arbour's personal life. For many years she has cohabited with Larry Taman,[17] formerly a professor at the Osgoode Hall Law School. Louise Arbour is, of course, entitled to make such domestic arrangements as she may wish. At the same time, judges do, surely, bear a responsibility for maintaining the appearance of their own independence. Arbour's domestic arrangements might conceivably have compromised, to some degree, the appearance that she was impartial. While she was a judge of the Ontario Court of Appeal, Taman was Ontario's deputy attorney general. I do not wish, in any way, to suggest that Justice Arbour might have been influenced in the making of her judgments by her connection with Taman. It is sufficient to note that such a relationship could well have led to questions being raised about the judge's impartiality.

It also emerged that Chief Justice Lamer had interfered in the political process in order to ensure Arbour's international appointment. When Lamer discovered some parliamentary opposition to Arbour's UN appointment, he was publicly critical of Parliament. He lobbied the president of the Canadian International Development Agency (CIDA) and the federal commissioner of judicial affairs to remove obstacles to Arbour's appointment.[18] This behaviour on the part of the chief justice of Canada was unprecedented. He should have been removed from office for this sort of political meddling.

It is difficult to think of a manifestation of judicial presumption and arrogance that comes close to certain statutory provisions enacted in 1996 and 1998. In 1997, Antonio Lamer decided there should be Judicial Compensation Commissions.[19] These were to be independent, autonomous bodies which would set salaries for the judges of the inferior courts in the provinces. In 1998, Bill C-37 to amend the Judges Act was introduced in Parliament. One provision of this bill would have created a Judicial Compensation and Benefits Commission to address the salaries and benefits of Superior Court Judges. A new section 26, creating such a commission, was to be added to the act. As Senator Anne Cools seems to have been the only member of either house of Parliament to grasp, this bill would have contradicted an important provision of the Canadian Constitution, found in section 100 of the Constitution Act, 1867, which states that the salaries of Superior Court Judges are to be fixed and provided by Parliament.[20]

Especially outrageous were statutory amendments dealing with individual pensions. One of these was called the "Lamer Amendment" because it created a special pension rule that could apply only to Antonio Lamer and his wife. This astonishing legislation created a special pension regime for judges, like Lamer, who were, in fact, married to another judge. Enacted in 1996, the other became known as the "judges' harem law."[21] This corrupt legislation would allow judges to confer pension benefits on both a spouse and a cohabitee. These two statutory amendments created special and unprecedented financial benefits for certain judges. The result of these amendments was that Antonio Lamer became able to confer pension benefits on a multiplicity of spouses and former spouses.

Although the current judges can hardly be viewed as political innocents, none had an active political career before being appointed to the Court. Ian Binnie was a practitioner and former associate deputy minister of Justice in Ottawa before he was appointed to the Court. He had no previous judicial experience. Frank Iacobucci served for a time as deputy minister of Justice. Chief Justice McLachlin may be the most experienced judge ever to have sat on the Court. She was a County Court judge in B.C. before being appointed to the province's Supreme Court and later Court of Appeal, becoming chief justice of the province in 1988, six months prior to her appointment to the Supreme Court.

It is interesting to look at the surnames of the judges who have sat on the Court since 1949. All their names are, with the exceptions of Laskin, Sopinka, and Iacobucci, either English, Scottish, Irish, or French. This makes it obvious that the Supreme Court is not representative of Canada's population as a whole. There is no reason the judiciary should be representative of a nation's population and many that it should not be. While the Supreme Court bench should not "represent" our whole population, it might be desirable if the bench "reflected" that population better than it does.

If the Supreme Court of Canada is to continue to play the dominant role in Canada's political system, it must be obvious that the current non-system for the appointment of judges will have to be changed. Leaving this completely discretionary power of selection in the hands of the prime minister should not be accepted.

There is a strange phenomenon at work in Canada today. The virus that has infected judges of the Supreme Court appears to have spread throughout the entire judicial structure. The virus manifests itself in two judicial predilections. First, the judges begin to become both oracular and sanctimonious. Intelligent and reasonable people are appointed judges and, at once, their minds seem to turn to jelly and they begin to imagine themselves to be inspired oracles.

Ted Matlow is a judge of the Ontario Superior Court of Justice. On 3 July 2001, he wrote an op-ed piece in the *Globe and Mail* in which he questioned the desirability of retaining the statement in the preamble to the Charter that "Canada is founded upon principles that recognise the supremacy of God." Matlow expressed opinions that would not have been out of place in a Grade Ten essay:

I believe in the existence of some supreme voice that was responsible for the creation of the universe. That force is called "God" in my religion and in many others. Some Canadians share similar beliefs. Others have very different ones. Persons who are atheists obviously do not share such beliefs; agnostics presumably do not get involved at all.

Although I have my own personal impression of some of my God's characteristics I am mainly unsure of them. And when I hear persons of other faiths speak about their God, I cannot tell for sure if theirs is the same as mine. I suspect that many people feel the same way I do.

We can all feel confident that Judge Matlow would never say or do anything that might cause anyone's feelings to be hurt.

The second manifestation of the virus causes judges to believe they are no longer bound by any rules. Rene Heikamp was the mother of Jordan Heikamp, a baby who starved to death in June of 1997 while in his mother's custody. Ms Heikamp was charged with criminal negligence causing death. Justice Mary Hogan, a Superior Court judge in Ontario, presided over the preliminary enquiry in late 1999 and discharged Heikamp. In July 2001 Heikamp showed up at the Old City Hall courts in Toronto and asked to speak with Hogan. The two chatted in Hogan's chambers, a meeting about which Heikamp said, "I just wanted to talk to her about stuff."[22] It appears a judge may now choose to be a social worker.

5

Judicial Review of Everything

The Supreme Court of Canada has been reluctant to accept that there can be any questions which are, by their nature, beyond its jurisdiction. It has been prepared to review foreign policy decisions of the Government of Canada.[1] The Court has also accepted that it may review the government's decisions dealing with abortion, euthanasia, and the details of the provision of medical treatment. I shall deal with each in turn.

ABORTION

Henry Morgentaler is undoubtedly Canada's best known abortionist. Under the newspeak of the orthodoxy, it is no longer permissible to say abortionist. Morgentaler is now to be described as an "abortion provider." I presume, further, that if one wished to refer to abortionists collectively, it would be necessary to speak of the "abortion provider community." Morgentaler has been to the Supreme Court several times.[2]

Prior to 1969, it was a crime to perform an abortion in Canada. In that year Parliament added section 251 to the Criminal Code. That section set out certain procedural and substantive conditions which had to be complied with before an abortion could be performed. An abortion performed in accordance with section 251 was lawful; to perform an abortion other than in accordance with section 251 was a crime. Morgentaler performed abortions in violation of the section, and in 1973 he was arrested and put on trial. The case ended up before the Supreme Court of Canada, where Morgentaler argued that section 251 denied rights set out in the Canadian Bill of Rights. The Bill of Rights purported to guarantee certain rights, but it had been enacted as an ordinary statute and not as a constitutional amendment. Primarily because the Bill of Rights was a statutory, rather than a constitutional, instrument, the Court upheld the validity of section 251.[3]

Morgentaler was originally tried by a judge and jury. The jury decided to acquit Morgentaler. The Crown appealed the acquittal to the Court of Appeal, which allowed the appeal and substituted a finding of guilty. Morgentaler's subsequent appeal to the Supreme Court of Canada was denied. This proceeding led to what has come to be known as the "Morgentaler amendment" to the Criminal Code. Under this provision, enacted after the Supreme Court had upheld Morgentaler's conviction, an appellate court might not substitute a conviction for an acquittal reached by a trial court where the trial court had been composed of a judge and jury.[4]

It took the adoption of the Charter to get Morgentaler back before the courts. Section 251, remember, was a long way from what Morgentaler and Canadian feminists wanted: abortion on demand – i.e., abortion not subject to any conditions or restrictions. In 1988, Morgentaler challenged section 251 on the basis of section 7 of the Charter.[5] While the Supreme Court generally accepted Morgentaler's arguments, it did not go as far as the U.S. Supreme Court had gone in *Roe* v. *Wade*, which was to find a constitutional right to have an abortion. The Court held, by a majority, that the conditions found in section 251 limited a woman's life, liberty, and security of the person in a manner which was not consistent with principles of fundamental justice, and it struck the section down.

The result is that in Canada today there is no legal control whatsoever on abortion. In *Roe* v. *Wade* the U.S. Supreme Court divided a pregnancy into three trimesters for legal purposes. In the first trimester, the state could not impose any limits on abortion, in the second trimester the state might create limits in the interests of the fetus, and in the third trimester the state could prohibit abortions. As a result of the Supreme Court's decision in *Morgentaler* (1988), abortion is now permissible at any stage in a pregnancy. This means that so-called "partial birth" abortions happen in Canada. In these circumstances, the woman is in the third trimester of her pregnancy. The cervix is dilated and the torso and limbs of the fetus are removed. The head is then destroyed. Canadian hospitals have seen the performance of a grotesque form of abortion in which a full-term fetus is delivered alive and simply left to die.[6]

Henry Morgentaler is at the cutting-edge of the privatization of health care in Canada. He operates a national chain of franchised abortion mills. These are free-standing "clinics," separate and distinct from state-run and state-funded hospitals. The Nova Scotia Medical Services Act sought to restrict the development of privatized for-profit health care in the province. The act prohibited the performance of abortions otherwise than in recognized hospitals. Once again, Morgentaler, seeing the operation of his private for-profit "clinics" under attack, challenged this legislation. Once again, the Supreme Court obliged him and struck the legislation down.[7] This third Morgentaler decision can be seen as a further example of the Court upholding freedom of commerce.

Since the Court was prepared to give every Canadian woman a right to kill a fetus which she might be carrying, it must follow that it would recognize a concomitant right to inflict injury on a fetus.[8]

EUTHANASIA

Susan Rodriguez was a forty-three-year-old woman living in Vancouver. She suffered from Amyotrophic Lateral Sclerosis (ALS). ALS is a degenerative disease of the central nervous system, and there is no cure or therapy for it. It leads inevitably to complete paralysis and death. Rodriguez wished to die. She might have taken her own life, but was not physically capable of doing so. If she were to achieve her goal of dying, she would have required the assistance of another person. Section 241(b) of the Criminal Code made it an offence to assist or abet anyone else in committing suicide. Rodriguez wished to challenge section 241(b) and advanced a strikingly farfetched argument: She argued that any able-bodied person who wished to commit suicide would be able to do so. Someone in her position who wished to commit suicide would not be physically capable of doing so and would therefore require the assistance of another person. Thus, section 241(b) of the Criminal Code "discriminated" against her. The fascinating thing about this argument is not so much that it is bizarre, but that several judges of the Supreme Court were prepared to accept it.[9]

Nine judges heard the Rodriguez appeal. Four judges were prepared to accept her argument. Justices McLachlin and L'Heureux-Dubé concluded that section 241(b) infringed rights guaranteed in section 7 of the Charter, arguing that "the security of the person" had an "element of personal autonomy, which protects the dignity and privacy of individuals with respect to decisions concerning their own body. A legislative scheme which limited the right of a person to deal with her body as she chose might violate the principles of fundamental justice under section 7, if the limit is arbitrary."[10] These four judges – McLachlin, L'Heureux-Dubé, Lamer, and Cory – would have invalidated section 241(b). Chief Justice Lamer would have suspended the declaration of invalidity for one year to permit Parliament to enact fresh legislation. Such a decision would have left the law on assisted suicide in precisely the same state as the law on abortion – there would have been none. The enlightened in Canada think that abortion is just swell[11] and have been organizing a determined campaign to have euthanasia recognized.[12] It is likely that no element of the orthodoxy is regarded as more fundamental and deeply-rooted than the belief in the desirability of abortion. To raise questions about abortion is to mark oneself in the eyes of the enlightened as hopelessly ignorant and uncivilized.[13] In the U.S., fundamental rights have regularly given way to the need to protect the sanctity of abortions.[14]

The case of Robert Latimer became very public and generated strong, if not particularly enlightened, feelings. Latimer had a twelve-year-old daughter, Tracy, who suffered from cerebral palsy. She endured great pain and suffering. Ostensibly to free Tracy from her travail, Latimer killed her. He was charged with second-degree murder and was convicted. Upon a conviction for second-degree murder, the trial judge is obliged by the Criminal Code to impose a sentence of life imprisonment without eligibility for parole for ten years. This sentence was passed on Latimer. He argued that his killing of his daughter was "compassionate homicide" and that the statutory minimum sentence was, in the circumstances of his case, cruel and unusual, contrary to section 12 of the Charter.[15]

Inevitably, Latimer ended up before the Supreme Court.[16] The Court succumbed to a rare outbreak of restraint and upheld the constitutionality of the minimum sentence in the Criminal Code. The judges also recognized that if "compassionate homicide" were to be recognized in Canadian law, the change would, properly, have to be made by Parliament. This decision was reached unanimously.[17] The Court's decision suggested that it believed the whole issue raised by the *Latimer* matter was one which should have been dealt with by Parliament. The Court said, in part:

While the test is one that attributes a great deal of weight to individual circumstances, it should also be stressed that in weighing the s. 12 considerations the court must also consider and defer to the valid legislative objectives underlying the criminal law responsibilities of Parliament (*Goltz*,[18] at p. 503). In this regard, Cory J., for the Court in *Steele v. Mountain Institution*, at p. 1417, stated:

> It will only be on rare and unique occasions that a court will find a sentence so grossly disproportionate that it violates the provisions of s. 12 of the *Charter*. *The test for determining whether a sentence is disproportionately long is very properly stringent and demanding*. A lesser test would tend to trivialize the *Charter*.

In emphasizing the deferential standard for the s. 12 review, this Court has repeatedly adopted the following passage from *R. v. Guiller* (1985), 48 C.R. (3d) 226 (Ont. Dist. Ct.) at p. 238, *per* Borins Dist. Ct. J. (cited at *Smith, supra*, at p. 1070; *Luxton, supra* at p. 725; *Goltz*, at p. 502):

> It is not for the court to pass on the wisdom of Parliament with respect to the gravity of various offences and the range of penalties which may be imposed upon those found guilty of committing the offences. Parliament has broad discretion in proscribing conduct as criminal and in determining proper punishment. While the final judgment as to whether a punishment exceeds constitutional limits set by the *Charter* is properly a judicial function, the court should be reluctant to interfere with the considered views of Parliament and then only in the clearest of cases where the punishment prescribed is so excessive when compared with the punishment prescribed for other offences as to outrage standards of decency.

Finally, before moving on to the applications of these principles to this appeal, we note that there are two aspects to the s. 12 analysis (*Goltz*, at p. 505). Specifically, the first aspect of the s. 12 analysis centres on the individual circumstances as set out above and is commonly known as the "particularized inquiry." If the particularized inquiry reveals that a challenged provision imposes a sentence that is grossly disproportionate in those particular circumstances, then a *prima facie* violation of s. 12 is established and will be examined for justifiability under s. 1 of the *Charter*. If, however, the particular facts of the case do not give rise to such a finding "there may remain ... a *Charter* challenge or constitutional question as to the validity of a statutory provision on grounds of gross disproportionality as evidenced in *reasonably hypothetical circumstances*" (*Goltz*, at pp. 505–6).

As is reflected in the constitutional questions before the Court, this appeal is restricted to a consideration of the particularized inquiry. In substance, the appellant concedes the general constitutionality of ss. 235 and 745(c) as these sections are applied in combination. Mr. Latimer's challenge to their overall constitutionality was put forward in the alternative, but was not pressed forcefully since no substantive argument on point was offered. Furthermore, no reasonable hypothetical situation was presented for the Court's consideration. In short, the appellant's arguments wholly centred on the effect of the sentence in this specific case on this specific offender. Consequently, only the individual remedy sought by the appellant, namely a constitutional exemption, is at issue.[19]

When euthanasia is recognized in Canada, I wonder whether physician/entrepreneurs like Henry Morgentaler will open euthanasia clinics. Such persons would likely be called "death-providers."

MEDICAL TREATMENT

In *Eldridge* v. *British Columbia (A.G.)*, the Court gave itself the authority to supervise the way health care is provided. Eldridge and his co-appellants were deaf patients in a B.C. hospital. Eldridge claimed that, by failing to provide signing services for deaf patients, hospitals in British Columbia were acting in a fashion which was contrary to the Charter's equality guarantee. Hospitals in Canada are largely publicly-funded but operate as autonomous institutions separate from the state apparatus. How, then, could the Charter apply to the medical operations of a hospital? Primarily, it seems, because hospitals in B.C. spent public funds and operated pursuant to provincial statutes. Eldridge's claim was upheld by the Court and B.C. hospitals thus found themselves under a constitutional obligation to make signing services available to deaf patients. In this case, the Court frustrated a policy of the provincial government aimed at controlling health care costs.

For reasons which are not immediately apparent, LEAF intervened in this appeal and, as has become commonplace, ended up on the winning side. I must assume that LEAF intervened in order to further its relentless pursuit of equality, at least as LEAF understands that term. Manfredi observed: "*Eldridge* illustrates how individual stakeholders can use rights-based claims to circumvent policy decisions made in the interest of the system as a whole."[20]

Thus, in both *Eldridge* and *Morgentaler* (1993), federally-appointed judges dictated to provincial governments the way to run their health care systems. One result in Ontario of the *Eldridge* decision has been a host of complaints being made against hospitals by deaf persons who were not provided with signing services. This is happening at a time when Ontario hospitals are in the midst of a financial crisis. One claim being made is that emergency rooms, which are experiencing severe staffing problems, should provide signing assistance as well as language interpreters.[21]

I cannot help wondering whether judges will one day don surgical greens over their ermine and scarlet and enter operating rooms to ensure that surgeons treat all their patients "equally." *Eldridge* makes clear that section 15 claims are not solely about equality, but often involve attempts by litigants to receive special treatment.

HOMOSEXUALITY V. HETEROSEXUALITY

There is a vast cultural debate going on in North America today over the relative merits and legitimacy of homosexuality and heterosexuality.[22] In 2001, the Supreme Court involved itself in this debate in the case of *Trinity Western University v. British Columbia College of Teachers*. The background to the litigation follows.

Trinity Western University (TWU) is a private institution in B.C., associated with the Evangelical Free Church of Canada. TWU established a teacher training program offering baccalaureate degrees in education upon completion of a five-year course, four years of which were spent at TWU, the fifth year being under the aegis of Simon Fraser University. TWU applied to the British Columbia College of Teachers (BCCT) for permission to assume full responsibility for the teacher education program. One of the reasons for assuming complete responsibility for the program was TWU's desire to have the full program reflect its particular Christian world view. The BCCT refused to approve the application because it was contrary to the public interest for the BCCT to approve a teacher education program offered by a private institution when the program appeared to follow discriminatory practices. The BCCT was concerned that the TWU Community Standards Agreement, applicable to all students, faculty, and staff, embodied discrimination against homosexuals. Specifically, the concern stemmed from the list of "PRACTICES THAT ARE BIBLI-CALLY CONDEMNED," which encompassed "sexual sins including ... homosexual behaviour."

The judges who took part in the majority judgment saw the issue this way.[23] The Court of Appeal was wrong in applying a lower standard to the findings of the BCCT regarding, first, the existence of discriminatory practices and, second, whether any such practices create a perception that the BCCT condones this discrimination or creates a risk that graduates of TWU will not provide a discrimination-free environment for all public school students. According to the judges, the existence of discriminatory practices is based on the interpretation of the TWU documents and human rights values and principles. This is a question of law that is concerned with human rights and not essentially educational matters.

At the heart of the appeal, the majority of the judges argued, is how to reconcile the religious freedoms of individuals wishing to attend TWU with the equality concerns of students in B.C.'s public school system, concerns that may be shared by society generally. While TWU is a private institution that is exempted, in part, from the B.C. human rights legislation, and to which the Canadian Charter of Rights and Freedoms does not apply, BCCT was entitled to look to these instruments to determine whether it would be in the public interest to allow public school teachers to be trained at TWU. Any potential conflict between religious freedoms and equality rights should be resolved through the proper delineation of the rights and values involved. Properly defining the scope of the rights avoids a conflict in this case: neither freedom of religion nor the guarantee against discrimination based on sexual orientation is absolute. The proper place to draw the line is generally between belief and conduct: the freedom to hold beliefs is broader than the freedom to act on them. Unless there is concrete evidence, therefore, that training teachers at TWU fosters discrimination in the public schools of B.C., the freedom of individuals to adhere to certain religious beliefs while at TWU should be respected.

As was probably predictable, Justice L'Heureux-Dubé dissented. In her words:[24]

This case is about providing the best possible educational environment for public school students in British Columbia. The *Teaching Profession Act* confers jurisdiction on the B.C.C.T. to consider discriminatory practices in evaluating T.W.U.'s application. The B.C.C.T.'s statutory mandate gives it a broad discretion to set standards for the approval of teacher education programmes, as well as for their graduates. The presence of discrimination is relevant and within the B.C.C.T.'s jurisdiction. ...

First, the B.C.C.T. has relative expertise in the area of setting standards for admission into the teaching profession. Deference should be accorded to self-governing professional bodies like the B.C.C.T. Second, on the question of the purpose of the Act as a whole and of the particular provision at issue, the B.C.C.T.'s decision concerning T.W.U.'s teacher education programme goes to the heart of the *Teaching Profession Act's* raison d'être and should only be disturbed by judges, who lack the specialized expertise of teachers, if it is patently unreasonable. The B.C.C.T. is entrusted with policy development. This policy-making mandate is reflected in the words of s. 4 of the Act. Moreover, the B.C.C.T. has wide discretion to review teacher training programmes under the Act. Its polycentric decision in this case was made pursuant to s. 21(i) of the Act, which involves the application of vague, open-textured principles, requiring curial deference. Finally, the B.C.C.T.'s decision is fact-based, concerning an issue the nature of which implicates the tribunal's expertise. Determining how T.W.U.'s programme may affect its graduates' preparedness to teach in the public schools is a factual rather than a legal inquiry and requires the specialized expertise of the B.C.C.T.'s members, the majority of whom have classroom experience.

The B.C.C.T. fulfills the role of gatekeeper to the profession of public school teaching. Statutory interpretation of the B.C.C.T.'s "public interest" responsibilities should be purposive and contextual, not nebulous.

It is a misconception to characterize the B.C.C.T.'s decision as being a balancing or interpretation of human rights values, an exercise that is beyond the tribunal's expertise. Equality is a central component of the public interest that the B.C.C.T. is charged with protecting in the classrooms of the province. The B.C.C.T. was required to consider the value of equality in its assessment of the impact T.W.U.'s programme will have on the classroom environment. The B.C.C.T. was not acting as a human rights tribunal and was not required to consider other *Charter* or human rights values such as freedom of religion which are not germane to the public interest in ensuring that teachers have the requisites to foster supportive classroom environments in public schools. The B.C.C.T.'s inquiry was reasonably limited to its area of educational expertise.

The B.C.C.T.'s decision not to accredit a free-standing T.W.U. teacher training programme should be upheld. The B.C.C.T.'s conclusion that T.W.U.'s Community Standards Agreement embodies a discriminatory practice is not patently unreasonable. Signing the contract makes the student or employee complicit in an overt, but not illegal, act of discrimination against homosexuals and bisexuals. It is not patently unreasonable for the B.C.C.T. to treat T.W.U. students' public expressions of discrimination as potentially affecting the public school communities in which they wish to teach. Although tolerance is also a fundamental value in the Community Standards Agreement, the public interest in the public school system requires something more than mere tolerance.

The B.C.C.T. was not patently unreasonable in concluding that, without spending a year under the auspices of S.F.U. [Simon Fraser University], T.W.U. graduates, due to their signature of the Community Standards contract, could have a negative impact on the supportive environment required in classrooms. The B.C.C.T. could reasonably find that without a fifth year of training outside the supervision of T.W.U. there would be an unacceptable pedagogical cost in terms of reduced exposure of T.W.U. students to diversity and its values. It is reasonable to insist that graduates of accredited teacher training programmes be equipped to provide a welcoming classroom environment, one that is as sensitive as possible to the needs of the diverse student body.

The modern role of the teacher has developed into a multi-faceted one, including counselling as well as educative functions. Evidence shows that there is an acute need for improvement in the experiences of homosexual and bisexual students in Canadian classrooms. Without the existence of supportive classroom environments, homosexual and bisexual students will be forced to remain invisible and reluctant to approach their teachers.

They will be victims of identity erasure. The students' perspective must be the paramount concern and, even if there are no overt acts of discrimination by T.W.U. graduates, this vantage point provides ample justification for the B.C.C.T.'s decision. The B.C.C.T.'s decision is a reasonable proactive measure designed to prevent any potential problems of student, parent, colleague, or staff perception of teachers who have not completed a year of training under the supervision of S.F.U., but have signed the Community Standards contract. The courts, by trespassing into the field of pedagogy, deal a setback to the B.C.C.T.'s efforts to ensure the sensitivity and empathy of its members to all students' backgrounds and characteristics.

The respondents' *Charter* claims should be dismissed. The effect of the BCCT's decision is to restrict T.W.U. students' expression. Assuming that T.W.U.'s expression is also fettered, these violations are saved under s. 1. First, the objective behind the B.C.C.T.'s decision to protect the classroom environment in public schools is pressing and substantial. Second, the B.C.C.T.'s decision satisfies the proportionality test. The burden placed on expression is rationally connected to the B.C.C.T.'s goal of ensuring a welcoming and supportive atmosphere in classrooms. By falling within an acceptable range of solutions, the B.C.C.T.'s decision also minimally impairs s. 2(b). The extent of the violations' deleterious effects on T.W.U. and its students is more than offset by the salutary gains that will plausibly accrue in classrooms. With respect to s. 2(d), since no unjustified individual rights violations were found in this case, and since T.W.U. students are not unconstitutionally restrained from exercising their individual rights collectively, the respondent students' 2(d) claim must also fail.

The distinction between the majority judgment and that of L'Heureux-Dubé can be summed up as follows. The majority, finding no evidence of actual discriminatory behaviour on the part of TWU graduates, concluded that the TWU course should have been recognized by the BCCT. L'Heureux-Dubé required no such evidence.[25] Her judgment, it seems to me, is the closest a Canadian judge has ever come to recognizing thought crime.

L'Heureux-Dubé's dissent merits an extended analysis. For her the teacher training program at TWU was not to be given official recognition. Why? Had any TWU graduate actually *done* anything wrong? No. She believed the strictures in the TWU. Community Standards Agreement could "potentially affect the public school communities" in which graduates might teach.

Justice L'Heureux-Dubé began her judgment by asserting that the case was about providing the best possible educational environment for public school students in British Columbia. Were the TWU graduates competent? Such considerations were irrelevant to L'Heureux-Dubé. What mattered was "the pressing need for teachers in public schools to be sensitive to the concerns of homosexual and bisexual students." Teachers, in her view, should be "equipped to provide a welcoming classroom environment, one that is as sensitive as possible to the needs of a diverse student body." In L'Heureux-Dubé's omniscience, the "educative functions" of a teacher were secondary. TWU argued that the BCCT decision infringed the Charter rights of its students. L'Heureux-Dubé simply defined this claim out of existence.

To cite a somewhat farfetched example, there is another issue, one with which L'Heureux-Dubé did not concern herself. The TWU Community Standards Agreement also obliged students to eschew "drunkenness." What about the equality concerns of alcoholics and of public school students from alcoholic families?

An important factor underlying L'Heureux-Dubé's dissent appears to be her belief that the bad thoughts harboured by TWU students might lead to homosexual students in their classes having their feelings hurt. She stated that "gay and lesbian students at all ages and all stages of schooling share an identity that has been bumped, bruised or completely ignored. That this personal identity crosses all ethnic, cultural, economic, geographic and gender boundaries makes gay and lesbian students universally present, yet easily invisible. I believe that the students' perspective must be the paramount concern and that, even if there are no overt acts of discrimination by T.W.U. graduates, this vantage point provides ample justification for the B.C.C.T.'s decision."[26] I can only interpret her words to mean the following: The fact that there is no evidence of improper behaviour by TWU graduates is irrelevant because they think bad thoughts and those bad thoughts might result in somebody's feelings getting hurt.[27]

Bearing in mind the many public speeches which L'Heureux-Dubé made on the importance of recognizing the equal status of homosexuals,[28] it seems reasonable to imagine that her mind might have been made up before the hearing of the appeal in the TWU case. Remarks she made during the hearing suggest that this may well have been the case. TWU attempted to argue that it was not against homosexuals, but against homosexuality. TWU asserted that its perspective was, "Love the sinner, hate the sin." L'Heureux-Dubé contemptuously dismissed this assertion, saying, "We have all this love stuff." She also stated that evidence of discrimination was to be found in the TWU program, adding, "What kind of other evidence do you want?"[29] Justice Binnie called the distinction advanced by TWU a "contradiction in terms."[30] If I lacked the wit to understand such a simple distinction, I would not admit to it in public.

To return to my farfetched example, what about the plight of alcoholic students? Surely, on the basis of the Court's own decisions about grounds analogous to those set out in section 15(1) of the Charter, alcoholics constitute a discrete and insular minority and thus deserve the Court's protection.

6

Making It Up as They Go Along: Herein of the "Unwritten Constitution" and Other Matters

The task and responsibility of judges is to expound the law. The judge should stand in the same relation to the constitution and the law as does a musician to a composer. The musician is expected to play the notes as they were written by the composer, not to rewrite the score at his or her fancy. Far too often the latter is precisely what judges of the Supreme Court have done. Rather than expounding established principles, they often appear to simply be making it up as they go along.

This practice can be seen in three contexts: the so-called "unwritten constitution," section 7 of the Charter, and section 15 of the Charter. I will deal with each in turn.

THE UNWRITTEN CONSTITUTION

There is no single document which can be called the Constitution of Canada.[1] Canada's Constitution is, in fact, an agglomeration from various sources. Section 52(3) of the Constitution Act, 1982 does attempt, in a fashion which is far from satisfactory, a definition of the Constitution. This section specifies certain statutes which are said to be part of the Constitution and it uses the word *includes*. This word makes clear that there is more to the Constitution than what the section specifies.

It is this lack of certainty as to the exact content of Canada's Constitution that has been exploited by the Supreme Court. In recent years, the Court has made much out of what it calls "the unwritten constitution," and reading the Court's decisions on the unwritten constitution led me to the conclusion that the best way to describe what the judges are doing in these decisions is through the phrase "making it up as they go along."

An important element of the unwritten constitution is the royal prerogative. The ambit of prerogative power has been much circumscribed, as the ambit of Parliamentary authority has increased, and it now extends only to such things as the conduct of foreign policy, the issuance of passports, and the conferring of honours and awards. The basis for most state power in Canada today is statutory, rather than being derived from the prerogative.[2] The Supreme Court has concluded that prerogative powers do continue to exist but that they must be exercised in conformity with the Charter.[3]

In *New Brunswick Broadcasting* v. *Nova Scotia (Speaker of the House of Assembly)*, the Supreme Court held that legislative privilege, including the right to exclude strangers from the legislature, was a part of the Constitution of Canada. The Court also concluded that, "given the clear and stated intention of the founders of our country in the *Constitution Act, 1867* to establish a Constitution similar to that of the United Kingdom, the Constitution may also include such privileges as have been historically recognised as necessary to the proper functioning of our legislative bodies."[4] Moreover, the Court held that section 52(3) of the Constitution Act, 1982 was not exhaustive. In this decision the court focused on the Preamble to the Constitution Act, 1867 as the basis of the common law of the Constitution, or the unwritten constitution. The Preamble does state that Canada is to have a constitution "similar in principle" to that of the United Kingdom and, thus, the Preamble can be seen as the basis for the incorporation into Canada's Constitution of certain principles derived from the UK. In subsequent decisions, the Court used the Preamble as the basis for a spree of inventing new constitutional principles.

The Court began to lose its direction in a 1997 decision called *Reference re Remuneration of Judges of the Provincial Court of Prince Edward Island*. This decision was a judicial response to the orgy of government cutbacks of the 1990s. Several provinces imposed across-the-board cuts and freezes on the salaries of all persons paid by the province. In three provinces these economies were to be applied to the salaries of judges in the lower courts of the province. The question of whether these salary reductions were an interference with the independence of the judiciary wound up before the Supreme Court. The judges were prepared to accept that they were. Chief Justice Lamer asserted that the independence of the judiciary was a basic principle of our Constitution and noted further that there is not an "exhaustive and definitive code for the protection of judicial independence" in our constitutional texts.[5] He also understood that, while sections 99 and 100 of the Constitution Act, 1867 did provide protection for the independence of superior court judges, formal protection for inferior court judges was decidedly thin. Finding no such constitutional protection, Lamer decided to invent it. For this purpose, he turned to the Preamble, finding in it a "deeper set of unwritten understandings which are not found on the face of the document itself." The Preamble contained what Lamer called "organizing principles." The Preamble, he said, actually "invited" judges to use "these 'organizing principles' to fill out gaps in the express terms of the constitutional scheme."[6] Here Lamer found that the provinces were under a constitutional obligation to create independent judicial compensation commissions. These commissions would set salaries for inferior court judges, thereby upholding one of the three pillars of judicial independence – financial security – which the Court had elaborated in its decision in *R. v. Valente*. Having invented judicial compensation commissions, Lamer also pulled out of thin air detailed rules concerning their composition, powers, and procedures. Most of Lamer's judgment was pure invention.

Lamer's judgment was also less than forthright. He managed to create the impression that the principles and doctrines which he was pulling out of the air were well-understood and accepted elements of Canadian constitutional law. He spoke as if courts had regularly "inferred" basic rules of Canadian constitutional law "despite the silence of the constitutional text."[7]

Lamer based much of his judgment on what he took to be the Constitution of the United Kingdom. Lamer's understanding of the UK Constitution, however, was no better than his understanding of the Canadian Constitution. There is only one principle of the UK Constitution. That sole principle is the unqualified supremacy of Parliament. Thus, if Parliament in the UK wished to do away with the independence of the judiciary, it would be constitutionally free to do so.

Lamer's colleague, Justice Gerard La Forest, delivered a scathing dissent. La Forest accepted that protection for the independence of the judiciary in our constitutional texts was incomplete. He also conceded that there were "unwritten rules" in our Constitution and that additional protection for the judiciary might be found in these rules. Despite these concessions, La Forest was ruthless in his criticism and rejection of Lamer's judgment. He stated that Lamer's view of the UK Constitution "entirely misapprehended" that Constitution and was based on a "historical fallacy."[8] He called Lamer's view of the Preamble to the Constitution Act, 1867 a "dubious theory" which "misapprehends" the Constitution Act, 1867.[9] La Forest went further and stated that the express provisions of the constitutional text were not, as Lamer had argued, "elaborations of the underlying unwritten and organizing principles found in the Preamble to the Constitution Act, 1867." On the contrary, said La Forest, the express textual provisions *are* the Constitution. To argue otherwise, he concluded, was to "subvert the democratic foundation of judicial review."[10] Shortly after excoriating Lamer's attempt to rewrite Canada's Constitution, La Forest resigned from the Court.

A year later, in *Reference re Secession of Quebec*, the court dealt with the question of whether and how a province might secede from Confederation. Once again, the Court indulged its predilection for rewriting the Constitution and making up new rules of constitutional law at its discretion. In this reference the Court was asked three questions:

1 Does Canada's Constitution permit the unilateral secession of Quebec?
2 Does international law allow Quebec to secede?
3 If there is a conflict between Canada's Constitution and international law, which should take precedence?

Turning to the first question, the Court recognized, sensibly and accurately, that "the Constitution is silent as to the ability of a province to secede from Confederation."[11] That was enough to answer the reference questions and the Court should have stopped there. The Court did not stop at that point, but went on to invent a series of rules and procedures to govern the secession of a province.

Chief Justice Lamer became positively mystical about the principles he was inventing. He allowed that "the constitution is more than a written text." Undertaking what he was pleased to call "a more profound investigation," Lamer discovered "underlying constitutional principles" which "infuse our Constitution and breathe life into it."[12] The Court then proceeded to invent detailed rules and procedures to govern the secession of a province. The judges of the Supreme Court went one better than Louis XIV's "L'état c'est moi." In this case they appeared to ordain that "the Constitution of Canada is whatever we judges say it is." The *Reference re Secession* is the clearest illustration possible of the predilection of the judges of the Supreme Court for treating the Constitution as if it were their personal possession. In this decision, Lamer invented four "underlying constitutional principles." One of these was "respect for minority rights." In a later decision, the Ontario Divisional Court followed the Supreme Court and used this so-called principle as the basis for inventing new constitutional rules about language use.[13] There is no mention in any of our constitutional texts of rules about the use of language in public institutions in Ontario. Basing itself on Lamer's musings in the *Reference re Secession of Quebec*, the Court persuaded itself that it had the authority to direct the Ontario government to operate a francophone hospital. This sort of lawless behaviour by our judges should no longer be tolerated by the Canadian people.

SECTION 7 OF THE CHARTER

The first case dealing with section 7 to reach the Supreme Court was *Reference re s. 94(2) (B.C.) Motor Vehicle Act*. This section had created an absolute liability offence of driving while prohibited or while one's licence was suspended. An individual could be convicted even though he or she had not been aware of the prohibition or suspension, and the statutory minimum punishment for this offence was seven days' imprisonment.

The issue before the Court was whether this coupling of an absolute liability offence with a minimum punishment of imprisonment violated section 7, which guarantees to everyone "life, liberty and security of the person and the right not to be deprived thereof except in accordance with principles of fundamental justice." The court was required to give a meaning to those words, especially "fundamental justice." Chief Justice Lamer made up a definition of *fundamental justice*. He grandly dismissed the evidence given by senior civil servants, including the one who had played a central role in drafting the Charter, that section 7 was intended only to guarantee procedural rights. Lamer concluded that section 7 did, indeed, guarantee substantive rights. By interpreting the section in this fashion, however, he was giving the judges the power to review statutes on the basis that they were not substantively fair. In giving itself the authority to review the substantive fairness of state acts, the Court was giving itself the same authority as the U.S. Supreme Court exercised in slaughtering much of Roosevelt's New Deal.[14] In elaborating his conclusions, Lamer became both lyrical and mystical. He clearly was not sure what the phrase "principles of fundamental justice" meant, but continued, "the principles of fundamental justice are to be found in the basic tenets of our legal system. They do not lie in the realm of general public policy but in the inherent domain of the judiciary as guardian of the justice system."[15] This formulation appears to me to be code for "Principles of fundamental justice mean whatever I say they mean."

If one actually looks at the text of the Charter, one sees that section 7 begins the "legal rights" part of the Charter. It seems obvious from its placement in the text, that section 7 was intended to guarantee basic procedural rights to persons caught up in the criminal justice system. Despite this, the judges transformed it into an independent basis for the exercise of judicial review powers. The judges gave themselves a further basis for reviewing the substance of state acts. The judges have used section 7 as the basis for reviewing foreign policy decisions,[16] the law on abortion,[17] and the law on assisted suicide.[18]

SECTION 15 OF THE CHARTER

Section 15 purports to prohibit the state from acting in a discriminatory fashion. Section 15(1) lists the precise grounds upon which the state may not discriminate. The Court has rewritten section 15(1), adding to it what the judges have been pleased to call "analogous grounds."

The Court invented the notion of analogous grounds in *Andrews* v. *Law Society of British Columbia*. Here, the Court decided that the anti-discrimination protection of section 15(1) would extend to cover persons who were members of any "discrete and insular minority."[19] What on earth is a discrete and insular minority? It is a social group whose members share a common characteristic that (a) sets them apart from the majority, and (b) imposes obstacles that render them incapable of defending or advancing their commonly shared interests through ordinary political action.

It should be observed that the existence of a discrete and insular minority could not be proven by the admission of what once was regarded as evidence by Canadian courts. This could only be established through "social science evidence" or judicial notice. Once again, the ambit of judicial discretion has been broadened substantially. In subsequent cases, such as *R. v. Turpin* and *Thibaudeau v. Canada*, the Court embroidered the notion of analogous grounds, without in any way making it more concrete. The Court's most recent statement on analogous grounds is *Corbiere v. Canada (Minister of Indian and Northern Affairs)*. Here the Court ordained that analogous grounds:

a identify groups that are discrete and insular minorities that lack political power, and are accordingly vulnerable to having their interests overlooked;
b identify groups that have experienced historical disadvantage, marginalization, and/or economic disadvantage;
c denote personal characteristics and are immutable, or unalterable except on the basis of unacceptable personal cost (i.e., constructively immutable);
d denote person characteristics that often serve as illegitimate and demeaning proxies for merit-based decision-making;
e denote personal characteristics that are important to identity, personhood, or belonging;
f are found in provincial and federal human rights legislation.[20]

Assuming that any of that has any meaning, it appears that the reach of section 15(1) is now limitless. All laws, by their nature, make distinctions. The new, judicially-redrafted section 15(1) will allow courts to determine that almost any conceivable distinction is "discriminatory" and, therefore, illegitimate.

The result of the Court's interpretations of the "unwritten constitution," the Preamble to the Constitution Act, 1867, and sections 7 and 15(1) of the Charter is to radically expand the scope for judicial review and judicial discretion. The Court may now overrule any state act which is "unfair" or which makes distinctions the judges do not like. Once again, the judges of the Supreme Court have acted to expand the ambit of their own power and their own discretion.

7

The Matriarchy in Change

This chapter looks at different ways in which feminists and feminist ideology have come to dominate our legal system.

INTRODUCTION

Feminist thought and ideology are central elements of the ruling orthodoxy. It thus stands to reason that the Supreme Court would have accepted feminist ideology in its decision-making. The Women's Legal Education and Action Fund (LEAF) has played a central role in this process. LEAF was formed after the Charter became part of the Constitution. The group's central goal is to use litigation, largely based on the Charter, as a means of advancing feminist goals. LEAF is a regular intervenor before the Court, having intervened in such appeals as *R.* v. *Morgentaler* (1988), *Andrews* v. *Law Society of British Columbia*, and, appropriately enough, *R.* v. *Seaboyer*. It has also been the most significant beneficiary of the Court Challenges Program and receives additional state support from another direction (see the discussion in R. Knopff and F.L. Morton, "Supreme Court as the Vanguard"). The university law schools, largely publicly-funded, provide LEAF with what amount to free research and training services. Since indoctrination in feminist ideology has become a major part of what the law schools do, there is a steady supply of persons who are willing to do research and provide legal services for LEAF. There is also a pool of law school graduates who are eager to apply for positions as judicial law clerks at the Court, positions from which they can begin to indoctrinate the judges in the kind of thinking espoused by LEAF. My own law school for several years offered a course called "Test Case Litigation." Courses like this provide fresh acolytes for LEAF. These courses attempt to indoctrinate students in the ideas espoused by LEAF and to train them in the kind of skills LEAF needs.

LEAF has had extraordinary success in the Supreme Court.[1] This success has been most apparent in cases involving sexual assault prosecutions and income taxation. I will discuss each category separately.

SEXUAL ASSAULT PROSECUTIONS

Catharine MacKinnon has had an extraordinary influence in the formulation of Canadian law on sexual assault. MacKinnon, as one writer put it, "was a child of privilege."[2] She was the third generation in her mother's family to attend Smith College. She is a graduate of Yale Law School and holds a Ph.D. in political science from Yale.[3] She was given tenure at the University of Michigan Law School in 1990[4] and has also taught at the Harvard Law School and the Osgoode Hall Law School. She has spent a large part of her adult life actively campaigning against pornography.[5] She has often expressed the view that sexual relations between men and women are inherently oppressive. In the early 1990s she announced that she was going to marry Paul Masson, a man who had publicly boasted of having slept with 1,000 women. Masson certainly admired MacKinnon. He said of her that, "She is the greatest mind at work in the world today" and "living with her is like living with God."[6] When asked why she would marry a man who had been so promiscuous with women, MacKinnon replied, "We do our best. He's not not a man and I'm not not a woman."[7]

Some of MacKinnon's views are unusual to say the least. Here are the opening words of *Only Words*: "You grow up with your father holding you down and covering your mouth so that another man can make a horrible, searing pain between your legs. When you are older, your husband ties you to the bed and drips hot wax on your nipples and brings in other men to watch and makes you smile through it. Your doctor will not give you drugs he has addicted you to unless you suck his penis."[8] MacKinnon has had her critics, including the highly respected legal scholar Ronald

Dworkin.[9] I once sent Dworkin a letter asking why he would write about Catharine MacKinnon. He replied that he thought it "important to make plain how shallow her position is."[10]

MacKinnon has been influential in Canada. She wrote the factum which LEAF submitted to the Supreme Court in the *R. v. Butler* appeal.[11] *Butler* was the decision in which the Court ruled on the constitutionality of section 163(8) of the Criminal Code, the section dealing with obscenity. The Court largely adopted a feminist analysis of pornography. Even more significantly, she played a major role in amendments to the sections of Canada's Criminal Code which deal with sexual assault.

In 1992, amendments to the Criminal Code to change the definition of "consent" in sexual assault were introduced in and enacted by Parliament. The amendments in Bill C-49 were largely the work of LEAF.[12] MacKinnon was a member of the LEAF Committee which consulted with the then minister of Justice about changes in the law, and she authored LEAF's submission to the House of Commons committee studying the bill. It is interesting that an American feminist legal academic who believes that the whole notion of a woman consenting to sexual relations with a man is "questionable" should have had an important role in amending Canada's Criminal Code provisions concerning sexual assault. It is a measure of the power of LEAF that it drafted a bill which, quickly and with little debate, became law.[13] The Criminal Code provisions dealing with sexual assault have been amended many times since 1983, largely in response to feminist pressure.[14] These amendments have gone a long way toward turning sexual assault into a reverse onus offence. They have also drastically circumscribed the ability of an accused person to defend himself and substantially limited the degree to which a sexual assault trial takes place in public. As a result, sexual assault is now a major exception to basic principles of Canadian criminal law.

Enacted in 1992, Bill C-49 made fundamental changes in the law with respect to the meaning and significance of consent in sexual assault prosecutions. The legislation created two new Criminal Code sections:

s. 273.1(1) Subject to subsection (2) and subsection 265(3), "consent" means, for the purposes of sections 271, 272 and 273, the voluntary agreement of the complainant to engage in the sexual activity in question.

(2) No consent is obtained, for the purposes of sections 271, 272 and 273, where

- (a) the agreement is expressed by the words or conduct of a person other than the complainant;
- (b) the complainant is incapable of consenting to the activity;
- (c) the accused induces the complainant to engage in the activity by abusing a position of trust, power or authority;
- (d) the complainant expresses, by words or conduct, a lack of agreement to engage in the activity; or
- (e) the complainant, having consented to engage in sexual activity, expresses, by words or conduct, a lack of agreement to continue to engage in the activity.

(3) Nothing in subsection (2) shall be construed as limiting the circumstances in which no consent is obtained.

s. 273.2 It is not a defence to a charge under section 271, 272 or 273 that the accused believed that the complainant consented to the activity that forms the subject-matter of the charge, where

- (a) the accused's belief arose from the accused's
    - (i) self-induced intoxication, or
    - (ii) recklessness or wilful blindness; or
- (b) the accused did not take reasonable steps, in the circumstances known to the accused at the time, to ascertain that the complainant was consenting.

While the presence or absence of consent has always been a central, perhaps *the* central, issue in rape or sexual assault prosecutions, the Criminal Code had not previously defined its meaning or its scope. Why, in 1992, was it felt necessary to do this? It must be assumed that Parliament enacted these provisions because it believed there were reasons which required the addition of such a definition to the Criminal Code.

More to the point, the approach in Bill C-49 is evidently one which seeks to narrow the effective ambit of consent. A "Background Information" paper prepared by the Justice Department to explain the bill to reporters when it was given first reading in December 1991 made this clear: "An accused person will not be able to use the defence of mistaken belief in consent if the mistake resulted from his or her self-induced intoxication, recklessness, or wilful blindness or where the accused took no reasonable steps to ascertain the complainant's consent."

I will later offer some detailed criticism of Bill C-49's approach to consent, but for now it must be assumed that Parliament believed these specific changes in the law governing consent to be necessary and desirable. That is, Parliament, or at least the Justice Department, must have believed that accused persons who were drunk, or reckless, or wilfully blind, or who had not taken reasonable steps to ensure that the eventual complainant was consenting were relying on the existing law to avoid conviction.

But was this in fact the case? Was the law about consent so loose that large numbers of sexual assaults were going unpunished? Did the urgent public interest in protecting women and children against sexual assault require these changes in the law?

Another feature of the changes raises one more question. Underlying the narrowing of the ambit of consent is a basic questioning of the legitimacy of what had hitherto appeared to be consensual sexual behaviour. Reading the new sections, one cannot avoid wondering whether the person who drafted them was fully convinced that most sexual or, at least, heterosexual acts are indeed consensual. The impression is created that far more sexual behaviour than we might have been prepared to imagine is non-consensual. Once again it must be assumed that Parliament was moved by a belief that substantial numbers of non-consensual sexual acts were occurring and that this situation should be addressed by the criminal law.

How did Parliament come to think these things? An analysis of the origins of Bill C-49 will address these questions.

The Genesis of Bill C-49

A useful starting point is Bill C-127,[15] which became law on 4 January 1983. The result of Bill C-127 was that the crimes of rape, attempted rape, and indecent assault against a male or a female were replaced with the new offences of sexual assault and aggravated sexual assault. It must be stressed that there is a fundamental difference between the prohibited conduct involved in rape and in sexual assault. Rape meant forced, that is non-consensual, intercourse; sexual assault includes what would have amounted to rape, but also extends to other assaults of a sexual nature. Changes in the procedure to be followed in trying sexual assault charges were also made.

The import of the 1983 reforms is well known and does not require further discussion.[16] Still, two of the underlying policy goals which motivated the 1983 amendments must be noted. First, the amendments were designed to achieve the "degenderization" of sexual assault.[17] The old offence of rape could only be committed by a man against a women; the new offence of sexual assault could, in theory, be committed by a person of either sex against a person of either sex. Second, a clear purpose of the amendments was to proscribe sexual assaults because they were seen to be acts of violence, not merely sexual acts.[18] To put the matter slightly differently and more directly, the new offence sought to punish violence, not sexuality.

Were the 1983 reforms successful? Were major problems left unaddressed?

The Department of Justice began a national research program in 1985 to evaluate the effect of the 1983 reforms. The program was completed in 1991. An "overview" report described it thus: "the Canadian evaluation initiative was substantial." The broad conclusion of this study was that the 1983 reforms had at least been successful in achieving an increase in reporting rates. This was a central aim of the reforms. As the overview noted, "national data confirm that there has been a general trend to higher rates of reporting sexual crimes since the introduction of Bill C-127."[19] Another aim was to bring about improvements in the way complainants in sexual assault cases were treated by persons in the criminal justice system. The Justice Department's report is more equivocal on this point, but there is a sense that, while more remained to be done, positive change had occurred.[20]

The multi-volume Justice Department report also sought to lay to rest a number of persistent myths about sexual assault which had arisen largely from an absence of information. One of them was that sexual assaults, once there had been a conviction, resulted in light or inconsequential punishments. A full volume was devoted to this question. The clear conclusion emerging from this volume is that the widespread perception of excessive leniency in sentencing in sexual assault cases was inaccurate.[21]

My point, however, is not to investigate whether the 1983 reforms were or were not effective. It is to note that a major official study based on the research of a number of consultants was carried out. While this study definitely pointed to shortcomings, these had to do largely with the way the criminal justice system dealt with both the accused and the complainant in sexual assault cases. There is absolutely nothing in the official study which suggested the need for a major substantive reform of the crime of sexual assault. There is no hint that the law needed to redirect itself from a concern with acts of violence, albeit of a sexual nature, toward a policy of questioning the legitimacy of consensual sexuality. There is not a word to suggest that the existing provisions concerning consent were in any way, let alone fundamentally, flawed.

All of this is to say there was nothing in the 1991 report which raised any of the concerns Bill C-49 apparently sought to address. If the issues relating to consent had become so serious by December 1991 as to require a legislative remedy, why is it that none of them was even mentioned in a major official study completed in the same year?

It is true that in a much criticized 1980 decision, *R. v. Pappajohn*, the Supreme Court of Canada accepted that an honest, if mistaken, belief that the victim had consented *might* be raised as a defence to a charge of rape. What often gets forgotten about *Pappajohn* is that the accused was convicted. And, indeed, a few years later, in *R. v. Sansregret*, the Supreme Court substantially restricted the availability of the "honest belief" defence.

Bill C-49, at least in the eyes of many of its supporters, purported to give legislative effect to the notion "No means no." As was further argued by its supporters, the bill was supposed to ensure that men charged with sexual assault would not be able to escape conviction by arguing, "I thought she meant 'Yes.'" But where are the cases in which this was actually happening? There is scant evidence to support the contention that significant numbers of assailants, or even any, were in fact being acquitted in Canada on this basis.

Indeed, none of the issues concerning consent which Bill C-49 purported to address has ever been the object of systematic empirical research in Canada. In a letter to the Honourable Kim Campbell, Minister of Justice, dated 12 March 1992, the Canadian Civil Liberties Association (CCLA) raised precisely this matter. Of the proposed changes to the meaning of consent, the CCLA observed, "To what extent, therefore, is such a change in the law necessary to provide adequate protections for the victims of sexual assault?"

The CCLA admonished the minister: "before making such changes in our criminal law, it would be wise to investigate more thoroughly than has apparently been done the community's actual experience with these sexual assault cases."

Bill C-49 did not arise as a response to concerns raised by the Justice Department's review of the existing Criminal Code, nor was it prompted by concrete, observed shortcomings in the law. Its true origins must be found in changing fashions in feminist ideology.

As I have already noted, a major goal of the 1983 reforms was to proscribe sexual assault primarily because it was seen as an act of violence. Lorenne Clark and Debra Lewis, two prominent Canadian feminists, expressed an extreme version of this view in their 1977 book, *Rape: The Price of Coercive Sexuality*: "So far as women are concerned, their sexual organs are no less, and no different a part of their person than their heads, eyes and limbs … Since sexual organs are just part of the body, an attack on the sexual organs is as threatening to life and health as an unprovoked attack on any of the other bodily parts … The same standards which apply to assaults against other parts of the body should also apply to attacks against the sexual organs."[22] Clark and Lewis were themselves simply repeating the point of view set out in Susan Brownmiller's influential 1975 book, *Against Our Will: Men, Women and Rape*.

But ideas began to change. The perception that the problem was violence began to give way to another approach which suggested that perhaps sexuality itself was the problem. We owe this new approach to Catharine MacKinnon. In her writing, the legitimacy and even the possibility of women consenting to heterosexual acts came to be questioned.

MacKinnon attempted to displace the focus on violence as the defining aspect of rape with the assertion that coercion, if not quite universal, is the norm in sexual relations between men and women. This point of view is set out most starkly in her two articles, "Feminism, Marxism, Method and the State: An Agenda for Theory" and "Feminism, Marxism, Method and the State: Toward Feminist Jurisprudence." MacKinnon's argument in these articles is clear enough. Sexual relations between men and women are about power, pure and simple. The essence of heterosexual relations is "male sexual dominance and female sexual submission."

She refers to "women as sexual objects for men, the use of women's sexuality by men."[23] In another work, MacKinnon dismissed the existence of an independent female sexuality: "Sex feeling good may mean that one is enjoying one's subordination."[24] She has argued for a "new paradigm,"[25] one that, in the words of a commentator sympathetic to her views, would treat "sexual coercion as the norm and mutual connection as the exception."[26]

This view of the inherently oppressive nature of heterosexuality has obvious implications for the law concerning both rape and sexual assault. It must be evident that Catharine MacKinnon would have reservations about the possibility of a woman ever freely consenting to a sexual act with a man. This is precisely her point of view. In 1992, she was quoted in a newspaper story as saying, "In the context of unequal power [between the sexes], one needs to think about the meaning of consent – whether it is a meaningful concept at all. I'm saying we need to think about it."[27] The implications for how the notion of consent would function seem clear. If the existence of consent is problematic, then logically the law should assume its absence and require the man accused of rape or sexual assault to prove that the consent of the woman was indeed given. MacKinnon herself has advocated this approach.[28]

My contention is that Bill C-49 did not arise as a response to concrete social reality in Canada, but as a manifestation of the extent to which feminist thought in Canada had adopted the ideas of Catharine MacKinnon. The events leading up to the introduction of the bill in the House of Commons on 12 December 1991 lend support to this contention.

After the Supreme Court of Canada's decision in *R. v. Seaboyer* (discussed below), Justice Minister Campbell initiated a process of consultation designed to lead to new legislation. During this process, the minister held five meetings with what she described as "national women's groups."[29] As mentioned earlier in this chapter, prominent among these groups was LEAF, and LEAF committee member Catharine MacKinnon. At these meetings, the idea of simply making minor changes in the law concerning sexual assault was rejected. "But, seizing the moment, the feminists pressed the minister for much more broad-ranging revisions of the rape law."[30] This direction was based, at least in part, on the approach which LEAF had decided to adopt. Its newsletter, *Leaf Lines*, stated in January 1992, "As a result of LEAF's legal opinion, the women's organizations recommended to the Department of Justice that it rewrite the law of sexual assault as a whole."[31]

Where the specific wording of Bill C-49 came from is not clear. Gwendolyn Landolt, an anti-feminist and vice-president of REAL Women, has claimed that Sheila McIntyre, a Queen's University law professor, feminist, and active member of LEAF, offered to draft the bill at the consultation held with national women's groups on 23 October 1991.[32] Kim Campbell denied this was true and asserted that the bill had been drafted by officials in the Justice Department.[33] While the bill as actually introduced in the House of Commons may well have been the result of technical work by the Justice Department, it seems obvious that Professor Sheila McIntyre played a role in its creation.[34] Throughout the early part of 1992 she was a leading public spokesperson on behalf of the bill, regularly defending its provisions and attacking its critics. Much more telling, however, is the fact that McIntyre, speaking on behalf of LEAF, and Judy Rebick, president of the National Action Committee on the Status of Women, held a press conference on 20 November 1992 at which they publicly announced details of the bill, *three weeks before it was introduced in Parliament*. If we ask the question, was Bill C-49 the Government of Canada's bill or LEAF's bill, the very fact of this unprecedented press conference strongly suggests an answer. And, if there could have been any remaining doubt at this point, Rebick dispelled it by adding, "We were delighted and surprised to find there has been a convergence between women's groups and the minister."[35] Rebick's statement confirmed that the views of LEAF, largely without change and largely without opposition, had become the views of the Department of Justice.

The Public Debate on Bill C-49

The public debate, or more accurately, the absence of public debate surrounding the passage of Bill C-49 is as clear a manifestation as one could wish of the power of interest groups in contemporary Canadian politics. LEAF and its allies got almost everything they wanted. Only a handful of critical voices was raised.

In Parliament itself there was no debate. The opposition parties proclaimed their support for the bill as soon as it was introduced. Indeed, if anything, opposition critics were more staunch in their support of the bill than the government. Liberal justice critic Russell MacLellan called it "basically a sound piece of legislation" and added, "I'm at a loss to see how we could do it any better." The NDP's Dawn Black said she had "difficulty understanding" the criminal lawyers who criticized the bill.[36] At one point a *Globe and Mail* editorial wondered why no criticism of Bill-C49 was being raised by members of Parliament.[37] The bill sailed through its three readings with all-party support.

The only public criticism of Bill C-49 came from outside Parliament. Lawyers, especially criminal lawyers, spearheaded this criticism. The Ontario Criminal Lawyers' Association (CLA) was particularly outspoken. Marlys Edwardh presented the association's main brief to the House of Commons Justice Committee. She, in common with all the lawyers who spoke against the original bill, saw it as shifting the burden of proof to the accused. She also observed that the most "frightening statement" made by supporters of the bill was that it would educate men about sexual assault. "I'm not sure that we want to put people in jail to educate them" was her response.[38] In saying this, Edwardh was simply recognizing that for the last several decades Canadian criminal law has been moving in the direction of restraint. MP Barbara Greene called the association's views on the bill "appalling."[39] Other lawyers also spoke out. Brian Greenspan, president of the CLA, and Michelle Fuerst, chair of the criminal justice section of the Canadian Bar Association (Ontario), expressed public reservations.[40] The CCLA, as noted earlier, raised serious questions about the bill. Gwendolyn Landolt appeared before the Justice Committee to attack the bill.[41] Professor Donald Stuart of Queen's University, a leading academic authority on criminal law, had concerns.[42] The *Globe and Mail* published a critical editorial. And Toronto lawyer Clayton Ruby wrote a *Globe and Mail* article about the bill in which he denounced it as "unfair."[43]

Reverse Onus

The various amendments to the Criminal Code were based on the perception that sexual assault was an "under-reported" offence and were designed to remove legal obstacles to the reporting of sexual assaults. One such obstacle was seen to be publicity. Since sexual assault trials – like all criminal trials – took place in open court, the complainant could, ordinarily, be identified in the media. Section 486(3) of the Criminal Code gives the trial judge the power to make an order prohibiting publication of the identity of the complainant or of any information that "could disclose" the identity of the complainant. The complainant is permitted to apply for such an order and, if she does, the judge *must* make it. A 1999 amendment would have provided the same protection to a witness (1999, c. 25). Section 486(1) gives the trial judge a very broad discretion to close the courtroom during "all" or "part" of the proceedings. Section 276 substantially limits the ability of the accused to cross-examine the complainant about her previous sexual history. Section 276 is usually referred to as a "rape-shield law." These provisions were designed to ensure that sexual assault hearings did not turn into a trial of the complainant. The point of a so-called rape-shield law is to limit the ability of the accused in a rape or sexual assault trial to cross-examine the accused about her previous sexual history. The section also lists certain circumstances under which such cross-examination may, nonetheless, be carried out. Companion provisions added to section 278 in 1997 restrict the ability of the accused to require production of the complainant's "medical, psychiatric, therapeutic, counselling" or related records (1997, c. 30). All these changes in the law might be seen as limiting both the extent to which a sexual assault trial takes place in public and, in addition, the right of an accused person to defend himself. This can be seen in three respects:

1 Sexual assault appears to have become a reverse onus offence.
2 The accused is not entitled to make a full answer and defence to the charge.
3 The trial does not take place in public.

All three results have been canvassed in proceedings before the Supreme Court, with, in each case, the statute which wrought these transformations being challenged. LEAF intervened in all these proceedings and usually ended up on the winning side: the Supreme Court, which often shows little deference to Parliament, was not prepared to interfere with legislation which substantially limited important Charter guarantees. Sexual assault thus remains an exception to basic principles of the Canadian criminal justice system.

Sexual Assault Appears to Have Become a Reverse Onus Offence   The 1992 Criminal Code amendments went a long way toward requiring the accused in a sexual assault proceeding to prove his innocence. In the original bill, as created by LEAF, the accused would have been obliged to show that he took "*all* reasonable steps to ascertain" that the complainant was consenting to the sexual activity in question. That formulation would have placed the burden of proof clearly on the accused. Before the bill was enacted the word *all* was removed. Why was this legislation adopted? The bill was often referred to as the "No means no bill," as if this principle had not been central to Canadian law on sexual assault law prior to 1992.

As mentioned earlier, a major study of Canadian sexual assault law carried out by the Department of Justice from 1985 to 1991 had not revealed deficiencies in the law which would have necessitated such changes.[44] That they were made is explicable only on the basis that LEAF had succeeded in capturing the policy-making process. These changes proceeded from the view that sexual relations between men and women are, by their nature, an abuse of power and a zero-sum game.

The Supreme Court's approach to this legislation has been enthusiastic and uncritical. In *R. v. Ewanchuk* the Court went even further in the direction of making sexual assault a reverse onus offence. The accused in this case tried to raise the defence of "implied consent," arguing that the complainant's behaviour had been such that he could imply from it that she was consenting to sexual activity with him. The Court emphatically rejected this defence. The accused also attempted the defence of "honest belief," arguing that he honestly believed the complainant was consenting. The court did accept that such a defence might be raised, but added that in order for the accused to raise the defence that he honestly, but mistakenly, believed the complainant was consenting, he must introduce evidence that would give an "air of reality" to the defence.[45] This approach has the effect of placing the burden of proof on the accused. The Court took a major step in this direction in a 1997 decision, *R. v. Esau.*

In *Esau* the accused and the complainant had sexual intercourse together after a party at her home. According to the accused, he and the complainant kissed each other and she invited him to her bedroom where the intercourse occurred. The complainant was drunk at the time and subsequently denied that she had consented. The accused was convicted at trial and appealled to the N.W.T. Court of Appeal. The Court of Appeal ordered a new trial so that the defence of honest but mistaken belief in consent could be put to the jury. The Crown appealed to the Supreme Court. The Court dismissed the appeal and ordered a new trial. Justice L'Heureux-Dubé dissented. She would have rejected the defence of honest but mistaken belief that the complainant had consented and would have required the accused to show that the complainant had "communicated" her consent to him. Again, the burden of proof is squarely on the accused.

The Accused Is Not Entitled to Make a Full Answer and Defence to the Charge The so-called "rape-shield" provisions in the Criminal Code were challenged in a case called *R. v. Seaboyer.* Seaboyer was charged with sexual assault. A major part of the Crown's case against him consisted of bruises on the complainant's body, bruises which, it was claimed, he had caused. Seaboyer wished to attack this Crown evidence by cross-examining the accused about her sexual activity with other men. This cross-examination, he believed, would show that not he, but someone else, had caused the bruises on the complainant's body. The majority held that section 276 – the section which shields the complainant's prior sexual history – "has the potential to exclude otherwise admissible evidence which may be highly relevant to the defence."[46] The majority struck section 276 down.

L'Heureux-Dubé dissented. She began her judgment by stating that, "Sexual assault is not like any other crime. It is for the most part unreported and the prosecution and conviction rates are among the lowest for all violent crimes."[47] As far as I can understand her judgment, L'Heureux-Dubé made that up. She began the next sentence of her judgment with the phrase "These statistics" and made no reference whatsoever to any statistics. The Justice Department report referred to above suggests that Justice L'Heureux-Dubé's guesses about the realities of sexual assault may be less accurate than she imagined. As in *Ewanchuk,*[48] L'Heureux Dubé declined to deal with the specifics of the appeal before her and delivered another sermon on "myths" and "stereotypes." She regarded the "principles of fundamental justice" as being of secondary importance in sexual assault prosecutions. This, of course, is an example of the "contextual" approach. As applied in criminal cases, this approach appears to mean that the substantive and procedural rights available to an accused person will vary according to the judge's personal opinion of the seriousness of the offence the accused is charged with. This amounts to yet another example of judges deciding cases on the basis of personal preferences and rewriting the constitutional text at their discretion. Section 11 of the Charter says that "Any person charged with an offence" has certain rights which are then enumerated. As I interpret it, L'Heureux-Dubé effectively rewrote the section to read, "Any person charged with an offence has such rights as a judge may think fit."

For her myths, L'Heureux-Dubé relied heavily on Catharine MacKinnon and the *Canadian Journal of Women and the Law* (CJWL), quoting articles from the latter. In 1992, the CJWL – which is heavily subsidized by public funds – published what must be the strangest article ever to appear in an ostensibly scholarly publication. The first sentence of this article read: "I am a white middle class Jewish radical lesbian feminist."[49] L'Heureux-Dubé also quoted articles from material written in social science periodicals by well-known feminist activists as if these, too, were completely unbiased sources which did nothing but state the truth. I wonder if counsel for *Seaboyer* was given an opportunity to challenge this "evidence"? While one assumes that a judge listens in an unbiased and objective fashion to the arguments advanced by both sides, L'Heureux-Dubé's behaviour suggested that this assumption, in her case, may have been unfounded.

Much feminist "research evidence" is fundamentally flawed, if not fraudulent. "This sort of advocacy research is in no way an attempt to discern truth, but instead, is directed towards the furthering of a political agenda."[50] The most fraudulent research in Canada in recent years has purported to address violence against women.[51]

The Panel on Violence against Women was established by the federal minister responsible for the Status of Women in August 1991. The panel was given a budget of $10 million in public funds, and the panel's report, *Changing the Landscape: Ending Violence – Achieving Equality*, was published in 1993. It is a vast confidence trick.

On the first page of the report the panel abandoned any effort at objectivity and affirmed that it intended rather to look at the issues it was to address through "a feminist lens." The panel stated that "violence against women is seen as the consequence of social, economic and political inequality built into the structure of society and reinforced through assumptions expressed in the language and ideologies of sexism, racism and class."[52] Why, one might ask, did the panel bother conducting any research at all? It could simply have stated the conclusions it had evidently reached before it began its inquiry and saved the Canadian people a lot of money.

There is a further methodological shortcoming concealed here. Because it adopted a "feminist lens" the panel looked only at violence against women. This is sufficient reason for rejecting the report. If you do not investigate violence against men at the same time as you investigate violence against women, you cannot say anything meaningful about violence against women. There must be some context.

This difficulty did not deter the panel. It made recommendations covering every aspect of Canadian life. To take but one example, the panel decreed that all religions in Canada should revise their doctrine and teachings to bring them into line with the orthodoxy. Religions were admonished to "review all basic materials, training programs, videos and texts used for religious and relationship instruction to eliminate sexist, racist and homophobic images and messages."[53] The panel also recommended "zero tolerance" of violence against women.[54] This is a phrase much-beloved amongst those who traffic in orthodoxy. If you are opposed to something, you must accept nothing short of "zero tolerance" of it.

Like the Bertha Wilson report,[55] the panel's report is littered with anecdotal statements. These are appropriately horrifying.[56] But, once again, they are unattributed and, therefore, unverifiable. Furthermore, the report is written in highly emotive language, language which suggests a reluctance to enter into careful investigation of social reality. Take, as an example, the opening sentence of chapter 1: "Every day in this country women are maligned, humiliated, shunned, screamed at, pushed, kicked, punched, assaulted, beaten, raped, physically disfigured, tortured, threatened with weapons and murdered."[57]

The passage just quoted points toward my main reason for describing the report as a confidence trick. The reason is its definition of *violence*, a matter that goes to the report's heart. How, then, did it define *violence*? Let us not forget, of course, that *violence* is not a neutral word. It is evocative and has decidedly negative connotations.

The panel decided that *violence* had five aspects or "dimensions." The first two were unexceptionable – "physical violence" and "sexual violence." But then the panel added "psychological violence." I would have thought this was a semantic impossibility, but no matter. "Psychological violence" was said to include "the deliberate withholding of various forms of emotional support." Then there was "financial violence," which could occur when men "withhold or maintain control over all or substantial amounts of money." And, finally, there was "spiritual violence," which might involve "the exclusion of women from key positions in some religious institutions."[58] I cannot avoid observing that many of the things the panel defined as "violence" are part and parcel of the normal wear and tear of human life. With this definition of *violence*, how could the panel have reached any conclusion other than that violence against women in Canada was "prevalent"? Indeed, I would venture to say that, based on this definition, there is not a woman or man alive who has not been a victim of violence.

A coroner's inquest held in Toronto in December 2001 and January and February 2002 actually saw some public questioning of the Can Pan report, as it came to be known. An Ottawa journalist questioned the scriptural status the report has achieved,[74] noting that "A newspaper editor would likely not accept any of the Can Pan report because it doesn't name sources and is packed with unattributed quotes."[59] The prominent psychiatrist Harold Merskey appeared as an expert witness at this inquest. When he attempted to question certain elements of feminist theology, the coroner instructed the jury to disregard his remarks.[60] Merskey's sin was that he had attempted to raise questions about the orthodoxy. For having done so, he was subjected to a vicious personal attack in the pages of the *Toronto Star*.[61]

The truly astonishing thing, however, is that having talked of the "prevalence" of violence, having gone so far as to repeat the phrase "war against women," in the very next paragraph of its report the panel stated, "Despite a wealth of research in the area, we have only educated estimates of the prevalence of violence against women in Canada today."[62] I take this as an admission that, even after cooking its definition, even after spending a full $10 million, the panel, at bottom, was relying on guesswork. More to the point, how on earth can recommendations based on "educated estimates" be justified?[63]

Parliament's response to the Supreme Court's decision in *Seaboyer* was to re-enact the Criminal Code section which had been struck down. In *R. v. O'Connor* the Court laid down an approach to the question of access by a person accused of sexual assault to the medical, therapeutic, and counselling records of the complainant. Not surprisingly, Justice L'Heureux-Dubé took a stricter approach than the other judges. Parliament subsequently legislated the L'Heureux-Dubé approach. What we have here is not the mystical "dialogue among the branches" which Justice Iacobucci spoke of in *Vriend* v. *Alberta*,[64] but clear evidence that LEAF has come to dominate the legislative agenda as fully as it dominates the judicial agenda.

The question of access to the complainant's counselling and therapeutic records can be important in a sexual assault prosecution. There is in Canada today a large and determined band of charlatans who call themselves counsellors and therapists. There is no licensing or certification process for such individuals: anyone who chooses may call herself a therapist and purport to give advice and counselling to women who present themselves at sexual assault crisis centres. The scriptural text for such persons is a strange little book called *The Courage to Heal*.[65] Access to a complainant's counselling and therapeutic records is important because there is a substantial likelihood that the therapist will suggest to her client that she has been sexually assaulted. The client, who is likely to be highly distressed, may be in an emotionally vulnerable state and very susceptible to suggestions made by the "therapist."

Given that there exist no enforceable ethical standards which might constrain therapists, there is nothing to prevent a therapist from manipulating a female client's emotional distress in order to convince her that she has been sexually assaulted. The true situation may well be worse. In 1996 the Canadian Psychological Association issued its "Guidelines for Therapy and Counselling with Women." These "guidelines" suggest that the CPA has accepted feminist ideology and is not averse to the notion of "therapists" manipulating their clients in order to support feminist goals.[66]

This issue becomes especially acute in relation to so-called recovered memory, which may result from a therapist suggesting to a woman that she was sexually assaulted at some distant point in the past. A leading Canadian psychiatrist had the following to say about such practices: "the reporting of sexual offences is currently confused and often misleading and exaggerated."

"The violation of scientific standards by those claiming to have the best interests of women at heart has been documented.[67] [Recovered memory] depends on implausible memories without corroboration and advances no criteria to distinguish true memories from fake memories. No formal restraint exists upon the practice of the RM therapist except for native good sense, which is frequently lacking."[68] In another public speech, Justice L'Heureux-Dubé gave her blessing to the whole notion of recovered memory and spoke ominously of "the important role that therapy often plays in coming to this understanding."[69] The Supreme Court has judicially accepted recovered memory.[70] There is currently a vast debate about "recovered memory" versus "false memory." It is a debate which represents the politicization of memory.

In 2000 the Supreme Court dealt with the question of old and uncorroborated evidence in sexual assault prosecutions in *R. v. A.G.* In this case the alleged sexual assault took place in 1986 or 1988. The complainant, who was between six and eight years old at the time of the alleged incident, disclosed her version of what happened to a school friend in 1993 or 1994 and told her mother in 1995. The mother informed the authorities and criminal charges were laid. The accused was convicted at trial, a trial at which both the complainant and her mother testified for the Crown. The accused appealed to the Ontario Court of Appeal, which dismissed his appeal. Justice of Appeal Finlayson dissented, stating, "there is not the remotest of supporting evidence that sexual acts took place," and he added of what he called "historical sexual abuse cases" that "they commonly involve allegations that are stale-dated and of a vague and unsubstantiated nature with the result that it is impossible for the person accused to give a detailed rebuttal to them without arousing suspicion as to why his memory is so precise." Finlayson concluded by expressing his concern that "the erosion and abolition of many traditional protections accorded to the accused in sexual assault cases threaten to render the concept of reasonable doubt a hollow invocation, rather than the shield against injustice."[71]

The Supreme Court dismissed the appeal by the accused, with Justice L'Heureux-Dubé having no reservations about the erosion of the presumption of innocence. She dismissed Finlayson's concerns, saying, "the justification for the law as it stands today is the need to affirm the principles of equality and human dignity in our criminal law by addressing the problem of myths and stereotypes about complainants in sexual assault cases."[72]

So much for the presumption of innocence.

She continued, "Our court has rejected the notion that complainants in sexual assault cases have a higher [sic] tendency than other complainants to fabricate stories based on 'ulterior motives' and are therefore less worthy of belief. Neither the law, nor judicial experience, nor social science research supports this generalization."[73] In support of this argument, she cited her own dissent in *Seaboyer*.

This decision made clear that the judges' knowledge of female anatomy was no better than their understanding of the law. The alleged acts which led to the accused's conviction were physical impossibilities. The Supreme Court accepted the complainant's testimony that "the accused touched and rubbed her vagina while she was fully clothed." It is not possible to touch someone's vagina while she is "fully clothed," the vagina being entirely internal. The correct term, which one might hope the judges were familiar with, for the external female genitalia is *vulva*.

A record of the exchanges between the therapist and the eventual complainant could be very relevant to an accused person's defence. Being largely a statutory reformulation of L'Heureux-Dubé's judgment in *O'Connor*, section 278 of the Criminal Code drastically restricts the ability of an accused person to require the production of counselling or therapeutic records in the possession of a third party – i.e., a sexual assault crisis centre or a "therapist." The Court dealt with these provisions in *R. v. Mills*, and L'Heureux-Dubé was sympathetic toward them, primarily, one suspects, because they were based on her judgment in *O'Connor* – where she spoke of "discrimination" in stereotyped lines of reasoning and of the importance of considering "privacy and societal interests" and referred also to "equality."[74] She believed that the relation between the courts and the legislature "should be one of dialogue."[75] She favoured non-disclosure, in part because "confidentiality" was essential to the "therapeutic relationship,"[76] as if "therapists" were properly certified and regulated professionals.

Inevitably, L'Heureux-Dubé made reference to "myths" and "stereotypes."[77] Chief Justice Lamer dissented and, in his dissent, was prepared to accord much greater significance to an accused person's right to attempt to defend himself. Lamer was prepared to alter section 278 by "reading down" and "reading in" so that the section would not apply in its full vigour to records already in the possession of the Crown. Such records, he concluded, should be disclosed to the trial judge.[78] Although Lamer's approach went some way toward restoring an accused person's right to defend himself, "reading in" and "reading down" of the same Criminal Code section meant redrafting it. Once again, L'Heureux-Dubé took a "contextual" approach which played down the significance of an accused person's right to make full answer and defence. One suspects that, if an accused person were female, L'Heureux-Dubé's analysis of the "context" might have been different.

The approach taken by the Supreme Court can be explained if one reflects on the orthodoxy and its obsession with victims. It is a fixation which has gone a long way toward corrupting our criminal justice system. The focus on "victims" has turned each criminal trial into a contest between an alleged victim and an accused person. In fact, a "victim" has no place in criminal litigation, which is entirely a matter between the state and an accused person. David Paciocco, a former criminal lawyer and now a professor at the University of Ottawa Faculty of Law, observed in April 2001 that "the Supreme Court has effectively removed the state from criminal trials and turned them into disputes between accused persons and complainants, with the defendant's rights 'neutralized.'"[79] It is, of course, misleading and dubious to speak of a "victim" of a crime until there has been a trial and a conviction. One can only speak of a victim after an accused person has been convicted by a court of competent jurisdiction. If sexual assault trials were, as they should be, solely a matter between the state and an accused person, then I suspect that L'Heureux-Dubé might have been capable of taking an impartial approach as between the state and the accused. But the entire matter becomes totally different when the trial is perceived as a contest between a female victim and a male aggressor. The pressures exerted by feminists may become impossible for a judge like L'Heureux-Dubé, who appeared to see herself as a delegate or representative of women, to resist. It is difficult to imagine that, in such a context, any accused man will receive a fair hearing.

The Trial Does Not Take Place in Public   Section 11 of the Charter guarantees everyone charged with an offence the right to a fair and *public* hearing. Our courts have long recognized the importance of the principle that courts be open to the public, stating that the openness of the courts is "one of the hallmarks of a democratic society,"[80] and that "openness" is the rule and "covertness the exception"[81] and, further, that the open court principle is "the very soul of justice" and "Courts are and have, since time immemorial, been public arenas."[82] But none of these considerations applies, in the view of the Supreme Court of Canada, to sexual assault prosecutions.

In *Canadian Newspapers* v. *Canada (A.G.)*, the Court upheld the constitutionality of section 486(3) of the Criminal Code which allowed a trial judge to make an order prohibiting the disclosure of the identity of the complainant in a sexual assault proceeding. Encouraging the reporting of sexual assaults was said by the Court to be a "social value of superordinate importance."[83] In *Canadian Broadcasting Corp.* v. *New Brunswick (A.G.)*, the Court considered the constitutionality of section 486(1) of the Criminal Code. The section allows a trial judge to exclude the public from all or part of a sexual assault trial. In this case, the judge had excluded the public and the media from the part of the proceeding which involved the sentencing of the accused who had pleaded guilty. This offence was, apparently, of a very delicate nature and involved young female persons. The argument raised by the CBC was that section 486(1) was a limit on the freedom of expression guaranteed in section 2(b) of the Charter. The Court upheld the constitutionality of section 486(1), concluding that its purpose was to "protect the innocent and safeguard privacy interests and thereby afford a remedy to the underreporting of sexual offences." The Court did not advert to any evidence which established that sexual offences were, indeed, underreported. The court also held that the "criminal justice system must be ever vigilant in protecting victims of sexual assault from further victimisation."[84] The Supreme Court did hold that the trial judge had not had sufficient evidence before him to reach the conclusion that an exclusion order was necessary to achieve this goal. Indeed, the Supreme Court quoted this statement from the trial judge: "I say some of the facts I knew beforehand or some I had some idea, I didn't know exactly what the facts were thus the order."[85] As if to make *Canadian Broadcasting Corp.* v. *New Brunswick (A.G.)* consistent with its other decisions, the Court, inevitably, talked about "values" and the need to place values in their "social context." There was also talk of "core values" as if these were different from ordinary values. The "context" appears to be that sexual assault is not like any other crime in Canadian criminal law and is not to be dealt with according to the usual rules. To be fair to Justice L'Heureux-Dubé, it should be noted that although she took part in hearing this appeal, she did not deliver her customary sermon about "myths and stereotypes."

This tendency toward holding secret trials in sexual assault prosecutions was again challenged unsuccessfully toward the end of 2000. In a sexual assault prosecution in Ottawa, the trial judge made an order banning publication of any details about the trial including his own name and the verdict.[86] Counsel for a newspaper attacked this unprecedented ban on the basis that it infringed the fundamental principle that criminal trials be held in public.

A crucial element of our system of open justice requires that the complainant in a sexual assault proceeding give evidence against the accused. In June 2001 a woman who had accused a man of sexually assaulting her refused to testify against him and was not charged with contempt of court. She had refused to testify because, as she stated, it would be "too painful." Bonnie Diamond, a director of the National Association of Women and the Law, sought to publicly justify the complainant's action on the ground that requiring her to testify would amount to "re-victimising" her.[87] This is another example of the courts' predilection for treating sexual assault prosecutions as an exception to the basic principles of our criminal justice system. The Supreme Court did so again in *R.* v. *Regan*, a judgment released on 14 February 2002.

On 15 March 1995, Gerald Regan, a former premier of Nova Scotia, was charged with a number of sexual offences, some of them involving events which had occurred in the 1950s. The investigation and prosecution of these alleged offences was decidedly unusual, verging in many respects on persecution. The police investigation may well have been triggered by a complaint to the RCMP made by one of Regan's political opponents. Despite a police policy of not revealing information about an investigation until charges had been laid, a member of the RCMP confirmed to a reporter that Regan was under investigation. From this point on things got worse. A strikingly zealous Crown attorney, Susan

Potts, engaged in "judge-shopping" in an effort to have the charges against Regan tried before a judge who would be sympathetic toward the Crown. The Crown also interviewed a number of possible complainants in an effort, as I interpret it, to encourage them to testify against Regan.

In April of 1998 a judge of the Nova Scotia Supreme Court issued a stay of proceedings for nine of the thirteen charges against Regan. The Crown appealed against the stay. The Nova Scotia Court of Appeal allowed the Crown's appeal and Regan appealed to the Supreme Court which, in a five-to-four decision, dismissed his appeal. The judge who granted the stay believed that the various Crown attorneys involved had allowed their role to get mixed up with that of the police, and thereby lost their objectivity, and concluded that there had been an abuse of process which was sufficiently serious to justify granting a stay. In upholding the Court of Appeal's decision to overturn the stay, the majority judges in the Supreme Court wrote: "Victims of sexual assault must be encouraged to trust the system and bring allegations to light. As the police saw it, there is evidence of a pattern of an assailant sexually attacking young girls and women who were in a subordinate power relationship with the accused, in some cases bordering on a relationship of trust. When viewed in this light, the charges were very serious and society has a strong interest in having the matter adjudicated, in order to convey the message that if such assaults are committed they will not be tolerated, and that young women must be protected from such abuse."[88] As I read those words, they strongly suggest that the judges had already decided Regan was guilty. The words quoted also appear to confirm my assertion that sexual assault is not to be dealt with according to the usual rules.[89]

Four judges dissented, concluding that Regan had been denied his constitutional right to a fair pre-trial procedure.

An editorial in the *Globe and Mail* applauded the Court's decision, believing that the decision would make the legal system "more responsive to the victims of sexual assault."[90] Other media coverage was less enthusiastic. An article in the *National Post* asserted that "the chances of a male accused of a sexual offence receiving a fair trial in Canada's matriarchal justice system are better than the chances of a Jew receiving a fair trial in Nazi Germany, but only just."[91] Another critic stated, "the trial of Mr. Regan reminds me of the 1930s trials of old Bolsheviks in Russia ... Mr. Regan's real offence is to have betrayed the feminist orthodoxy."[92]

INCOME TAXATION

Domestic Servants

One result of the triumph of feminism in North America has been the rebirth of the domestic servant class.[93] This phenomenon makes clear a fact which feminists have laboured mightily to obscure: women belong to classes.[94] It has become commonplace for women who are lawyers, or members of other professions, to have nannies[95] to look after their children. In 1993 a Toronto lawyer went to the Supreme Court of Canada in an attempt to force Canadian taxpayers to subsidize the salary she paid to her full-time nanny.[96] Elizabeth Symes enjoyed a family income of about $200,000. She attempted to challenge the constitutionality of a provision in the Income Tax Act which prevented her from deducting her nanny's salary from her own income for tax purposes. Symes's litigation was supported by the Court Challenges Program. A founder of LEAF, Symes was represented by another LEAF founder, Mary Eberts.[97] In her attempt to deduct her nanny's salary as a business expense, Symes had won in the Federal Court, Trial Division, and then lost in the Federal Court of Appeal.

She also lost in the Supreme Court of Canada. The Court split between male and female judges, with both Justices L'Heureux-Dubé and McLachlin writing judgments in favour of Symes. A crude class analysis of the decision would suggest that it only makes sense that two bourgeois female judges would side with a bourgeois female litigant. The decision is, in addition, odd, in that it stands as one of the few appeals in which LEAF intervened and did not end up on the winning side.

Justice L'Heureux-Dubé's judgment was predictable, and it was so in three respects. First she imagined herself to have an oracular knowledge of "societal" reality in Canada. Second, she based her conclusions on a great deal of highly questionable research. Third, she rejected the notion of judicial impartiality and revelled in her own biases. I will deal with each in turn.

On the first, she observed, "women, rather than men, fulfil the role of sole or primary caregiver to children" and "the male standard now forms the backdrop of assumptions against which expenses are determined to be, or not to be, legitimate business expenses." And further, "the proportion of responsibility borne by women lawyers for their children is almost double that borne by male lawyers."[98] One assumes that L'Heureux-Dubé *just knew* these things. Second, she quoted the Bertha Wilson report on gender equality in the legal profession as if it were revealed truth rather than a highly-biased and methodologically flawed statement of ideology. As in her judgments in sexual assault cases, L'Heureux-Dubé quoted Catharine MacKinnon with approval. Third, she dismissed the "myth" of neutrality in judging.[99] Once again L'Heureux-Dubé revealed that she perceived herself, in her judging, to be a delegate or a representative of women. Finally, L'Heureux-Dubé sought to justify her conclusion by reference to Charter "values." To put the *Symes* case in "context," it must be noted that it was decided in late 1993 at a time when the Canadian government was in the throes of an orgy of cutbacks. Funding for health care and other social programs was being slashed in an inhuman fashion. It is obscene that at such a time judges of the Supreme Court were prepared to deny revenue to the state by allowing privileged middle-class women to deduct from their incomes the costs of maintaining domestic servants. Only a judge blinded by ideology could have been prepared to accept that a nanny's salary was a "business expense."

Support and Maintenance Payments

Given that divorce and separation are widespread, if not universal, many men in Canada are supporting ex-wives and children. It is common for women to be awarded custody of any children of a marriage on divorce and for the father of the children to be required to make payments to her for their support. Important tax issues arise concerning such payments. Who should be responsible for paying the income tax on such payments – the man who makes them or the woman who receives them?

For many years, Canada's Income Tax Act dealt with such payments on a basis known as "deduction/inclusion." The payments would be deducted from the payor's income and included in the payee's income. Thus, the man making the payments would not have to pay tax on them, while the woman receiving the payments would have to.

This deduction/inclusion system was challenged in a case called *Thibaudeau* v. *Canada*. Suzanne Thibaudeau claimed that the fact that she was required to pay tax on the child support payments she received from her ex-husband was a denial of the equality rights in section 15(1) of the Charter. She was joined by a host of intervenants, including, inevitably, LEAF. Indeed, there were so many intervenors that the report of the decision in the Supreme Court Reports referred to them collectively as "the coalition."[100]

Justices Cory and Iacobucci began the Court's majority judgment in a reasonably concrete fashion, noting that the deduction/inclusion system had the effect of "promoting the best interests of the children by ensuring that more money is available to provide for their care. If anything, the inclusion/deduction regime confers a benefit on the post-divorce family unit." The two male judges held that the inclusion/deduction approach of sections 56(1)(b) and 60(b) of the Income Tax Act did not infringe section 15(1) of the Charter. Justice L'Heureux-Dubé dissented. Her judgment was abstract and ideological. She eschewed a concrete analysis of the inclusion/deduction scheme, stating, "An analysis that looks only to whether actual harm has been suffered is too narrow." She moved thence to abstractions, observing that "a distinction will be discriminatory within the meaning of s. 15 where it is capable of either promoting or perpetuating the view that the individual adversely affected by this distinction is less capable or less worthy of recognition or value as a human being or as a member of Canadian society." She added that "Adverse legislative distinctions on the basis of membership in [the group of separated or divorced custodial spouses] are therefore very likely to be perceived to have a discriminatory impact by members of this group."[101]

Justice L'Heureux-Dubé came very close to saying, if you *feel* you were discriminated against, then you were. She would have declared the relevant sections of the Income Tax Act to be unconstitutional. Parliament obligingly amended the act, so that, today, spousal payments are deducted from the income of the payor and become part of the income of the payee. Child support payments remain part of the payor's income, but do not become part of the payee's income.[102]

Typically, the judges of the Supreme Court declined to consider the practical effect of their decision. In contemporary Canada, it appears that the worst social miscreant of all is the so-called "deadbeat dad." A deadbeat dad is a divorced or separated husband/father who fails to make required support payments to his former wife, either for her support or the support of their children. In Ontario, "deadbeat dads" can be imprisoned and have their driver's licences and passports taken away. The effect of the current sections, 60(a) and 56(1)(a) of the Income Tax Act, may often be to double the financial burden of support payments on the payor. The current, post-*Thibaudeau* regime may have the effect of forcing men into deadbeat-dadism.

THE BATTERED WOMAN SYNDROME AND A JUDICIAL LYNCHING

Perhaps the most extreme way in which the Supreme Court has denied the legal existence of men has been in its adoption of the "battered woman syndrome" in murder prosecutions. In August 1986 Lyn Lavallée murdered the man she lived with, Kevin Rust.[103] Kevin Rust was a vicious brute who had been beating and abusing Lavallée for years. At her trial, Lavallée sought to extend the defence of self-defence by relying on the "battered woman syndrome." The essence of this was to argue that Lavallée had been abused to the point where she was so psychologically traumatized that she could not respond rationally and she truly and reasonably believed she had to use extreme force to defend herself against further abuse.[104] On this basis, Lavallée was acquitted at trial and her acquittal was upheld by the Supreme Court.[105]

The "battered woman syndrome" was created by an American psychologist named Lenore Walker. Walker also started the Super Bowl Sunday hoax in which she claimed that violence against women increased dramatically on Super Bowl Sunday. This fairytale was widely accepted until Christina Hoff Sommers demolished it.[106] David Paciocco has observed that "Social science is, by its nature, soft science, and the battered woman syndrome is weak social science," adding that "it is not at all difficult to find 'experts' who are prepared to diagnose virtually any woman who kills her abusive spouse as suffering from battered woman syndrome."[107] The battered woman syndrome has been raised by women who were not physically abused and who murdered their husbands when the husband was in bed asleep. Lilian Getkate shot her husband in 1998 when he was asleep.[108] Her defence was based on "psychological abuse." She was convicted of manslaughter and spent eleven days in jail.[109]

Canadian courts have proved helpless in the face of "experts" like Lenore Walker. The battered woman syndrome is an extreme manifestation of victimology, turning women into helpless, irrational, sub-humans. In *R. v. Malott* a woman who killed her husband and then tried to murder his girlfriend raised the battered woman syndrome in her defence. Malott was convicted of second-degree murder and the Supreme Court dismissed her appeal. The victimology of the battered woman syndrome proved too much even for Justice L'Heureux-Dubé. She spoke of "myths and stereotypes" about battered women and asserted that the mere fact that the accused was a battered woman did not entitle her to an acquittal. She, nonetheless, revealed herself to be mesmerized by "experts."

The acceptance of the battered woman syndrome defence could be described as a contextual approach to murder. Adopting this approach, the judge says, "If someone I like kills someone I don't like, she walks."

A further example of the matriarchal domination of the legal system occurred in 1993. Walter Hryciuk was a judge of the Ontario Court (Provincial Division). Certain complaints about his behaviour were made to the Ontario Judicial Council. As a result, a commission was established to enquire into whether Judge Hryciuk should be removed from office. Madam Justice Jean MacFarland of the Ontario Court (General Division) was appointed commissioner. She held hearings from July to October 1993 and reported on 24 November 1993.[110] Her report recommended that Hryciuk be removed from office. She made this recommendation even though, as she stated in her report, "[Judge Hryciuk] has been described not just as a good judge, but, rather, an excellent judge."[111] A lengthy parade of witnesses spoke against Hryciuk at the inquiry. The commissioner accepted the evidence of all those witnesses who spoke against Hryciuk and rejected the evidence of those who testified on his behalf, largely on the basis of Hryciuk's boorish behaviour at two Christmas parties, each of which took place more than two years before the inquiry. The commissioner recommended that he be removed from office, largely it seems, because he "consistently made sexist and demeaning comments to women," and on one occasion made a woman feel "very uncomfortable."[112] Hryciuk applied for judicial review of the commissioner's findings. The Divisional Court, by a majority, upheld the commissioner's findings.[113] The Court of Appeal then allowed Hryciuk's appeal and quashed the commissioner's findings,[134] primarily because the commissioner had not followed the law in hearing evidence concerning the complaints against Hryciuk: as required by the Courts of Justice Act, the complaints should first have been made to the Ontario Judicial Council.

Reading the commissioner's decision, as well as the decisions of the Divisional Court and the Court of Appeal, it seems to me that it is fair and reasonable to describe the whole matter as a lynching.

It is instructive to compare the treatment of Judge Hryciuk to that given to Judge Leslie Baldwin in 2002. In 1999 Baldwin was given leave from her judicial duties to chair something called the Joint Committee on Domestic Violence. This committee made a series of highly political recommendations to then attorney general Charles Harnick, and Baldwin returned to her judicial duties. Unhappy, however, with the dilatory fashion in which the Ontario government was dealing with her recommendations, in July 2000 she wrote a letter to the new attorney general, James Flaherty. She demanded more funding for domestic violence groups and called upon Flaherty to organize a "summit" on domestic violence. She added that she had not seen a change in the way domestic violence cases were being handled in the courts.

This letter was more the work of a political activist than a judge. The Criminal Lawyers' Association made a complaint about Baldwin to the Ontario Judicial Council, and in May 2002 the council held a "public" hearing about her. The lawyer retained by the council, ostensibly to present the case against Baldwin, did not identify the lawyers who had made the complaint, nor did he put the letter from the Criminal Lawyers' Association on the record, nor did he call any evidence. On 10 May the Ontario Judicial Council decided that Baldwin had done nothing improper.[115]

A comparison of the Baldwin and Hryciuk matters makes the matriarchal domination of Canada's legal system unmistakably clear.

Any possible doubt that the matriarchy is in complete control of our legal system should have been removed as a result of a 2002 decision of the Ontario Court of Appeal.[116] In this decision the court decided that when registering a child's birth under the Vital Statistics Act a mother was not obliged to acknowledge the child's father.[117] In February 2003, an application for leave to appeal was denied by the Supreme Court.

CONCLUSION

This chapter has attempted to outline some of the concrete results of the feminist domination of Canada's legal system. Amongst those results have been a substantial politicization of judicial proceedings as well as the abandonment of what were once thought to be fundamental principles. The judges of the Supreme Court of Canada have become, in my opinion, eager acolytes of feminist thought.

It is difficult to think of a writer with feminist credentials as impeccable as those of Doris Lessing. Yet even she recently denounced feminist excesses.[118]

8

Is the Supreme Court Still a Court?

It is legitimate to ask whether it is still possible and accurate to call the Supreme Court a court. This question can be raised from two perspectives. First, the Supreme Court has trespassed to an extraordinary extent on the proper constitutional role of the legislature and, second, it no longer seems to feel constrained to behave like a court.

THE JUDICIAL ROLE

Canada's Constitution does not include a complete separation of powers,[1] at least not to the degree that separation of powers is a defining feature of the U.S. Constitution. Separation of powers can have a variety of meanings.[2] The concept can mean separation of personnel or simply separation of functions. In a parliamentary system a separation of personnel between the legislature and the executive is impossible. What exists in Canada is a separation of functions, to a degree, amongst the legislature, the executive, and the judiciary.

Canada's Constitution does not contain a formal declaration that the legislative function is vested in the legislatures, nor that the judicial function is vested in the courts. Thus, it is possible for the legislature both to create administrative tribunals and to delegate some or all of its law-making authority to the executive. In fact, during both world wars, Canada was largely governed under the War Measures Act.[3] While this act was repealed in 1988, Parliament, by invoking the act during the world wars, delegated much of its law-making authority to the executive, if it did not indeed effectively abolish itself.[4]

Since we have a parliamentary system in which the executive is, in effect, a committee of the legislature, a complete separation of powers is not feasible. Our judges have not always understood this point. In one decision Antonio Lamer stated, "There is in Canada a separation of powers among the three branches of government – the legislature, the executive and the judiciary."[5] This is not accurate. It is discouraging that a chief justice of Canada could have had such a flawed understanding of our Constitution. We do not, in Canada, have either a separate executive branch or judicial branch of government. As has been noted, the executive is made up of members of the legislature. While we do have an *independent* judiciary, we do not have an *autonomous* judicial branch. An autonomous judiciary is one which is fully responsible for its own budgeting and internal administration. This is not the case in Canada.

The point of a separation of powers is to limit the power of the state and to thus prevent the state from becoming a despotism. The theory is that if the totality of powers exercised by the state be divided functionally amongst three separate branches, these branches will check and balance each other, thereby creating an institutional bulwark against despotism. Since constitutional government is, by definition, limited government, it is possible to argue that some notion of separation of powers must inhere in all systems of constitutional government. A monumental constitutional battle occurred in the Union of South Africa in the 1950s as the courts resisted certain initiatives taken by the National Party government to implement its policy of apartheid. The so-called Coloured Voters cases were a landmark effort by the courts to require the legislature to act within the Constitution.[6]

Canada does have a limited separation of powers which recognizes that certain decision-making functions are reserved to the judiciary.[7] This means that no other organ of the state may purport to exercise these decision-making functions. This principle has been recognized even in the constitutional law of states whose constitutional texts make no express provision for a separation of powers. A series of Judicial Committee decisions interpreting the Constitution of Ceylon in the 1960s explored the extent to which a legislature might be permitted to vest judicial functions in decision-making bodies which are not courts.[8] One result of these decisions was that in 1971 Ceylon became a republic with the name Sri Lanka, abolished appeals to the Judicial Committee, and adopted a constitution which formally vested the "judicial power of the state" in the legislature.[9]

The textual bases for Canada's limited separation of powers are section 96 of the Constitution Act, 1867 and section 11 of the Canadian Charter of Rights and Freedoms. Section 96 states that the governor-in-council is to appoint the judges of the county, district, and superior courts in the provinces. A body of case law has developed which appears to establish that there are certain kinds of decisions which may be made only by a judge appointed under section 96. This body of case law has the practical effect of limiting the kinds of decision-making functions which the legislature may vest in administrative tribunals. Section 11(e) of the Charter states that anyone charged with an offence is entitled to a fair and public hearing before an "independent and impartial" tribunal. This suggests that determinations of guilt or innocence of criminal charges may be made only by a court.

To the extent that our Constitution does recognize some degree of separation of powers, it would be reasonable to assume that the legislative function might be vested in the legislatures. This is not the way the Supreme Court has always seen the matter. While in one case, former chief justice Antonio Lamer did seem to accept this point of view – he claimed that the "role of the legislature is to decide upon and enunciate policy"[10] – in a number of decisions the Supreme Court has been prepared to exercise legislative power, using a doctrine it invented for this purpose and to which it gave the name "reading in." Now, when a court exercises its judicial review function, it is, to a degree, interfering with the legislature. Invalidating a statute or a portion of a statute is clearly an interference. But in addition to striking down invalid legislation, the Supreme Court of Canada has been willing to amend legislation, that is, to add words not placed in the statute by the legislature.

The Court invented "reading in" in 1992 in a case called *Schachter v. Canada*. Chief Justice Antonio Lamer, whom we have to thank for this development, was not entirely candid about what he was doing. He reviewed various interpretive techniques the Court had used in the past, including one called "reading down." He then leaped quickly to "reading in," creating the impression that this was an old, familiar, and well-established technique. The *Schachter* litigation involved a question of the constitutionality of provisions in the Unemployment Insurance Act dealing with parental leave. Different periods of leave were provided for natural parents and for adoptive parents. By distinguishing between natural and adoptive parents, this legislation, it was argued, amounted to a denial of the equality rights guaranteed in secton 15 of the Charter. The Court was prepared to accept this argument and conclude that the provision in the act establishing differential leave periods was invalid. This created a dilemma. If the Court had struck down the offending provision in the act, this would not have assisted Schachter, nor anyone else for that matter. Striking down this provision would have led to the result that no parent, natural or adoptive, would have been entitled to parental leave. To avoid doing this, the Court decided it had the authority to amend the legislation by "reading in" to the act new periods of parental leave. There can be no doubt that to alter the terms of a statute is to exercise an expressly legislative function.

For arrogant and presumptuous ignorance of the proper role of legislatures and of the basic features of Canada's Constitution, it would be difficult to top a statement made by Justice L'Heureux-Dubé in 1994. She wrote, "In a complex society with increasingly involved rules and interrelationships, it is no longer acceptable for courts to foist the entire responsibility of lawmaking upon the legislature."[11] This suggests that L'Heureux-Dubé believed that the judiciary was the primary law-making body and that, from time to time, the judiciary might fail in its duty and allow the legislature to engage in law-making.

What happened in *Schachter* was an unmistakable example of a Court deciding and enunciating policy, something which, as Antonio Lamer himself had observed, is "the role of the legislature." "Reading in" is thus condemned in the words of the judge who invented it. Judicial review involves measuring legislative acts against the Constitution to determine if they are valid, and striking them down if the legislature has exceeded the constitutional authority conferred upon it. Judicial review does not involve rewriting statutes. It does not involve filling in gaps in legislation. To do so is to trespass on territory which should be reserved to the legislature. If separation of powers demands that the judiciary respect and act within the functional limits placed on its authority, a further form of judicial restraint which reinforces the principle of separation of powers is a "political questions" doctrine – i.e., a doctrine which implies a recognition by the judges that certain questions are not properly within their jurisdiction and should be dealt with only by the political organs of the state. The Supreme Court has refused to accept that the scope of its authority may be limited by a political questions doctrine.[12] The Court has refused to accept that there can be questions or issues which are, by their nature, beyond its jurisdiction. A separation of powers must also require that the judiciary behave in a judicial fashion. If the judicial function is vested in the judiciary, it must be assumed that the judges will also discharge the judicial role – that is, that they will act like judges.

ACTING JUDICIALLY

Only the judges may perform judicial functions and they must do so in a judicial fashion. That assertion is utterly obvious and likely beyond argument. The fact that it needs to be made makes clear the extent to which the judges of the Supreme Court have abandoned their proper constitutional role. The judges must act like judges and they must preside over a body which is recognizable as a court. It had been understood that courts existed to resolve concrete issues between parties and that these issues were to be resolved based on established legal principles. A court hearing a matter is not a legislative committee, nor is it a law reform commission. Just as it has decided not to be constrained by any functional limits on its authority, however, the Supreme Court of Canada appears to have also abandoned the notion that it is obliged to act like a court.

The most obvious manifestation of this abandonment has been in the Court's approach to the issue of intervenors. There was a time when the Court heard appeals and the only parties before it were the appellant and the respondent, which is to say that it heard only the two parties directly involved in a particular appeal. The Court now allows just about any person or organization, which so desires, to be granted intervenor status. There once were limits on who might be allowed to intervene. These have, as a practical matter, been abandoned.[13] Intervenors are permitted to file written facta with the Court and to make oral arguments before it. Indeed, organizations seeking to advance political agendas appear regularly before the Court.

The problem, as I see it, is that intervenors can distort or pervert the concrete litigation actually before the Court. A clear example of this is *Andrews* v. *Law Society of British Columbia*. In this case, Andrews, who was not a Canadian citizen, was challenging a section of the Law Society Act of British Columbia which said that he could not become a lawyer in the province because he was not a Canadian citizen. LEAF intervened. It must be clear that the Women's Legal Education and Action Fund had no interest in the outcome of the concrete litigation. It clearly could not have cared whether Andrews became a lawyer in B.C. or not. LEAF's aim, I surmise, was to persuade the Court to adopt its feminist, some-people-are-more-equal-than-others interpretation of section 15(1) of the Charter. LEAF's intervention politicized a fairly concrete appeal and transformed it into an abstract, ideological battle. The Supreme Court obliged LEAF and adopted its interpretation of the section. The Court rejected the clear meaning of the opening words of section 15(1) – "Every individual is equal" – and decided that only those persons it approved of might claim equality rights.

Unlimited intervention guarantees that the Court will behave less and less like a court and more and more like an oracular censor of ideological disputes. Certain organizations have become regular intervenors, and in many cases these interventions are funded by the state.[14] Most prominent amongst the regular intervenors is LEAF, which as previously mentioned has had extraordinary success, ending up on the winning side in many decisions. It would be fascinating to compare the judgments written by certain judges with the facta filed by LEAF. It would be an overstatement to suggest that certain organizations have "hijacked" the Court, although LEAF has almost always been on the winning side when it has intervened. If the same organizations appear as intervenors with considerable regularity – they do – it can only be assumed that these organizations intervene as often as they do because they are confident they will get the results they are looking for, namely those they could not have achieved through the democratic process.

Since intervenors are not parties to the dispute which led to an appeal, the presence of a substantial number of intervenors tends to lend an abstractness to Supreme Court hearings. The court is less and less directed toward the resolution of concrete legal issues between real parties, but more and more toward abstract speculation on broad issues of public policy. Because it has relaxed earlier rules about standing[15] and because it allows persons to raise Charter claims based on alleged violations of other persons' rights, the Court has contributed substantially to making its proceedings highly abstract.

It would be wrong to blame the abstractness of Supreme Court proceedings entirely on the judges. Reference cases are an important and special feature of Canada's constitutional system.[16] Section 53 of the Supreme Court Act permits the governor-in-council to refer "questions of law or fact" to the Supreme Court. The Court invariably hears such references, although, by their nature, there is no concrete dispute between parties in a reference case. Thus, the very existence of the reference procedure lends an abstractness to the work of the Supreme Court.

An extreme example of the way intervenors can transform a proceeding can be found in the 1999 decision *R. v. Ewanchuk*.[17] This was a criminal appeal in which LEAF and other organizations intervened. How can an accused person receive a fair trial and enjoy the right to attempt to defend himself or herself when the Crown is joined by a collection of likely publicly-funded intervenors? In such a situation the accused person might well feel ganged-up against. To permit this to happen amounts to the abandonment of what had been a defining feature of Canadian judicial proceedings – their adversarial nature. In *Ewanchuk*, one party – originally the accused – was confronted not only by the state, but, in addition, by a selection of intervenors, all of whom were probably funded by the state. It is difficult to characterize such a proceeding as "fair."

It used to be thought that the proper place for special interest organizations, such as LEAF, was before legislative committees and law reform commissions. It was once thought that in seeking to resolve outstanding issues between parties a Court should restrict itself to the information and the arguments actually presented by the parties themselves. In *Ewanchuk*, Justice L'Heureux-Dubé actually declined in her judgment to address the specific legal issues which had been raised before the Court and contented herself with delivering a sermon apparently dispelling what she described as "myths" and "stereotypes." In her judgment L'Heureux-

Dubé cited articles by Catharine MacKinnon, who, as noted in chapter 7, has argued that the notion of a woman consenting to sexual relations with a man is "very questionable."[18] I cannot grasp how a judge who is prepared to accept this point of view can deal in a judicial fashion with the issues raised in a sexual assault prosecution, especially when, as in this case, the major issue raised by the defence was consent – the accused person's defence was that the complainant had consented to engaging in sexual relations with him. By quoting MacKinnon, L'Heureux-Dubé appeared to be admitting that she had closed her mind to the arguments being raised by the appellant.

The Supreme Court no longer addresses only the facts and arguments advanced by the parties. Each judge now has three judicial law clerks – recent law school graduates. These clerks do independent research for their judges and write memoranda for them setting out the results of their research as well as arguments as to how the judge should decide a particular matter. It thus is possible for a judge to reach a decision on the basis of facts and arguments not raised in open court. Once again, the worst offender in this regard was Justice L'Heureux-Dubé. She went to great lengths in an attempt to justify reliance on material not introduced by the parties to an appeal.[19]

An apologist for law clerks has written that they "give the law the needed capacity for change, bringing knowledge from excellent professors in demanding law schools."[20] I doubt whether either of these latter things exists in Canada.

A disturbing manifestation of this predilection for deciding cases based on more than the submissions of the parties was revealed in a newspaper article published in late 2000.[21] The article made known that a judicial chat site had been created on the Internet. Judges may now consult electronically with other judges as to how to decide cases, thereby obviating the need for such tedious exercises as listening to what the parties have to say. Add to this the fact that the aforementioned clerks occasionally draft judgments for their judges.[22] When, from time to time, they abdicate the judgment-writing function to their clerks, the judges further abandon the judicial role.[23]

While organizations may not have "hijacked" the Court, clerks have occasionally managed to "capture" their judges. Justice L'Heureux-Dubé was the most actively feminist judge on the

Court. She was born in 1927 and finished law school in 1952. It is, therefore, difficult to imagine how, in the normal course of events, she might have been so rigorously instructed in feminist ideology. In 1986, when her appointment to the Court was announced, L'Heureux-Dubé stated, "I can tell you I'm for justice. Whether it be left, right or centre, that's all that counts."[24] This, to use the hideous jargon of the orthodoxy, is a completely "decontextualized" approach to justice. By 1999 L'Heureux-Dubé's commitment to the orthodoxy was so well known that a reporter could say about a case before the court, "The firm hand and feminist perspective of Madam Justice Claire L'Heureux-Dubé are expected to guide tomorrow's Supreme Court of Canada ruling."[25] What had happened? How had L'Heureux-Dubé moved from an abstract commitment to justice to being so publicly and obviously biased? This, I believe, must have come about through the efforts of judicial law clerks.

Many years ago, Canadian law schools eschewed the teaching of law and have since contented themselves with indoctrinating students in the orthodoxy.[26] Getting the kind of law school grades which allow a graduate to be hired as a clerk at the Supreme Court may well depend on how completely the student demonstrates his or her commitment to the orthodoxy. Once in Ottawa it is not difficult for such a graduate to convert the judge he or she is ostensibly working for. This is evident in the degree to which the law schools' latest ideological fashions, as well as their grammatical and syntactical infelicities, find their way into Supreme Court judgments.[27] This surmise that the clerks serve as the conduit from the law schools to the judges was confirmed in a minor scandal which erupted in March 2000. It transpired that law professors had been sending manuscripts to clerks in the hope that the clerks would attempt to influence their judges to decide cases in a particular way. The incestuous connection between the Court and the law schools is also apparent in the number of former judicial law clerks now teaching in university law faculties.

While the practice of law professors sending their writings to law clerks, one assumes, ended after Chief Justice McLachlin denounced it in a letter to Canadian law schools,[28] one can only assume that the unscrupulous law professors had some success. The decisions of the Supreme Court in recent years have become harder and harder to recognize as "judgments." They are invariably lengthy and often involve self-indulgent excursions by the judges into history, psychology, or sociology. These do little beyond demonstrating the banality of the judges' minds.[29] Many of these decisions are nearly impossible to understand. They often lack the defining element of a judgment in that, in many cases, they do not actually decide anything. It has also become commonplace for every judge who hears a particular appeal to write a decision. Reading these prolix and self-indulgent essays, it is not always possible to determine what, if anything, the court actually decided.[30] Professor Albert Abel once accused the Court of "shoddy craftsmanship," "floundering," and "ragged exposition."[31]

The most extreme recent manifestations of the Court's predilection for trespassing on the territory of the legislature can be seen in decisions involving gay rights. In *Vriend* v. *Alberta* a man had lost his job after publicly announcing that he was homosexual. He wished redress, but was denied this because Alberta's human rights legislation, the Individual Rights Protection Act, did not list sexual orientation or sexual preference as prohibited grounds of discrimination in employment. Vriend argued that by failing to so specify, the Alberta legislature was denying rights guaranteed in section 15 of the Charter. The Court accepted that, in not prohibiting discrimination on the basis of sexual orientation, the legislature had denied Vriend the equal benefit of the law. Even though sexual orientation is not listed as one of the prohibited grounds of discrimination in section 15 of the Charter, the Supreme Court has judicially amended the section by recognizing what are called "analogous grounds."[32] The Alberta act was found to be in contravention of the Charter. If the Court had struck down the act this would not have benefited Vriend. Instead, the Court accepted that it possessed the jurisdiction to alter the act by "reading in" sexual orientation, even though the Alberta legislature had expressly rejected precisely that idea on an earlier occasion.

A similar example of judicial infringement on legislative territory can be found in *M. (K.)* v. *M. (H.)*. In 1994 the Ontario legislature rejected a government bill which would have given statutory recognition to same sex unions. The judges were prepared to "read in" to the legislation, contrary to the express wishes of the legislature, in such a way as to legally recognize same-sex unions. Once again the Court was prepared to exercise a legislative function and amend a statute. In a constitutional democracy it is the province of the people's elected representatives to enact legislation. This is not part of the judicial function. Constitutional government requires that all organs of the state accept the constitutional limits within which they are bound to act. "Reading in" is an example of the refusal on the part of the Supreme Court of Canada to accept that it, too, is constrained by the Constitution.

One function which our Constitution reserves exclusively to the legislatures is that of amending the Constitution.[33] But even here, in some cases, the Court has altered the constitutional text in order to reach the result which accorded with the personal preferences of the judges.[34]

Given its abandonment of the judicial role and its willingness to arrogate to itself the performance of specifically legislative functions, it is difficult to continue to describe the Supreme Court of Canada as a "court." There is one decision in which the Supreme Court, to be fair, was prepared to show respect for the legislature. In *New Brunswick Broadcasting Co. v. Nova Scotia (Speaker of the House of Assembly)*, a broadcaster attempted to interfere with the workings of a provincial legislature, arguing that the Charter could be the basis for forcing the legislature to have its proceedings televised against the wishes of its members. The Court concluded that "legislative privilege" was part of the Canadian Constitution and was, thus, constitutional. The attempt on the part of a broadcaster to defeat the wishes of the legislature failed.

9

Encore une Trahison des Clercs

Canadian law professors have played a central role in the subversion of our law and our democracy. This chapter addresses different aspects of that role.

Julien Benda was a French writer of the twentieth century. In 1927 he published *La Trahison des clercs* (*The Treason of the Intellectuals*). This book accused intellectuals of abandoning the search for truth and succumbing to their personal political predilections. The approach of Canadian legal academics to the Charter and the Supreme Court is a further manifestation of the treason of the intellectuals. Canada's law professors have contented themselves with being cheerleaders. To return to Benda, the central point of *La trahison des clercs* was to criticize Henri Bergson, a French philosopher who had retreated into mysticism and a fascination with the self, failings which are reminiscent of Supreme Court Charter decisions.

While there have been Canadian intellectuals with sufficient courage and integrity to be critical of the Court, these people have largely been political scientists – Ted Morton of the University of Calgary, Ian Brodie of the University of Western Ontario, Rainer Knopff also of the University of Calgary, and Chris Manfredi of McGill University. Only two law teachers, the most prominent being Michael Mandel of the Osgoode Hall Law School, have been publicly critical.[1] Professor Kent Roach of the Faculty of Law at the University of Toronto recently attempted some mild criticism of the Court.[2] Roach's book is interesting in that at the same time as he questioned the behaviour of the judges he expressed his support for the orthodoxy. Consequently, Roach was critical of my earlier writing about the Court, simultaneously calling me both a "left-" and a "right-wing" critic.[3] In fact, the writing of legal academics about the Court and the Charter has been both sycophantic and unprincipled.

SYCOPHANTIC

James MacPherson took sycophancy to new heights. His article "Canadian Constitutional Law and Madame Justice Bertha Wilson – Patriot, Visionary and Heretic" is a masterpiece of grovelling unctuousness. It is also laughable. He stated, "The tides of time will wash against her immense judicial footprints." He continued, "But many of her footprints will endure."[4] MacPherson did not seem to grasp that there is only one thing tides do to footprints, judicial or otherwise. They expunge them. MacPherson has a strong claim to membership in Canada's ruling clique. He was the executive legal officer at the Supreme Court from 1985 to 1987, moving from there to be dean of the Osgoode Hall Law School at York University from 1988 to 1993 and thence to the Ontario Court of Appeal as a judge, having stopped along the way at the Ontario Superior Court.

UNPRINCIPLED

When it comes to unprincipled, one must never forget an extraordinary article by Dale Gibson. Gibson noted that some of the Supreme Court's decisions interpreting section 15(1) of the Charter amounted to "judicial amendments" of the Constitution. He applauded the Court for doing so. He expressed a lack of sympathy for the "democratic process" and concluded his article by asserting that his sole concern was with "getting the answers right."[5] If the only thing we care about in the way that a final constitutional court interprets a constitution is getting the answers right, we would be well-advised to do away with constitutional government and adopt Chief Justice Lamer's benevolent absolute monarchy.

While I am on the subject of unprincipled academics, I must refer to an article in the *Globe and Mail* by Osgoode Hall Law School professor Allan Hutchinson. In the article, Hutchinson revealed that "judges cannot avoid making political choices." He added that "In a vibrant democracy [whatever that might be], it is political justice and not legal dogma that we are after."[6] Hutchinson, in his public utterances, usually describes himself as a "Professor of Law." If he really means it when he asserts that "politics is law" and "law is politics," I must ask myself, What precisely is it that he professes? Does York University pay him a handsome salary as his reward for telling students that "law is politics" and "politics is law"?

Hutchinson's final assertion about "vibrant democracy" is, surely, just another way of saying that all that matters is getting the answers right. To get the full flavour of how unprincipled Canadian legal academics have become, we must return to the 1992 volume of the *Dalhousie Law Journal*.

Christine Boyle of the Dalhousie Law School contributed a rhapsodic piece entitled "The Role of the Judiciary in the Work of Madame Justice Wilson." Boyle applauded Justice Wilson's behaviour as a judicial delegate or representative of women. She also expressed her approval for the notions of gender apartheid expressed by Carol Gilligan.[7] Gilligan's work, which seems to suggest that human males and females belong to different species, is the source of the solipsistic views about gender expressed by Justice Wilson in *R. v. Morgentaler* (1988).

Professor Mary Jane Mossman of Osgoode Hall Law School contributed something called "The 'Family' in the Work of Madame Justice Wilson." Mossman managed to be both sycophantic and unprincipled. She was unprincipled in taking a purely ideological view of her subject matter and sycophantic in her fulsome praise of Wilson both for politicizing family relations and for subjecting them, through law, to more and more state control.

The article "Equality and Access to Justice in the Work of Bertha Wilson" is a defining statement of everything that is wrong with Canadian legal "scholarship" today. Its author, Hester Lessard of the University of Victoria Law School, wrote in almost purely ideological terms. The article was largely a statement of the extent to which Lessard has surrendered her mind to the orthodoxy. Her work was an expression of the neo-apartheid epistemology which is central to the orthodoxy. She also manifested the depressing predilection of legal "scholars," borrowed from Supreme Court judges, for simply making things up to fit their preconceptions. Lessard revealed that the doctrine of precedent and the rules of statutory interpretation were "racist,"[8] although no hint was given as to how she had reached those conclusions. She also asserted that "Increasingly, Canadians have sought to understand themselves as a community through the language of equality rights."[9] I can only assume that Lessard made that up since no reference was supplied to suggest where she might have discovered this truth. There is a certain bizarre logic here. If one believes that reality is socially constructed and that the emotional should have precedence over the intellectual, there is no good reason that one should not simply make things up. Translated, I assume that Lessard's assertion means, "The other professors and feminist lawyers I talk to think this way." Lessard was once a judicial law clerk at the Supreme Court.

The main reason I speak of Canadian legal scholarship as "intellectually corrupt" lies in its disregard for the methodological imperatives which should inform academic writing.[10] Canadian university law professors have largely abandoned any pretense at being scholars and have turned themselves into propagandists – propagandists for the ruling clique and for the orthodoxy. The true state of the corruption of legal education was revealed in a scandal which rocked the University of Toronto Faculty of Law in February 2001. A detailed discussion of the events which took place follows. This is presented both because it is interesting and for what it says about legal education in Canada today.

It was alleged that thirty-odd first-year law students had falsified their December grades in applications for summer jobs which were sent to leading Toronto law firms. A common explanation for this behaviour was that a law professor had actually encouraged the students to lie about their grades. An orgy of finger pointing and rationalization ensued. The attempts to explain away the students' cheating and lying became increasingly bizarre. It was suggested that a highly competitive job market and aggressive recruiting by law firms, rather than the students themselves, were to blame. Also blamed were the Americanization of the law school and the attempt by the dean to build what he called "a truly great global law school."[11] No one seemed inclined to say publicly that what the students had done was dishonest and dishonourable, and intolerable in prospective lawyers.

The dismal business at the University of Toronto percolated on, reaching a contested and unsatisfactory apotheosis in May 2001. Everyone involved in the whole sorry matter tried to blame other people for what had happened.

The behaviour of thirty-four students was investigated by the law faculty. The reason for this was that there were thirty-four cases of "discrepancies between students [sic] official academic records and the marks they submitted to the law firms."[12] These thirty-four students were invited to meet with a law professor who concluded that in nine of the cases there were "reasonable and valid" explanations for the discrepancies.[13] Thus, twenty-five students met with the dean to "provide an explanation."[14] Twenty-five students admitted that they had misrepresented their grades. Seventeen students received one-year suspensions plus notations on their academic transcripts, while seven received lesser sanctions and three were to face formal charges before a university disciplinary tribunal.[15] The recriminations and finger pointing did not end there. Prominent Toronto lawyer Clayton Ruby represented twenty of the twenty-five students who had admitted to misrepresenting their grades. He wrote a letter to the *Globe and Mail*, a letter which I interpret as an attempt to lay the blame for the students' misbehaviour at the feet of the law school dean. Ruby referred to "the influence of the big Bay Street firms and their millions of dollars of donations heaped upon the law faculty" and added that the "harsh and unconscionable penalties" meted out to the students by the dean were "the dean's attempt to prove his loyalty and toughness to the big firms."[16]

There was one final, bizarre twist to the whole little drama. In the early stages of the unfolding of the saga, the University had suggested that Professor Denise Réaume of the law faculty might have counselled her students to misrepresent their grades. The university began an enquiry into Réaume's conduct and she filed a grievance against the university. The university eventually suspended its enquiry and apologized to Réaume. She dropped her grievance.[17] Réaume made a final comment on the whole business: "Everybody knows that the fundamental concept involved in legal education is the tension between the aspirations to be a proper university program and the fact that most of our graduate students [sic] go into the practice of law."[18] Réaume called for a comprehensive enquiry into job recruitment practices at law schools.

As a further manifestation of its apparent determination to become Canada's leading American law school, the University of Toronto Faculty of Law has changed the designation of its first law degree from "LL.B.," the more traditional Bachelor of Laws, to "J.D.," the standard American Juris Doctor. Each fresh piece of news out of the U. of T. law faculty makes the situation look worse. In December 2001 Dean Daniels announced that, as part of his goal of "standing among the world's top five law schools," he would increase tuition fees to $25,000 per year.[19] On 17 December, Daniels took to the pages of the *National Post* to set out his perception of the whole question.[20] His statement was, as might be expected, self-serving. It was also rambling and less than convincing. He was rhapsodic about the direction in which the U. of T. law school was heading, beginning his remarks, "Imagine a law school in Canada where the very best students from across the country and the world receive an education that is in every dimension equal to or better than, the leading law schools of the world." To the extent that I can grasp Daniels's thinking, it appears to me that he believes there exists, somewhere or other, an international body which rates law schools and determines which ones are "truly great" or "world-class." A similar skepticism was expressed by one of the U. of T. law professors. James Phillips was quoted as saying, "While looking to the United States is often justified as part of becoming a 'great' law school, what great means is never articulated."[21]

While concern over the tuition business continued, the fiasco about students inflating grades refused to die. One student who, so it was claimed, had admitted to falsifying her grades was suspended. She challenged this suspension in the Divisional Court, which overturned her suspension on the ground that, in suspending her, Dean Daniels had acted in excess of his authority.[22] This result moved two professors at the law school to take to the pages of the *Law Times* to express their views. They asserted that the dean had acted in a way that was "patently unreasonable" and "contrary to the basic values of our legal system."[23] Not all Canadian legal scholars were prepared to accept Ronald J. Daniels's protestations about his law faculty. Professor Peter Hogg, then dean of the Osgoode Hall Law School, said of the notion that the U. of T. Faculty of Law was "Canada's pre-eminent law school" that "this viewpoint is a highly contested one." Hogg made this trenchant observation: "Pre-eminence cannot simply be asserted – or purchased."[24] It is an interesting footnote to this sorry saga that in the *Canadian Lawyer* annual survey of Canadian law schools for 2002 the University of Toronto ranked eighth in Canada.[25] A reasonable conclusion to be drawn from Daniels's actions and remarks is that he believes money to be the key to offering a solid legal education. Put simply, the goal appears to be to establish a law school in Canada which will have the same reputation and the same endowment as the most prestigious law schools in the U.S.

An unusually forthright book by a Canadian law professor is University of Ottawa law professor Constance Backhouse's *Petticoats and Prejudice: Women and Law in Nineteenth Century Canada*. In this book, Backhouse admitted that her overriding goal in writing was to create propaganda. She stated that her purpose was to "locate" "heroines" and to "forge a new definition of heroine."[26]

What has driven Canadian law professors to become propagandists? The motivating force, I would suggest, is fear. What exactly are these people afraid of? They can have nothing concrete to fear. They mostly have tenure and are well paid, often supplementing their official salaries through moonlighting. The thing they seem to fear most is being caught thinking bad thoughts. Once again, Constance Backhouse has been remarkably forthright. In one article she expressed her terror at the possibility of being viewed publicly as thinking bad thoughts. She stated that her reaction to the suggestion that she might have written something which was anti-Semitic was a certain "weak-in-the-knees, wet-under-the-armpit adrenalin rush which visits me … when I find myself characterized this way, or in parallel ways, in print."[27]

Canadian law professors exemplify the observation which Marx and Engels made: "inside this class [the ruling class] one part appears as the thinkers of the class, its active conceptive ideologists, who make the perfecting of the illusion of the class about itself their chief source of livelihood."[28] The legal academics play this role by applauding everything the Supreme Court does and constantly telling Canadians what swell people the judges are.

In the fall of 2000, the Supreme Court organized a conference to celebrate its own 125th anniversary. This was a publicly funded love-in. While no critics were invited, many academics were – each one was a cheerleader.[29]

Where law professors have dared to breathe a word of criticism, they have usually suggested that the Supreme Court does not go far enough. David Beatty of the University of Toronto law faculty has regularly attempted to urge the Supreme Court on to ever greater excesses.[30] In *R. v. Oickle*, the Court actually showed some restraint and, in response, Osgoode Hall Law School professor Alan Young accused the judges of "cowardice."[31]

As would be expected from priests and priestesses of the ortho-doxy, Canadian legal academics are not enthusiastic about democracy. John D. Whyte is a leading Canadian constitutional scholar. Professor Peter Russell, not someone usually given to overstatement, once wrote of Whyte's "disdain for democracy."[32]

Not only are they unenthusiastic about democracy, but our law professors have a decidedly unusual understanding of how democracy is supposed to work. James MacPherson offered this fantastic explanation of how democracy operates: "However, [major political issues] no longer stay or end in the political arena. They move from there to the courts, especially the Supreme Court of Canada, because the Charter gives people unhappy with a result in the political arena an opportunity to challenge that result in the judicial arena."[33]

In addition to being sycophantic and unprincipled, Canadian legal scholars have also been lazy. Chief Justice Brian Dickson once wrote, "If I were to venture any criticism, it would be that the quality of good academic writing, published in any year, is meagre in relation to the number of legal scholars to be found in the law schools of the nation."[34]

Two superb sources for understanding the sorry state of university legal education in Canada today are volume 15, number 1 of the *Dalhousie Law Journal*, published in 1992, and an article by Alan Hunt of the Department of Law, Carleton University, in a 1988 issue of the *Osgoode Hall Law Journal*. The *Dalhousie* issue is a collection of essays written in honour of Bertha Wilson. The various authors appear to fall over themselves in an effort to demonstrate both their love for and admiration of Bertha Wilson and their contempt for the basic principles of our legal system. The Hunt article made clear the barrenness, the anti-intellectualism, and the anti-rationalism of post-modernist thought.[35] Hunt was at pains to emphasize the importance of attacking "truth, logic and objectivity."[36] He made clear the strong Nazi drift of post-modernist thought, if it can be called thought. Hunt's analysis of Hutchinson's work strongly suggested that post-modern intellectual work is a dialogue with the self and affirmed that what we are dealing with in this genre is a politics of style. Once again, aesthetics subsumes politics. This systematic anti-rationalism accompanied by an overriding emphasis on style is the very essence of Nazism.[37]

It is worth noting that, at the same time the *Osgoode Hall Law Journal* published a laudatory review of one of his books, Allan Hutchinson was the journal's Book Review editor.

10

One Tiger to a Hill

The phrase "One Tiger to a Hill" is taken from Robert Ardrey's *African Genesis: A Personal Investigation into the Animal Origins and Nature of Man*.[1] Ardrey's central analytical concept is "territoriality"; this is the notion that much animal behaviour can be explained as a struggle over territory. A tiger must hunt to survive and the idea is that any single hill will provide only sufficient hunting opportunities for one tiger to be able to survive. The idea of territoriality, as applied to human behaviour, connotes that human life is a process of constant struggle and that, within any human population, some group of individuals or some individual is bound to become dominant.

Applied to human societies, the same concept suggests that in each society some institution must be dominant, must play a directing role. That institution could be the monarchy; it could be the apex of a religious hierarchy; it could be a gang of generals, or the central committee of a dominant party, or, as used to be the case in Canada, the people's assembled elected representatives. The dominant institution in Canada today is the Supreme Court.[2] As Peter McCormick, who is generally sympathetic toward the Court, put it, "The Supreme Court's evolution from bit player to leading actor is one of the most important developments in the past few decades."[3] It achieved this position by superseding Parliament.[4] How the Supreme Court became the one tiger on the Canadian hill is not clear. The Canadian people were not consulted about this transformation.

Canada may be the first country in the world to have experienced a judicial *coup d'état*. In writing about the Supreme Court,

McCormick noted that the "expansion of judicial power" is a "global" phenomenon.[5] Senator Anne Cools stated that "In fact, the forays of justices into the legislative function, complete with judgments and inevitable negative consequences, can only be described as a judicial coup d'état. This is a judicial usurpation of legislative power and function. It is a diminution of Canadian citizens' representative rights in public policy. It is constitutional vandalism."[6] After the Russian Revolution of October 1917, an important slogan used by the Bolsheviks was, "All power to the Soviets." The slogan of Canada's ruling clique today appears to be, "All power to the judges."[7]

The Supreme Court's status as the dominant institution in Canadian society is not immutable. The Canadian people could recover the power which has been usurped by the judges. This will require some struggle, but it is plausible to imagine that ordinary Canadian people might once again become the tiger on the Canadian hill and that they might actually displace the clique on whose behalf the Court rules.

Despite judicial obfuscation of how the 1982 constitutional changes came about, the Canadian people were unaware of the revolution which had occurred. Former chief justice Antonio Lamer described the adoption of the Charter as a "revolution on the scale of the introduction of the metric system, the great medical discoveries of Louis Pasteur and the invention of penicillin and the laser."[8] In a similarly effusive fashion, Lamer later added, "Thank God for the *Charter*."[9] The Charter, despite whatever fantasies Antonio Lamer might have wished to indulge himself in, did not come from God. It came from the UK Parliament acting in response to a decision that was not taken by Canadians, but by the prime minister and eight provincial premiers. If Canadians had a better understanding of how the Charter came to be part of our Constitution, they might be less enthusiastic about it.

Having been, as I believe, the first country to experience a judicial *coup d'état*, Canada might well become the only country other than the United States in which there has been a popular democratic struggle against the judges. A major popular struggle against the courts occurred in the United States in the 1930s. Franklin Roosevelt was elected president in 1932. He promised a new deal of progressive economic and social reforms. The Supreme Court of the U.S., acting in accordance with a half-century-long tradition of reaction, attacked Roosevelt's reforms.[10] The Court, in Alexander Bickel's words, waged war on Franklin Roosevelt's New Deal.[11] Aligning themselves with the rich and the powerful, the judges struck down much of Roosevelt's economically and socially progressive legislation. During the 1936 election campaign, Roosevelt ran, to a large extent, against the Supreme Court. He denounced the judges for their reactionary decisions and vowed that if he were re-elected he would re-introduce New Deal legislation in the Congress. He added that if the Supreme Court interfered again with this legislation he would ask Congress to enact legislation giving him the authority to appoint new judges to the Court and he would continue appointing judges until he was sure that the majority of them would not interfere further with New Deal reforms. Roosevelt handily won re-election. He did not carry out his "court-packing" threat because, by 1937, the Supreme Court appeared to have got the message and to have changed direction.[12]

Another major struggle between the judges and a government broke out in the Union of South Africa in the early 1950s. A newly-elected National Party government was determined to press ahead with the implementation of its policy of apartheid. This required, amongst other things, taking away the right to vote of certain "coloured" voters in the Cape Province. In South African parlance, *coloured* meant persons who were of mixed African and European ancestry. There were not many such persons entitled to vote, but the National Party's apartheid policy demanded that only persons of European ancestry should be allowed to vote. In 1951 the legislature enacted a statute, called the Separate Representation of Voters Act, which stripped the franchise from coloured voters. The Appellate Division of the Supreme Court of South Africa decided that the procedure by which this statute had been enacted was unconstitutional and struck it down.[13] The governmental response to this decision took the form of constitutional sleight of hand which attempted to circumvent the decision. Once again, the Appellate Division was not impressed and invalidated the government's constitutional hocus-pocus.[14] The government was determined to overrule this second decision and took a series of questionable steps, including increasing the number of judges on the Appellate Division from five to eleven. At this point the judges realized they were beaten and capitulated.[15]

I do not wish to suggest any parallel between the situation in Canada in 2003 and that in South Africa in the 1950s. The current government of Canada has been, unlike the government of South Africa fifty years ago, democratically elected. And it would be insulting to the courageous and principled judges of the Appellate Division of the Supreme Court of South Africa in the 1950s to suggest similarities between them and the judges of today's Supreme Court of Canada. While today's Canadian judges subvert constitutional government, the South African judges fought a good fight in an attempt to uphold it. Erwin Griswold, then dean of the Harvard Law School, described one of the Appellate Division's decisions as "a great judgment, deserving to rank with the best work of the judges who have contributed to the field of constitutional law."[16]

Canadians have quietly acquiesced in the judicial *coup d'état*. It is worth remembering that the only Canadians who have spoken out against this *coup d'état* have been political scientists. As noted in the previous chapter, lawyers and law professors have, with few exceptions, either maintained a pusillanimous silence or been cheerleaders for the Court. This acquiescence has happened largely because Canadians have been seduced by the orthodoxy and its apparent worship of human rights. An essential element of the orthodoxy is the belief that human rights will be better protected by the judges than by wicked "politicians."[17] Many Canadians appear to believe that the sole point of constitutional government is the protection of human rights. It is conveniently forgotten that self-government is also a human right. Mesmerized by human rights rhetoric and the blandishments of lawyers and law professors, Canadians have stood by quietly and meekly while the judges hijacked their country.

Montesquieu published his influential essay *L'Esprit des Lois* in 1748. This essay is considered to be the origin of the notion of separation of powers. Montesquieu argued that the exercise by one state institution of executive, judicial, and legislative powers was bound to lead to despotism. The Supreme Court now exercises all three sorts of power and, on the basis of Montesquieu's analysis, must be regarded as despotic. Absolute power, in Lord Acton's aphorism, corrupts absolutely and the Supreme Court is now absolutely corrupt. This distressing situation will exist only so long as Canadians continue to tolerate it, and Canadians are probably the most tolerant people on earth. There is no virtue in tolerating the intolerable.

In 1982, the Government of Canada published a pamphlet called *The Constitution and You*. The opening words of the pamphlet claimed that it was "published in the interest of contributing to public understanding and awareness of the constitutional resolution approved by Parliament in December of 1981." The pamphlet noted that to the extent Canadians were involved in the process at all that involvement was passive and reactive: "1,200 briefs and letters [were submitted] to a Special Joint Committee of the Senate and House of Commons." Thus, Canadians were allowed to react to proposals for constitutional change which had been developed and adopted by others. The pamphlet obfuscated the adoption of the Charter. Under the heading "Transferring Power to the People," the pamphlet stated that the Charter "gives people the power to appeal to the courts."[18] The pamphlet makes clear that the Charter cast the Canadian people in the role of supplicants, supplicants at the feet of the judges. It is difficult to characterize the ability to hire a lawyer in order to "appeal" to the courts as a "power."

It is not my purpose to suggest that the Supreme Court has become the dominant institution in Canada because the judges are particularly venial and wicked people. It would be inaccurate to think such a thing. It is our national obsession with rights which has impelled the judges toward their current position of dominance. The judges have been as mesmerized by the quest for human rights as have other Canadians. One other thing which should be clear from this book is that our national quest has not been for *all* human rights, but, almost exclusively, for "equality." A central point which de Tocqueville made in *Democracy in America* was that the quest for equality would eventually subvert democracy.[19]

Not only has the obsession with human rights been the pretext for the subversion of democracy in Canada, it has become the mechanism of choice for subverting the sovereignty of states throughout the world. Human rights is the banner under which a recolonization of Africa and Asia is taking place. Human rights has become the twenty-first century equivalent of the nineteenth century "civilizing mission." As the devotees of human rights have championed the Supreme Court as the dominant institution in Canada, likewise they are committed to transferring as much power as possible to things like the International War Crimes Tribunal in the Hague.

Persons who wish to see this doubtful goal achieved see the creation of a permanent international criminal court (ICC) as a desirable means of doing so. As one devotee put it, "When states are unwilling or unable to prosecute – the I.C.C. steps in."[20] The ICC would, presumably, end the bad old days of state sovereignty and ensure the universal predominance of right-thinking lawyers.[21]

Historian Eric Hobsbawn is not convinced that international tribunals offer a complete solution to all the world's ills.[22] The movement toward a government of lawyers, by lawyers, for lawyers is not uniquely Canadian; it is also an international phenomenon.

Canadians who imagine themselves to be not-right are regularly critical of globalization. They are happily unaware that their obsession with human rights has become a major globalizing force.

11

What Is to Be Done?[1]

This chapter discusses courses of action which might be adopted to address the issues identified in this book. It begins by canvassing the causes of the current situation and turns then to possible remedies.

HOW DID WE GET INTO THIS MESS?

The Supreme Court of Canada has not always been an institution in which Canadians could take immense pride,[2] but it should be clear that the Court has been reduced to a level which is intolerable. In my opinion, the main causes of the Court's subversion are feminism and feminists. Modern Canadian feminism began in the 1970s, encouraged by the report of the Royal Commission on the Status of Women in 1970 and by the United Nations' declaration of 1975 as "International Women's Year." For the feminists of the 1970s, the Supreme Court of Canada and the legal system were the primary enemies.[3] This was so largely because of three decisions of the Supreme Court – *Lavell*, *Murdoch*, and *Bliss*.[4] These decisions galvanized the women's movement in Canada and feminists began to wage war on the Supreme Court.

Elizabeth Fox-Genovese has offered a cogent explanation for why feminists should attack legal, and all other, forms of order. As she put it, "rationality, reason and justice – the pre-eminent attributes of the public sphere – appear hopelessly compromised by their association with men." She continued, "By thus insisting upon the essential gendering of all modernist thought, postmodernist feminists equate the revolt against illegitimate authority with a revolt against all forms of order." Fox-Genovese encapsulated and dismissed post-modernist orthodoxy in a telling phrase: "a flagrant nihilism passes into a transparent totalitarianism."[5]

As if to confirm Fox-Genovese's analysis, the National Film Board of Canada produced a film called *In the Face of Justice: Women's Challenge to Law in Canada*. This received its first public screening on International Women's Day in 2002 at an event sponsored jointly by LEAF and the Law Society of Upper Canada.

Canada (A.G.) v. *Lavell* involved section 12(1) of the Indian Act, which dealt with the legal consequences of marriages between Indians and non-Indians. Under section 12(1)(a), if an Indian man married a non-Indian woman, she would thereby acquire Indian status and any children of the marriage would have Indian status. Under section 12(1)(b), if an Indian woman married a non-Indian man, she would thereby irrevocably lose her Indian status and children of the marriage would not have Indian status. Jeannette Lavell was an Indian woman who married a non-Indian man. Shortly after the marriage she received notification that she had lost her status and would be required to leave the reserve where she lived and had grown up. She challenged section 12(1)(b) on the basis of the equality guarantee in the Canadian Bill of Rights. In a judgment which is close to incomprehensible, the Supreme Court rejected her challenge.

Murdoch v. *Murdoch* involved a farm wife who had spent her adult life working to build up the farm. Upon divorce, she claimed that she should get a share of what she regarded as the joint property of herself and her husband. Her claim was denied.

In *Bliss* v. *Canada (A.G.)*, Stella Bliss challenged a section of the Unemployment Insurance Act under which she had been denied unemployment benefits after having given birth to a child. Bliss's challenge was to section 46 of the act. The Court dismissed her challenge, stating, "If section 46 treats unemployed pregnant women differently from other unemployed persons, be they male or female, it is, it seems to me, because they are pregnant and not because they are women."[6]

Lynn McDonald is a sociologist, feminist, and former member of Parliament. Her comments about *Lavell*, *Murdoch*, and *Bliss* amount to a complete statement of the feminist view of these cases:

Section 15(1) initially had the same "equality before the law" wording as the *Canadian Bill of Rights*, which the Supreme Court of Canada had interpreted narrowly and stupidly. According to the Supreme Court, the provision meant only that laws could not be *applied* unequally in the ordinary courts; inequalities, except for the creation of a criminal offence, were legitimate if written explicitly into the law. ...

Women's groups had no confidence in the Supreme Court of Canada, and pressed hard for changes in the wording. The word "individual" was changed to "person" because there had been a judicial interpretation that person did not include a foetus. ...

Next, there has been a remarkable number of judicial errors in dealing with women's equality cases. The Supreme Court of Canada is supposed to *correct* errors made by lower courts. Instead, it makes its own, misunderstanding the simplest evidence before it and betraying flagrant inconsistencies. Let me skip over the "persons" cases at the end of the last century, for the point can be made with more recent examples. ...

In *Lavell* and *Bedard*, the Supreme Court of Canada condemned native women to a status not equal to that of native men. Legally, the decision was just as devastating, ending the court's brief flirtation, in *Drybones*, with giving the *Canadian Bill of Rights* precedence over other federal legislation.

The decision at the county court level in *Lavell* astonishes both for its illogic and its mis-statements of fact. ...

The *Murdoch* case is one of the worst in Canadian judicial history, but *Leatherdale*, decided in 1982, shows that its lessons were only half learned, even *after* the *Charter*. ...

The fact that the wife had performed various services in connection with the husband's ranching activities did not give her any beneficial interest in the property claimed. ...

Murdoch was decided by the Supreme Court of Canada only six weeks after *Lavell* and *Bedard*, and in the same spirit. It is marked just as much by illogic, lack of respect for the facts, and inhumanity. The great difference between *Murdoch* and *Lavell* and *Bedard* lay in the political results. *Murdoch* provoked an enormous outcry, bringing vast numbers of articulate, middle-class women into the women's movement. Within five years most provinces had, in response, changed their matrimonial property laws. Equality has yet to be attained, but enormous improvements have been made. At the time of writing, however, the discrimination continues for native women. As a result of pressure from women's organisations, the evictions were stopped, but repeal of section 12(1)(b) is still only a promise, and re-instatement of those women, and their children, who lost their status is still in dispute. ...

The *Bliss* case, concerning discrimination in unemployment insurance, outdoes even *Murdoch, Lavell* and *Bedard* in double-speak. ...

So, the Supreme Court of Canada believed that it was nature that wrote the *Unemployment Insurance Act*. Apparently judges could not understand that nature made Stella Bliss quite able to work several weeks after having her child, a point never contested in the proceedings. It was a thoroughly arbitrary *statute* that denied her unemployment insurance benefits.[7]

Feminist hostility toward "incorrect" decisions by the Supreme Court carried over into an intense lobbying campaign designed to ensure that the 1982 constitutional reforms contained the right wording.[8]

The story of contemporary North American feminism is an extraordinary one. Seldom in human history can a political movement have achieved so much success so quickly and at so little cost to itself. A court which thirty years ago was, in the eyes of some, the very personification of evil has been transformed into a feminist instrument.

Parallels between the political styles of Nazis and feminists can be seen in an incisive observation made by the Canadian historian Modris Eksteins, who spoke of the "pursuit of authenticity" and added, "what was important was constant confrontation, an unflinching adversarial posture and not the details of that posture."[9]

Feminists began their assault on the Supreme Court out of a deep hostility toward our law and our legal institutions. A basic principle of our criminal justice system is the notion of *mens rea* – the idea that before someone may be convicted of a crime, the state must prove that he or she meant to commit the crime. One feminist "scholar" recently commented, "The doctrine of *mens rea*, understood in law as neutral and objective, has been unmasked as partial and privileging a particular (male) viewpoint."[10] No evidence was presented to support this assertion which was, of course, pure ideology.

Canadian feminists attacked legal education with as much enthusiasm as they did the Supreme Court. And here, again, the feminist victory has been complete. At my own law school there were, at one time, three different feminist courses offered: "Women and the Law," "Sex Discrimination," and "Test-Case Litigation" – this last presumably designed to train fresh lawyers for

LEAF. A student who was a friend of mine described "Women and the Law" as "part way between a cult and a therapy group." One instructor would begin her first class by announcing, "My name is Professor X; I am a lesbian; each one of you was conceived as a result of a rape." Students were not required to write essays or exams, since such things were considered to be "patriarchal and linear." The usual requirement was for students to keep journals which the instructor would grade. The same friend who I mentioned above had her journal returned once with critical comments. The gist of these comments was that the journal should not contain analysis of the course, but was to be a record of "how the course has changed your life." One year the final mark in one of these courses was based on the students' participation in a car wash organized to raise money for a women's shelter. These, of course, are things which could have happened in any Canadian law school over the last twenty years. As a general observation, feminists dominate post-secondary education in Canada today. The results of this domination are not encouraging.[11]

Some insight into the intellectual level of feminist legal education can be gained from the following story. In 1996, the annual meeting of the Canadian Association of Law Teachers was held at Brock University from 2 to 5 June. As a preliminary, a "Feminist Perspectives Workshop" was conducted in January 1996. Participants were asked to discuss the problem which follows under the heading "Establishing an Open, Mutually Respectful Climate":

As some of you already know, at some point in the future, Whosits from the planet Who have come to live on Earth. Relations between Human Beings and Whosits have not always been positive. Whosits need to replenish their bodily fluids on a regular basis; not all Human Beings believe that they really need to do this and think that it is just an excuse to avoid having to follow Earth practices. There have been incidents in which Whosits have felt that Human Beings have been guilty of speciesism because of comments they have made or actions they have taken against Whosits. In one incident, occurring in a workplace, a Human Being said to a Whosit who was leaving the office for the afternoon to undergo the replenishment of bodily fluids: "Why do you have to do this now? Isn't there some other time you could arrange it?." The Whosit said: "Are you questioning my motives? I don't have to explain to you." The Human Being did not say anything and the Whosit left.

The incident has affected the co-workers of the Whosit and the Human Being. Some of the other Whosits feel that they cannot assert their need for replenishment openly and some Human Beings feel that they cannot say anything about their concern that they have to cover work which the Whosits would be doing during this period. A few Whosits do try to explain, but they feel as if they are betraying the Whosit who was challenged; other Human Beings agree with the Whosit or the Human Being, but do not want to get involved. Finally, a small delegation of Whosits and Human Beings come to see you to ask you to help them get over the negative climate in the workplace by facilitating the dispute.

How do you approach this facilitating function? What questions might you ask? How might you ask the Whosit and the Human Being involved in the original exchange to participate. What about other Whosits and Human Beings in the workplace? Might there be other issues underlying their disagreement which have not surfaced and if so, should you raise them and if so, how would you raise them?

A further example of feminist approaches to education occurred in Winnipeg in June 2001. High-school girls who took a one-week course called "Women and Art" at the University of Winnipeg were taught to masturbate with fruits and vegetables.[12]

One further example of feminist thought is necessary.

Sheila McIntyre is a professor in the Faculty of Law at Queen's University. Some of her thoughts on "anti-feminism" follow:

Consciousness of my own ill health caused me to register how many feminist scholars are struggling with serious illness. I know two other feminist legal scholars with rheumatoid arthritis. Among my academic acquaintances are feminists suffering from lupus, Epstein-Barr, serious insomnia, cancer, candida and cluster migraines. Given how few feminist scholars there are, it is difficult to throw this off as mere coincidence.

I think anti-feminism plays a significant role in triggering or aggravating such diseases, not least because acute stress and exhaustion have been medically linked to all these illnesses.[13]

The main vehicle for the feminist assault on the Supreme Court has, of course, been LEAF. LEAF's interventions before the Supreme Court have not always been principled: the organization has worked both sides of the street on the question of pornography. In *R.* v. *Butler*, LEAF was against pornography and used the

Catherine MacKinnon argument that pornography is, by its nature, violence against women. *Butler* involved a constitutional challenge by the owner of a video shop in Winnipeg to the anti-obscenity provision in section 163(8) of the Criminal Code. The essence of the Court's decision in *Butler* was as follows:[14]

Section 163(8) of the *Criminal Code* was authoritatively interpreted by this Court in *Butler, supra*. Parliament, it was held, had distanced itself from the old common law *Hicklin* test which defined obscenity in terms of whether the material in question would result in the "corruption of morals." See *R. v. Hicklin* (1868), L.R. 3 Q.B. 360. "The prevention of 'dirt for dirt's sake'", Sopinka J. for the majority said at pp. 492–93, "is not a legitimate objective which would justify the violation of one of the most fundamental freedoms enshrined in the *Charter*." For ease of analysis, Sopinka J. divided potentially obscene material into three categories at p. 484:

a explicit sex with violence,
b explicit sex without violence, but which subjects participants to treatment that is degrading or dehumanizing *if the material creates a substantial risk of harm*,
c explicit sex without violence among adults that is neither degrading nor dehumanizing.

In applying the community standard of tolerance to each of these categories, *Butler* concluded (at p. 485) that the first category – the depiction of explicit sex coupled with violence will "almost always" constitute the undue exploitation of sex. The second category – explicit sex that is "degrading or dehumanizing" – may be undue "if the risk of harm is substantial." The third category – explicit sex that is not violent and is neither degrading nor dehumanizing – is "generally tolerated in our society and will not qualify as the undue exploitation of sex unless it employs children it its production."

The key word in the statutory definition – 'undue' – was interpreted to incorporate an assessment of the broader community's tolerance of harm. As Sopinka J. stated at p. 479:

This type of material would, apparently, fail the community standards test not because it offends against morals but because it is perceived by public opinion to be harmful to society, particularly to women.

Again, at p. 481, after citing Wilson J. in *Towne Cinema Theatres Ltd v. The Queen*, [1985] 1 S.C.R. 494, 18 D.L.R. (4th) 1,18 C.C.C. (3d) 193, Sopinka J. emphasizes that "[t]he community is the arbiter as to what is harmful to it." And, at p. 485, he says:

> The courts must determine as best they can what the community would tolerate others being exposed to on the basis of the degree of harm that *may* flow from such exposure. (Emphasis added.)

This approach was accepted by Gonthier J., concurring, who said at p. 520:

> In this context, tolerance must be related to the harm. It must mean not only tolerance of the materials, but also tolerance of the harm which they *may* bring about. (Emphasis added.)

In the result, *Butler* affirmed constitutional protection for sexually explicit expression and drew the boundary only where harm exceeded the community's level of tolerance. Section 163(8) of the *Criminal Code* was upheld on the basis that (i) the definition, as interpreted, was sufficiently certain to be "prescribed by Law," and (ii) being defined as a harm-based obscenity provision, it addressed a substantial and pressing social objective in a rational and proportionate way.[15]

Little Sister's Book and Art Emporium v. *Canada (Minister of Justice)* is worth looking at. Little Sister's is a gay and lesbian bookshop in Vancouver. It challenged the action of customs officials in seizing certain material it wished to import and an extended discussion from the *Little Sister's* case follows:

The appellants question the correctness of *Butler* and say, in any event, that its approach cannot be freely transferred from heterosexual erotica to gay and lesbian erotica. No constitutional question was stated regarding the validity or constitutional limits of s. 163 of the *Criminal Code*. The absence of notice of such a constitutional question precludes the wide-ranging reconsideration of *Butler* sought by the appellants and some of the interveners (even if the Court were to conclude that such a reconsideration is either necessary or desirable). On the more specific issues, the appellants, and the interveners in their support, argue that in the context of the Customs legislation a "harm-based" approach which utilizes a single community standard across all regions and groups within society is insufficiently "contextual" or sensitive to specific circumstances to give effect to the equality rights of gays and lesbians. The appellants, supported by the interveners LEAF and EGALE, contend that homosexual erotica plays an important role in providing a positive self-image to gays and lesbians, who may feel isolated and rejected in the heterosexual mainstream. Erotica provides a positive celebration of what it means to be gay or lesbian. As such, it is argued that sexual speech in the contest of gay and lesbian culture is a core value and *Butler* cannot legitimately be applied to locate it at the fringes of s. 2(b) expression. Erotica, they contend, plays a different role in a gay and lesbian community than it does in a heterosexual community, and the *Butler* approach based, they say, on heterosexual norms, is oblivious to this fact. Gays and lesbians are defined by their sexuality and are therefore disproportionately vulnerable to sexual censorship.[16]

The appellants' criticisms of *Butler* can, for present purposes, be grouped under the following headings.

(a) The Community Standard of Tolerance is Majoritarian and Suppresses Minority Speech, Including Homosexual Expression

The appellants contend that importing a majoritarian analysis into the definition of "obscenity" (e.g., what the broader Canadian community will tolerate), inevitably creates prejudice against non-mainstream, minority representations of sex and sexuality. They argue that the "national" community is by definition majoritarian and is more likely than the homosexual community itself to view gay and lesbian imagery as degrading and dehumanizing. The whole idea of a community standards test, they say, is incompatible with Charter values that were enacted to protect minority rights. The fact that no particular evidence to define the community standard is required to support a successful prosecution heightens the vulnerability of minorities (B. Cossman, et al., Bad Attitude/s on Trial: Pornography, Feminism, and the Butler Decision (1997) , at pp. 107–108). What makes this standard even more problematic in the context of gay and lesbian erotica is that where expression is suppressed on the basis of sexual orientation, so goes the argument, it silences voices that are already suppressed and subject to discrimination. Professor Richard Moon says that in Butler "[j]udicial subjectivity (value judgment) is simply dressed up in the objective garb of community standards" ("R. v. Butler: The Limits of the Supreme

Court's Feminist Re-interpretation of Section 163" (1993), 25 Ottawa L. Rev. 361, at p. 370).[17]

This line of criticism underestimates *Butler*. While it is of course true that under s. 163 of the *Criminal Code* the "community standard" is identified by a jury or a judge sitting alone, and to that extent involves an attribution rather than an opinion poll, the test was adopted to underscore the unacceptability of the trier of fact indulging personal biases, as was held to have happened in *Towne Cinema*. A concern for minority expression is one of the principal factors that led to adoption of the national community test in *Butler* in the first place, *per* Sopinka J., p. 484:

> Some segments of society would consider that all three categories of pornography cause harm to society because they tend to undermine its moral fibre. Others would contend that none of the categories cause harm. Furthermore there is a range of opinion as to what is degrading or dehumanizing. See *Pornography and Prostitution in Canada: Report of the Special Committee on Pornography and Prostitution* (1985) (the Fraser Report), vol. 1, at p. 51. Because this is not a matter that is susceptible of proof in the traditional way and because we do not wish to leave it to the individual tastes of judges, we must have a norm that will serve as an arbiter in determining what amounts to an undue exploitation of sex. That arbiter is the community as a whole.[18]

The protective character of the national standard requirement is readily apparent from the summation of the test in *Butler* (at p. 485):

> If material is not obscene under this framework, it does not become so by reason of the person to whom it is or may be shown or exposed nor by reason of the place or manner in which it is shown.

In other words, a person's constitutionally protected space does not shrink by virtue of his or her geographical location or participation in a certain context or community, or indeed by the taste of a particular judge or jury. It is not necessarily in the interest of the minority to disaggregate community standards. The appellants have in mind a special standard related to their lesbian and gay target audience. The fact is, however, that they operate a bookstore in a very public place open to anyone who happens by, including potentially outraged individuals of the local community who might wish to have the bookstore closed down altogether. If "special standards" are to apply, whose "special standard" is it to be? There is some safety in numbers, and a national constituency that is made up of many different minorities is a guarantee of tolerance for minority expression.

Butler affirmed that Parliament had successfully criminalized harmful sexual expression, that is to say, sexual expression that is shown to be incompatible with society's proper functioning, but Canadian society also recognizes as fundamental to its proper functioning the *Charter* rights to freedom of expression and equality. The standard of tolerance of this same Canadian society cannot reasonably be interpreted as seeking to suppress sexual expression in the gay and lesbian community in a discriminatory way.

It may serve repeating that the national community standard relates to harm not taste, and is restricted, *per* Sopinka J., at p. 485, to "conduct which society formally recognizes as incompatible with its proper functioning." The test is therefore not only concerned with harm, but harm that rises to the level of being *incompatible* with the proper functioning of Canadian society. The Canadian Civil Liberties Association argues that "for gays and lesbians erotica and other material with sexual content is not harmful and is in fact a key element of the quest for self-fulfilment" (factum, at para. 14). So described, the CCLA has defined the material safely outside the *Butler* paradigm. *Butler* placed harmful expression – not sexual expression – at the margin of s. 2(b).

(b) The Degrading or Dehumanizing Test is Open to Homophobic Prejudice

The appellants argue that the "degrading or dehumanizing language in *Butler* is highly subjective and encouraged Customs, for example, to prohibit depictions of anal intercourse long after the Department of Justice advised Customs to the contrary. This argument seems to ignore that the phrase "degrading or dehumanizing" in *Butler* is qualified immediately by the words "*if* the risk of harm is substantial" (p. 485) (emphasis added). This makes it clear that not all sexually explicit erotica depicting adults engaged in conduct which is considered to be degrading or dehumanizing is obscene. The material must also create a substantial risk of harm which exceeds the community's tolerance. The potential of harm and a same-sex depiction are not necessarily mutually exclusive. Portrayal of a dominatrix engaged in the non-violent degradation of an ostensibly willing sex slave is no less dehumanizing if the victim happens to be of the same sex, and no less (and no more) harmful in its reassurance to the viewer that the victim finds such conduct both normal and pleasurable. Parliament's concern was with behavioural changes in the *voyeur* that are potentially harmful in ways or to an extent that the community is not prepared to tolerate. There is no reason to restrict that concern to the heterosexual community.[19]

LEAF argued a pro-pornography line in *Little Sister's*. Thus, heterosexual pornography, as in *Butler*, was bad and homosexual pornography, as in *Little Sister's*, was good.[20] In the *Little Sister's* case, the Supreme Court, once again, manifested its attachment to an apartheid view of the world. Reading the decision, one might conclude that homosexuals and heterosexuals inhabited different planets. A further blow is, thereby, dealt to the notion of common citizenship.

In the matter of pornography, as in many other instances, LEAF has let Catharine MacKinnon do its thinking for it. MacKinnon reveals herself in her writing to be fixated on pornography.[21] Some of MacKinnon's statements could lead reasonable persons to question her sanity. Consider this statement about physicians which was quoted in chapter 3: "Your doctor will not give you drugs he has addicted you to unless you suck his penis."[22] Notice that even MacKinnon is not above making sexist assumptions. Had it never occurred to her that a woman might possibly consult a physician who did not have a penis? MacKinnon is by no means the most extreme feminist teaching in an American university. Others have observed that Newton's *Principia Mathematica* is a "rape manual" and Beethoven's Ninth Symphony expresses "the throttling murderous rage of a rapist incapable of attaining release."[23]

While modern feminism was, and perceived itself as, a progressive social movement when it emerged in the 1970s, it has since degenerated into female tribalism. Female tribalism is largely indistinguishable from what Christina Hoff Sommers described as "gender feminism."[24] Twenty-five years ago feminists did address social issues in a progressive fashion, but as litigation such as *Symes* v. *Canada* makes clear, feminists today are largely devoted to the narrow concerns of bourgeois women. Feminists once sought to address broad social issues. A thoughtful observer, I believe, would see feminism as, from the outset, a massive power grab. This basic truth has been obfuscated by an unrelenting rhetoric of morality and justice.[23]

HOW DO WE GET OUT OF THIS MESS?

In this section I will discuss, first, steps which the Parliament and government of Canada might take and, second, steps which the Canadian people might take.

The Parliament and Government of Canada

Parliament could abolish the Supreme Court by the simple act of repealing the Supreme Court Act, but that would be unnecessary and undesirable. There are certain things which Parliament could and should do. The non-method for the appointing of judges could be changed, which is to say that a procedure could be established for the selection of judges. I do not favour aping the current U.S. approach, nor do I favour direct parliamentary involvement. Giving Parliament a role in the selection of the judges could well give the judges a greater degree of democratic legitimacy, thereby encouraging them to even greater excesses. This should be avoided.

It might be useful to establish an independent judicial nominating commission, much like the Judicial Service Commissions which exist in many other Commonwealth states. The really difficult question would be to determine the membership of such a commission.

I do not favour giving an important role to the Canadian Bar Association (CBA) in appointments. In 1967 Justice Minister Pierre Trudeau gave the CBA a role in the appointment of judges to the superior courts of the provinces. The CBA is little more than a social club which likes to imagine that it speaks for all Canadian lawyers. Its letterhead describes it as "the voice of the legal profession," which it is not.

Parliament could adopt measures designed to turn the Supreme Court back into a court. Legislation could seek to address the question of standing and to limit the number of individuals and organizations which might be permitted to intervene in a particular appeal. Tightening the rules on standing and limiting intervenors would have a significant effect in depoliticizing the work of the Supreme Court. Both steps would encourage the Court to hear only cases which involve concrete issues between parties.

Parliament votes the money which allows the Supreme Court to operate.[26] Parliament could limit the money available to the Court in two important ways. First it could reduce, if not eliminate, the judges' travel budget.[27] If the judges were no longer able to swan around the world and the country, they might be inclined to refrain from being oracles and begin to act like judges again. The second step would be to eliminate the funding which allows the judges to hire law clerks. Doing away with judicial law clerks would have a very positive and beneficial effect on the Court, by forcing it, once again, to act like a court. The average salary for judicial law clerks is $41,662.00, giving a total, for twenty-seven clerks, of $1,124,874.[28] Without the law clerks, judges might be forced to confine themselves to the arguments and the material actually presented by the parties appearing before them and to write their own judgments. (I do not believe that the law clerks and judicial travel are the cause of most of the deficiencies which I have identified. I do believe, however, that getting rid of both would be beneficial. Nor do I imagine that travel by the judges causes these same deficiencies. I believe, likewise, that limiting the temptations for the judges to become oracles would be salutary).

The Government of Canada could also pull the plug on the Court Challenges Program. The Mulroney government ended the program in 1992, but in 1994 the Chrétien government, then in the midst of a savage process of budget-cutting, reinstated the program with increased funding.[29] The program now operates as an independent corporation, something which might make shutting it down difficult. It is difficult to understand why the people's money should be used to pay wealthy and privileged lawyers to attempt to increase their wealth and privilege.[30]

Some further funding cuts would be highly desirable. Canadian feminism is almost entirely state-funded.[31] The major national feminist organization – the National Action Committee on the Status of Women – receives most of its funding from Ottawa. Both LEAF and the Canadian Journal of Women and the Law are heavily subsidized, and it would be a great benefit for Canadians if all this funding were to end. It is deplorable that in a democracy the people's money is used to fund sectarian political organizations.

A degree of public openness would be highly desirable. Parliament could amend the Access to Information Act by adding the Court Challenges Program, the Canadian Judicial Council, the

National Judicial Institute, and the Supreme Court of Canada to Schedule 1 to the act as the right of access created by the act only applies to organizations listed in this schedule. If an organization is not listed, there is no right of access to its records.

The Government of Canada could also make a major effort to rehabilitate section 33 of the Charter, the so-called override provision, which could be used to reassert Parliamentary control over public policy.[32]

The Canadian People

Canadians could begin to free themselves from the orthodoxy. An important point which this book has attempted to suggest is that the avatars of orthodoxy are best understood as a gang of Nazi bullies. Canadians have not always been intimidated by Nazi bullies. Between 1939 and 1945, 41,000 Canadians were willing to lose their lives in the struggle to defeat Nazi bullies. Bullies rely on intimidation and the most basic lesson is that, in resisting bullies, a little bit of backbone goes a long way. Canadians might be amazed to discover how much benefit would flow from rediscovering their collective backbone. Defeating the hegemony of the orthodoxy would be a significant step toward reclaiming our country from the Court.

The Effluxion of Time

It should be obvious to anyone who has read this far, that I regard the tenure of Claire L'Heureux-Dubé as a judge of the Supreme Court as a major national disgrace. It has not been my aim to suggest that Justice L'Heureux-Dubé is a particularly bad person. After careful study and reflection, it is my honest opinion that she was given responsibilities which made demands that transcended both her intellectual and her moral capacities.[33] There is hope, however.

The year 2002 was a great year for Canadians who believe in the rule of law and constitutional government. On 7 September in that year, Claire L'Heureux-Dubé turned seventy-five and was obliged, under section 9(2) of the Supreme Court Act, to retire.[34] *The Canadian Journal of Women and the Law* had already announced plans for a special issue to mark Justice L'Heureux-Dubé's work. In a similar vein, Chief Justice McLachlin turned sixty in

September 2003. Canadians should continue to hope that she takes care of her health and looks carefully in both directions before she crosses the street. If we had lost McLachlin, the result would have been disastrous.[35] The convention is that the position of chief justice alternates between an anglophone and a francophone.[36] L'Heureux-Dubé was the senior francophone judge on the Court. If McLachlin had ceased to hold office, L'Heureux-Dubé would, by convention, have been appointed chief justice of Canada.

The year 2002 saw one particularly awful event. Wednesday, 17 April 2002, was the twentieth anniversary of the adoption of the Charter. This event was marked by an orgy of sanctimonious self-congratulation. Lawyers, law professors, and judges told Canadians how grateful they should be for the Charter and elaborated all the wonderful things the Charter has allowed lawyers, law professors, and judges to do for Canadians.

Many who spoke about the Charter reified it into an entity possessing the capacity to do wondrous things on its own. Of all the rhapsodies composed on the Charter, none could equal the remarks of Madam Justice Abella of the Ontario Court of Appeal: "Twenty years from now a new generation of children will have grown up with the values of the Charter as their moral tutors and the preeminence of rights as the core of their civic curriculum."[37]

This dismal celebration seems to have begun on 27 December 2001 when Mark L. Berlin, National Director of Outreach and Partnerships in the Department of Justice in Ottawa, wrote to all the deans of Canadian law faculties to inform them of a joint project of the Department of Justice and the Canadian Bar Association. This project involved "collaborative sponsorship of a National Essay Contest celebrating the 20th anniversary of the Charter of Rights and Freedoms."[38] The letter announced that "the author of the essay selected as the overall winner will receive a book prize, commemorative trophy and a trip to Ottawa to meet with the Minister or Deputy Minister of Justice." A skeptical person like myself might suggest that second prize would be a meeting with *both* the minister and the deputy minister. Likewise, third prize would be dinner with the two of them.

APPENDIX

Social Context Education Program of the National Judicial Institute

T. Brettel Dawson, the director of the Social Context Education Program at the NJI refused to let me have the syllabus for the program. I was able to piece this together from the institute's bulletins and various press releases and public statements. The model of social context education which the NJI has developed is focused on:

- Understanding changing social and demographic structures, experiences of inequality, disadvantage, difference and points of contact with law;
- Understanding changing legal values and jurisprudential evolutions;
- Examining the Judicial role, judicial independence, judicial notice, fact finding, decision-making and discretion; and
- Examining issues related to access/accessibility to justice.

PROGRAMMING PRINCIPLES

Needs Assessment and Advice

The Social Context Education Program has worked to ensure that judicial education in the area of social context addresses judicial learning needs in planning, design, delivery, and content.

Local Input

SCEP has worked in close partnership on individual program development with local judicial education planning committees. This element has fostered judicial ownership and ambassadorship for the program, and ensured that local programming needs are met.

Focus on Judicial Role and Tasks

Social context education is developed in a manner that understands and respects the role of the judiciary and the complexity of the issues judges face. Emphasis has been given to practical examples relevant to the everyday work of judges.

Adult Learning Principles

Social context education is developed to reflect adult education principles fostering active learning through engagement/discussion, problem-based learning, and carefully planned small group work.

Trained Faculty and Planning Committees

Social context education is supported through faculty development of members of judicial education committees and the judges responsible for small group and workshop settings. Faculty development has examined substantive social context themes, introduced facilitation and program design skills, and addressed the role of community involving judicial education.

Program Design Principles

Social context education encourages judicial planners to set clear learning objectives; match resources and instructors to meet those objectives; collaborate with instructors on the content to meet those objectives; develop a delivery plan that can meet these objectives; and set out an evaluation plan (for participants and instructors) after delivery to see if those objectives were met.

Judicial, Academic, and Community Input

Social context education is judge-led. The involvement of academic and community leaders familiar with disadvantage and diversity is encouraged in the planning of the content and delivery of programs as appropriate. The role of community input is to make available soundly based information in a setting where it can be the subject of questions and discussion.

Feedback

Consistent with good pedagogy, education should be evaluated on a confidential basis to allow assessment and adjustment of programming as appropriate.

A guiding principle has been that social context education is a long-term process which involves both an intellectual component and education in new analytical approaches. While our long-range goal has been to ensure that relevant social context issues can be effectively integrated into judicial education, we have realized since the outset that it would be first necessary to create a common base of information and understanding through offering introductory social context programming to a large number of judges.

We have been reassured in our efforts to this end by the overwhelmingly positive evaluations which have been received from judges who have attended social context programs. Many judges have remarked on the relevance of the social context issues raised in the programs to their daily work. Not atypical have been comments such as "Great seminar. At the start I was not sure it would be of much help. I was wrong." Others have appreciated that the conferences have "opened for consideration a very broad range of concerns which have direct bearing on the daily exercise of our functions" and provided "much food for thought." Judges have also found useful the opportunity for exchange between themselves. The inclusion of small group discussion and workshops has allowed judges to "share experiences and gain experience with fellow judges." When all three levels of court were gathered together, a frequent remark was that it was "particularly enjoyable to have all three levels of court together to share views" and "observe the viewpoint of members of different benches." It was not uncommon to hear judges requesting more participatory small group time in follow-up programming. Unsurprisingly too, judges have emphasised the importance of practical approaches, and requested opportunities for more in-depth consideration of applied topics. In this regard, it is notable that the Supreme Court of Quebec has moved quickly to work with SCEP to develop two follow-up programs.

Now, with the strong support of the National Judicial Institute's Board of Governors and renewed funding from the Department of Justice, we are commencing a second phase of the project. A number of components are under development but two elements will play a central role in the second phase: first, integration of social context issues, and secondly, a more in-depth faculty and program development process. The central importance of continued faculty development in the next phase was emphasized by participants at a consultation held in June with members of our Advisory Committee and judicial educators from across Canada. The focus will be on advanced training in principles of adult education, program design and integration with substantive attention to the developing scope and implications of equality jurisprudence. Participants will work closely with leading faculty to develop social context education modules which can be incorporated into local and/or national judicial education programming.

Each program will be offered in two parts. The emphasis in the first residential course will be on substantive teaching. During the break before the second residential course, judges will be assigned the task of developing a teaching module using local issues and resources. The second course will be to provide teaching practice and feedback. We hope that participating judges will become a resource for their own court education planning committees and that national programming resources and modules will be developed. The first faculty development program is scheduled to begin with an intensive course February 13, 14, and 15, 2001 at Lake Louise and a second course in the Victoria area in June 6–7, 2001. Judges who wish to be more involved in judicial education and who wish to enhance their skills should contact us about participating in this program.

Other elements of Phase II will include further modeling of appropriate community involvement in judicial education including the use of community consultations. We plan to develop an enhanced resource capacity through providing independent study materials and acting as a National Clearing House for initiatives in the area. The resources and expertise developed in the SCEP are also available to any court developing a program.

At the outset of this initiative, the Honourable Justice Elizabeth Roscoe commented that the purpose of social context education is "to increase awareness and understanding of principles of equality and fairness in an era of rapid change within the society in which judicial duties are performed. The ultimate goal," she said, "is to become better judges." These remarks were echoed by the keynote speaker at the January intensive program of the Court of Queen's Bench of Alberta, the Right

Honourable Ted Thomas of the New Zealand Court of Appeal. "The challenge for judging at the outset of the twenty-first century," he argued, is "to adopt a functional and practical approach which will promote justice and equality in the law and better ensure that the law meets the needs and reasonable expectations of the community."

Notes

Case references in the notes have been shortened. The complete case reference for each case appears in the Table of Cases following the notes.

INTRODUCTION

1 See Margaret Wente, "Global Warming: A Heretic's View." In this context, Jean Bethke Elshtain has spoken of "liberal monism" (Elshtain, "The Bright Line," 148).

2 This book is very critical of feminism and feminists. The main thing I dislike about feminists is their contemptuous attitude toward women. See George F. Will, "Feminism Hijacked."

3 The notion "least dangerous branch" appears to have been used first by Alexander Hamilton in the *Federalist*, paper no. 78. See Alexander Hamilton, James Madison, and John Jay, *The Federalist*. See also Geoffrey Marshall, *Constitutional Theory*, 105.

4 See, especially, *Brown v. Board of Education*.

5 Bickel, 16, 21.

6 Ibid., 25–7.

7 Ibid., 59.

8 Ibid., 64.

9 Ibid., 30, 246.

10 Ibid., 4–5.

11 Manfredi, 22n14.

12 See *Cuddy Chicks Ltd.* v. *Ontario*; *Tetreault-Gadoury* v. *Canada*; and *Weber* v. *Ontario Hydro*. As with many Supreme Court decisions, it is impossible to extract any clear principle from these cases. It

appears that some tribunals may exercise constitutional review powers and some may not.

13 Manfredi, *Judicial Power and the Charter*, xi, 196.

14 The Republic of Zimbabwe was once governed according to the Rule of Law. See *Smith v. Mutasa*. Beginning in the year 2000, the government of Zimbabwe began to destroy the Rule of Law. See International Bar Association, *Report of Zimbabwe Mission, 2001*.

15 While nearly every state possesses a constitution, by no means all of them have a constitutionalist system of government in the sense that the state regularly acts in accordance with the constitution. See Karl Loewenstein, "Reflections on the Value of Constitutions in our Revolutionary Age," 149.

16 See *Edwards v. Canada (A.G.)*.

17 See Anne F. Bayefsky, *Canada's Constitution Act 1982 & Amendments: A Documentary History*.

18 Macklem, Risk, et al., *Canadian Constitutional Law*, vol. 1, 3.

19 Gertrude Himmelfarb has criticized the U.S. Supreme Court for "the abandonment of a strictly constitutional principle of interpretation and the arrogation to the judiciary of powers properly belonging to the legislative branch of government" (Himmelfarb, *One Nation, Two Cultures*, 68).

20 Hugh Segal, President, IRPP, letter to author, 21 March 1999.

21 See Joseph E. Fletcher and Paul Howe, "Canadian Attitudes toward the Charter and the Courts in Comparative Perspective." Unfortunately, the report's usefulness is severely compromised by the fact that it is both jargon-ridden and ungrammatical. See also Gregory Hein, "Interest Group Litigation and Canadian Democracy," and Howard Leeson, "Section 33, the Notwithstanding Clause: A Paper Tiger?"

22 Fletcher and Howe, *Canadian Attitudes*, 15.

23 Ibid., 55.

24 *Vriend v. Alberta*. This case is discussed more fully in chapter 8.

25 Fletcher and Howe, *Canadian Attitudes*, 42.

26 Ibid., 43.

27 Fletcher and Howe, *Canadian Attitudes*.

28 A compelling statement and critique of the orthodoxy can be found in Robert Fulford, "From Delusions to Destruction."

29 The *Toronto Star*'s attachment to the orthodoxy is discussed in Robert Fulford, "What's Wrong with Welsh on a Bet?" The Canadian Radio-Television and Telecommunications Commission

(CRTC), in recent decisions renewing the broadcasting licences of the CTV and Global networks, appears to have decreed that these broadcasters adhere to the orthodoxy. See CRTC decisions 2001–457 and 2001–458. CTV was ordered, as a condition of its broadcasting licence being renewed, to ensure that its portrayal of "all minority groups" be "accurate, fair and non-stereotypical." The network was also directed to ensure that "stories about ethnic communities do not appear solely within the context of coverage of cultural celebrations or reporting of negative stories" (CRTC decision, 2001–457).

So powerful is the devotion of the so-called mass media to the orthodoxy, that it often seems to me that we have but two newspapers in Canada. One should be called *The Daily Orthodoxy*, even though it is published in different places and under different names. Sometimes it is called the *Globe and Mail*, sometimes the *Toronto Star*, and sometimes the *London Free Press*, the *Kitchener-Waterloo Record*, or the *Edmonton Journal*, but even clothed in these ostensibly different appellations, it is always the same. The other newspaper, the only daily which takes a distinctively and consistently counter-orthodox approach, is the *National Post*. While *The Daily Orthodoxy* gives the impression that every word is written by the same person, it is a welcome change to be able to find independent thought in the pages of the *National Post*.

The one other bright spot in the Canadian media landscape is *Frank*. While *The Daily Orthodoxy* grovels in sycophancy toward the members of the ruling clique, *Frank* revels in muck-raking, never hesitating to reveal the dishonesty and venality of those who rule us.

A comment made about *New York Times* columnist Anthony Lewis in the *New Criterion* effectively sums up the sort of writing that appears constantly in *The Daily Orthodoxy*. One of Lewis's columns was described as "an excruciating compendium of politically correct clichés that seamlessly blends smug self-satisfaction and unrelenting disdain" ("The Struggles of Anthony Lewis," *New Criterion*, January 2002).

The CBC could fairly be described as the "state-funded electronic orthodoxy." A judge of the Ontario Superior Court of Justice recently described the behaviour of a CBC producer during an examination for discovery conducted as part of a libel action against "The Fifth Estate" as "self-righteous arrogance" (*Leenen*

v. *Canadian Broadcasting Corporation*). It would be difficult to imagine a better three-word description of "The Fifth Estate."

30 See Robert Martin, "Social Conservatism and Economic Radicalism: An Agenda for a Revived Canadian Left" and, in response, see Ian Malcolm, "Letter."

31 T. Brettel Dawson, letter to the author, 26 June 2001.

32 These include National Judicial Institute, *Bulletin* (2000) vol. 13, no. 2 and National Judicial Institute, Social Context Education Project, *Principles of Operation*, May 2001.

33 Despite the fact that the NJI refused to let me have detailed information about Social Context Education, I was able to obtain paper copies of slides used at an NJI seminar held in Banff in May 2000. The seminar was called "Building a Human Rights Culture: Tools for Transformation." A brief summary of the content of the slides will make clear that this seminar was devoted to relentless indoctrination. The focus of the seminar was on "equality." Equality was seen as relating largely to gender, race, and aboriginal peoples. Professor Lynn Smith of the University of British Columbia Faculty of Law stressed that Social Context Education should emphasise "analytical approaches which may be new to many judges." That last observation seems to me to be about as close to a definition of indoctrination as anyone could ask for. The advisory committee and the Program Development Group for the seminar included Smith, Juanita Westmoreland-Traore, former Ontario "Employment Equity" commissioner, Professor Sheila Martin of the University of Calgary, another feminist law professor, and Professor Joanne St. Lewis of the Faculty of Law at the University of Ottawa. (St. Lewis was the major author of the Canadian Bar Association's 1999 *Report: Racial Equality in the Canadian Legal Profession*.) (See *R.* v. *Sharpe*, D.L.R. at 49.) Reading through this material I can understand why the NJI wants to keep it secret. On 4 September 1998, former chief justice Antonio Lamer wrote to Gwendolyn Landolt of REAL Women in answer to concerns which she had raised about Social Context Education. The text of the letter follows:

Thank you for your letter of July 29, 1998. I regret the delay in responding.

As I indicated, I asked my Executive Legal Officer, Mr. James O'Reilly, to review the NJI materials on Gender Equality in light of your group's concerns. His conclusion was that the materials give considerable attention to the subject of domestic assault and that the perspective of women who are victims of such assaults is given primacy in the materials. However, he felt this was a product of the timing of the preparation of the materials rather than bias. The materials were put together just after this Court's decision in *R. v. Lavallée*. Quite naturally, the manner in which the issue is addressed is affected by the legal issues that arose in that case. As you know, the case centred on the perspective of a battered woman. The fact that the materials look at the issue from that perspective as well does not necessarily mean that they are biased. Rather, they reflect a natural desire to explore legal issues that were very topical at the time. I have no doubt, however, that if the materials were to be updated and revised, they would reflect a subtler and more sophisticated understanding of domestic assault as the understanding of this issue has evolved considerably since 1990.

Other areas addressed in the materials include sentencing of a person convicted of a spousal assault, custody of children, sexual assault trials and the credibility of women in the courts. Again, there is a good deal of consideration of the perspective of women in these areas. Such issues as the need to take account of the reality of working women, the prevalence and effect of sexual assault on women, the need to use gender neutral language and the reality of young women practising law in a male-dominated profession are addressed. Mr. O'Reilly concluded that there was nothing improper about the manner in which these issues were presented. It brings to the attention of judges a perspective that may assist them in better dealing with these issues fairly.

As for the excerpts from articles written by Shelagh Day and Gwen Brodsky, who are founders of LEAF, as you know, these excerpts provide background on equality cases decided under the *Canadian Bill of Rights* and a discussion of this Court's first decision under s. 15: *Andrews*. Both are critical. The first criticizes this Court's judgments in *Lavell* and *Bliss*. The second is critical of the equality analysis provided by this Court in *Andrews*. Mr. O'Reilly informs me that the excerpts are very short and do not present any overall thesis, if one exists, of the authors. All that one can glean from these passages is that the authors are critical of the analysis contained in the above-mentioned cases. While in principle it might have been better to include some commentary that praised the Court's decisions, given the brevity of the articles, such a measure was not strictly necessary in the circumstances.

In summary, Mr. O'Reilly's conclusion was that the materials do not reflect a feminist bias. At the same time, he felt that the materials should be improved. They very much need updating. In fact, I am told that the materials will be revised and updated within the framework of the NJI's Social Context Education Project. No doubt, the new version will be more relevant and current, as well as balanced.

A final point – my consideration of your concerns and the conclusions of my Executive Legal Officer convince me of the importance of dealing with these kinds of issues in substantive programs as well as in discrete capsules. For example, if the discussion of domestic violence took place in the context of a program on substantive criminal law (*i.e.* homicide or self defence), the perspective of both women and men would be equally relevant and would be discussed side by side. Taken out of that context and dealt with alongside other issues relating to women, one may get the mistaken impression that judges are only getting the point of view of women on such issues. I know that the NJI works very hard to ensure that these matters are not just dealt with in isolation but as part of their overall programming. I can well see the need to do so.

I very much appreciate your having raised your concerns with me. As I have said before, and now repeat, I believe that the NJI should be developing and delivering programmes that are relevant, informative and balanced. Comments that assist us in achieving those goals are welcomed.

This letter suggests further reasons for the NJI wishing to keep its activities secret.

34 National Judicial Institute, "Social Context Education: A Retrospective and Prospectus."
35 Schmitz, "Top Judge Views Social Context Training as Threat," 14.
36 See Senate, Standing Senate Committee on National Finance, *Second Report*, 4–10.

37 Anyone wishing to catch the flavour of the orthodoxy can do so
by reading any issue of *Canadian Forum* or watching *Vision TV* for
an hour or so.

38 Anderson, *Judging Bertha Wilson*.

In asserting the immanence of post-modernism, Anderson
claimed that "contingency" and "contextuality" run deep in the
history of Western civilization (136). She also spoke of the "infinite
variability of legal subjects," "legal texts," and "legal facts." She
also denied the possibility of certainty and objectivity in law (137).
She described Canada as a "post-Charter, post-modern society"
(139). She sees the Charter as a kind of post-modernist manifesto
(145). Anderson described Wilson as "the most post-modern of all
Canadian judges" (165).

39 The *Oxford English Dictionary* (Compact Edition, 1971) defines
hagiography as "The writing of the lives of saints; saints' lives as a
branch of literature or legend." Some examples from Anderson's
book about Bertha Wilson will illustrate the hagiographical character of Anderson's writing. Anderson described a reunion
dinner which Wilson arranged in 1991 for her former judicial law
clerks: "Typically, Wilson had selected the sumptuous menu
(crabmeat and avocado, veal marsala, strawberry mousse) and
the wines and then picked up the costs herself. The warm and
affectionate letters of thanks which came in afterwards indicated
that this was an absolute surprise and very much appreciated.
Clerk after clerk invited her to visit them [sic] at home when
next she happened to be visiting in their [sic] cities; clerk after
clerk mentioned how grateful they [sic] had been to work with
her during their [sic] year at the Supreme Court and that in
retrospect the gruelling workload they [sic] helped shoulder had
offered them [sic] the experience of a life time" (329). Littering
these sentences with *sic* may appear to be arch. This was done in
order to draw attention to what I regard as the most barbaric
aspect of our reigning newspeak, that is, the use of *they* as a
third-person singular pronoun.

This was the way Anderson described a visit Wilson paid to
Lord Denning in England: "And Wilson, who was within months
of announcing her own retirement and had long been considered
something of a Canadian Denning herself, paid Denning the highest tribute in her brief remarks. She was thoroughly thrilled and

did not mind at all sounding just as starstruck as she genuinely
was" (324).

Prior to a visit to the Soviet Union in 1989, Wilson decided to
present her Soviet hosts with photo albums to commemorate their
earlier visit to Canada. She dispatched her court attendant, Jean
Plourde, to buy the albums. Plourde went off to Zellers, bought
the albums and set them all up in his tidy manner to show to his
judge. She had to tell him gently, "That is not quality enough." But
Wilson knew exactly where to get the right kind of albums to
mark a state visit and it was a simple matter to transfer Plourde's
work to the more appropriate bindings (322).

Anderson quoted James MacPherson's adoring view of Wilson:
"Accordingly, he concluded, she was a perfect judge for her time.
What made it possible for her to do so much were three qualities
which he considers her to possess to an unusual degree: a
formidable intellect, a profound compassion, and a passionate
boldness" (133).

Of the Charter, Anderson opined: "Wilson's influence on the
Canadian legal landscape has been pervasive. Of course not all of
the cases in which Bertha Wilson participated at the Supreme
Court of Canada were concerned with Charter issues. But as we
will see, Charter considerations have become inextricably linked
with every area of Canadian experience as Canadians have come
increasingly to identify Canadian law with Canadian national feeling. Charter values, explicitly or implicitly, form the backdrop of
expectations shaping our society" (147).

The cutline on a photo of a sixteen-year-old Wilson described
her as "beautiful Bertha Wernham."

40 Martin Loney has attempted to set out the central elements of
the orthodoxy. See his *The Pursuit of Division: Race, Gender and
Preferential Hiring in Canada*, 3–21.

41 There is no canonical statement of the orthodoxy, but there is a
growing body of literature from both the U.S. and Canada which
criticizes the orthodoxy. See Gertrude Himmelfarb, *On Looking into
the Abyss: Untimely Thoughts on Culture and Society*; Jean Bethke
Elshtain, *Democracy on Trial*; Christina Hoff Sommers, *Who Stole
Feminism? How Women Have Betrayed Women*; Neil Bissoondath,
Selling Illusions: The Cult of Multiculturalism in Canada; and John
Fekete, *Moral Panic: Biopolitics Rising*. The endemic intellectual corruption of our universities is wittily and scathingly elaborated in

Malcolm Bradbury's *Mensonge*. The most original critique of the orthodoxy is found in Christopher Lasch's *The Revolt of the Elites and the Betrayal of Democracy*. Lasch characterized the orthodoxy as "a form of class warfare, in which an enlightened elite (as it thinks of itself) seeks not so much to impose its values on the majority (a majority perceived as incorrigibly racist, sexist, provincial and xenophobic), much less to persuade the majority by means of rational public debate, as to create parallel or 'alternative' institutions in which it will no longer be necessary to confront the unenlightened at all" (ibid., 20).

42 For daring to depart from the orthodoxy to the extent of being critical of feminism and feminists, La Framboise was the object of a vicious attack in the *Toronto Star* in January 2002. She was lumped together with Karla Homolka and accused of being "anti-female" (Giese, "Vancouver Feminists and Gender Politics").

43 See Dave Brown, "Men Challenge 'Bible' of Violence Against Women," "Burying Ghosts of a Violent Past," "'I Learned It's a System that Doesn't Listen,'" and "Turning Domestic Violence into a Religion."

44 Canada is, I believe, unique in being the only state in the world to have enshrined a commitment to relativism in its constitution. See section 27 of the Canadian Charter of Rights and Freedoms.
A superb and convincing critical analysis of relativism can be found in Keith Windschuttle, *The Killing of History: How Literary Critics and Social Theorists are Murdering our Past*.

45 Lasch called "the social construction of reality – the central dogma of post-modernist thought." (Lasch, *Revolt of the Elites*, 20n44).

46 A sound critique of the obsessive attachment to abstractions is Mark Steyn, "Pacifists' Ill-Breeding Scorns Actual People."

47 The fatuity of this mode of thought was made clear by Martin Loney when he spoke of "epistemological equity" (Loney, *Pursuit of Division*, 316).

48 Farber and Sherry have argued that relativism renders the making of moral judgments nearly impossible. See Farber and Sherry, *Beyond All Reason*, 105, 118. Gertrude Himmelfarb has noted that students in U.S. universities now regard the making of any judgments as "arbitrary, intolerant and authoritarian" (Himmelfarb, *One Nation, Two Cultures*, 122). She also quoted a student's view of the Nazis: "Of course I dislike the Nazis, but who is to say they are morally wrong?" (Ibid.). Hilton Kramer and Roger Kimball

have referred to "a permanent incapacity for critical judgment" (Kramer and Kimball, eds, *The Betrayal of Liberalism*, 11).

A decision of the Ontario Court of Appeal, released on 19 June 2002, suggests that the judges of that court do not grasp the distinction between truth-telling and lying. In her judgment in *Kreklewetz v. Scopel*, Madam Justice Feldman stated, in part, that "It is possible for a person to acknowledge something to be true in one context, but to decline to do so in another context" (D.L.R., at 398). For comment on this judgment, see the editorial "In the Name of the Father," *National Post*, 22 June 2002. (The Supreme Court of Canada denied leave to appeal on 6 February 2003.)

49 Windschuttle observed that "Without a claim to be pursuing truth, writing history would be indistinguishable in principle from writing a novel about the past" (Windschuttle, *Killing of History*, 203). Farber and Sherry have observed that "if there's no historical truth, there's no difference between a bad historian and a competent one" (Farber and Sherry, *Beyond All Reason*, 120).

50 Hadley Arkes made this observation about American judges: "the modern judges, the products of the best law schools in the land, affirm the right of a person to make up his own version of the universe" (Arkes, "Liberalism and the Law," 96).

51 Deconstructionist thought has done much to promote subjectivity and a lot of other nasty habits. For a searching critique, see David Lehman, *Signs of the Times: Deconstruction and the Fall of Paul de Man*.

52 To Windschuttle, relativism obscures any distinction between knowledge and ignorance and, in its final *reductio*, suggests the impossibility of ever knowing anything (Windschuttle, *Killing of History*, 226).

53 See William A. Henry III, *In Defense of Elitism*.

54 Windschuttle described this sort of relativism as "the return of tribalism in thinking and politics" (Windschuttle, *Killing of History*, 308).

55 A convincing explanation of the Nazi roots of much post-modernist thought can be found in Modris Eksteins, *Rites of Spring: The Great War and the Birth of the Modern Age*. An especially astute observation made by Eksteins: "Nazism took as its point of departure the subjective self, feeling, experience, *Erlebnis*, and not reason and the objective world" (311).

56 See the discussion in T.R.H. Davenport, *South Africa: A Modern History*, 336–40. The theory of Separate Development, which was

rooted in the Tomlinson report, emphasized "group identity" and "awareness of the role of cultural differences" (Randall, ed., *Anatomy of Apartheid*, 63).

57 See especially vol. 2.

58 The Royal Commission spoke of the notion that an Aboriginal nation enjoying self-government would "foster and protect its language, culture and identity" (Royal Commission on Aboriginal Peoples, *Report*, vol. 2, *Restructuring the Relationship*, 223). Concern has been raised about the integrity of the processes of the Royal Commission. See Gerard I. Kenney, *Arctic Smoke and Mirrors*.

59 *Van de Perre v. Edwards.*

60 In dealing with custody disputes, Canadian courts are required to seek "the best interests" of the child. In this respect the question of the adoption of aboriginal children by non-aboriginal parents has been a particularly difficult one. The Supreme Court dealt with this issue in *Racine v. Woods* where the Court did not find the question of "racial heritage" to be determinative (Ellen Anderson, *Judging Bertha Wilson*, discusses this case at 189–91).

61 *Van de Perre v. Edwards*, S.C.R. at 1036.

62 See Christopher Lasch, *Revolt of the Elites*, 184–7.

63 Farber and Sherry, *Beyond All Reason*, 134.

64 Lasch, *Revolt of the Elites*, 20.

65 Christopher Lasch addresses this question in *The True and Only Heaven: Progress and its Critics*, 412–75.

66 See her *Petticoats and Prejudice: Women and Law in Nineteenth Century Canada*. The current government of Ontario appears to have adopted the "bad thoughts cause bad behaviour" analysis and has announced a program of setting up re-education centres for offenders. See Dave Brown, "Provincial Ridicule, at Your Own Expense."

This view of the world may usefully be described as the *All in the Family* theory of history. *All in the Family* was a very successful U.S. television sitcom of the 1970s. Most episodes focused on the juxtaposition of Archie Bunker and his son-in-law Michael Stivic (Meathead). Archie was the archetypal unenlightened person. Meathead was undeniably enlightened. It was clear that Archie thought bad thoughts and Michael thought good thoughts. It was often suggested that many of the serious social ills of the United States were the result of people like Archie thinking bad thoughts. And, the remedy appeared to be, if only everyone would learn to think good thoughts, everything would be fine. The clear message of *All in the Family* was that ordinary, working-class people like Archie were irredeemably bad.

67   See *R.v. Keegstra* (1990) and *Eldridge* v. *British Columbia (A.G.)*. As I understand the dissent of Justice L'Heureux-Dubé in *Trinity Western University* v. *British Columbia College of Teachers*, the judge appears to have been motivated by outrage at the possibility that students might get their feelings hurt. Much of her dissent was taken up with expressions of her concern that certain students might have low "self-esteem" (at 844). In this decision Justice L'Heureux-Dubé discovered a new category of victim – those who suffer "identity erasure" (at 848). This case is discussed fully in chapter 5. Robert Fulford argued in "From Delusions to Destruction" that the fear of doing anything that might offend anyone is what gives the orthodoxy its power.

68   Matsuda, "Public Response to Racist Speech," 2323.

69   Mallick, "Read my Lips."

70   Cabral, *Revolution in Guinea*, 74. Rosa Luxemburg was equally unimpressed with this sort of politics. She spoke of "a vain effort to repair the capitalist order" (Howard, ed., *Selected Political Writings of Rosa Luxemburg*, 53).

71   Greene, *Charter of Rights*, xx.

72   The *Canadian Lawyer* annual survey of Canadian law schools for the year 2002 began with the statement "the majority of the 200 or so respondents stated they are sick and tired of political ideology in the classroom" (McMahon, "Making the Grade," 36). It is not just law schools that have abandoned education in favour of indoctrination. Canadian universities today are largely devoted to indoctrination (Loney, *Pursuit of Division*, 288–9, 321). A detailed picture of the dismal state of Canadian universities is presented in Peter C. Emberley, *Zero Tolerance: Hot Button Politics in Canada's Universities*. The rigour of graduate and undergraduate studies has declined at all levels. See Linton Weeks, "You're the Dr."

73   A good introduction to the intellectual cesspool that is Canadian university legal education today is provided in (1992) 15:1 *Dalhousie Law Journal*. An article by Hester Lessard, formerly a judicial law clerk at the Supreme Court and now a professor at the Faculty of Law of the University of Victoria demonstrates the depths to which discourse about Canadian law has sunk. In her contribution to this volume she expressly argued against "principle and reason" (Lessard, "Equality and Access," 41).

74 Wente, "Food, Sex and Racism."

75 She probably did not understand the nature of criminal prosecutions because the people teaching her did not either. Kent Roach is a professor of law at the University of Toronto. In 1996 he published an article in which he flaunted his ignorance of our criminal justice system. See Kent Roach, "For a Victim Rights Model of Criminal Justice," 17. Wayne N. Renke is a law professor at the University of Alberta. In 1996 he manifested a similar enthusiasm for the involvement of "victims." See Wayne N. Renke, "Should Victims Participate in Sentencing?" 13.

76 William Ryan's *Blaming the Victim* is the origin of this bit of idiocy.

77 There is a large and bizarre literature on this point. Its flavour can be gleaned from Rosemary J. Coombe, "The Properties of Culture and the Politics of Possessing Identity: Native Claims in the Cultural Appropriation Controversy."

78 Justice Bertha Wilson of the Supreme Court of Canada gave judicial blessing to this sort of thinking in her judgment in *R. v. Morgentaler* (1988).

79 Loney, *Pursuit of Division*, 12.

80 Jean Bethke Elshtain's *Democracy on Trial* is very good on the politicization of everything. Paul Fussell explains how we have come to adopt the rhetoric of warfare in *The Great War and Modern Memory*.

81 Fox-Genovese, "From Separate Spheres," 235.

82 Lasch, *True and Only Heaven*, 17. See also Mary Zeiss Stange, "The Political Intolerance of Academic Feminism." In a similar vein, Jean Bethke Elshtain spoke of "a form of pluralism that requires uniformity" (Elshtain, "The Bright Line," 149).

83 Fussell's *The Great War and Modern Memory* is very good at explaining the deep cynicism of contemporary society. This point is elaborated in Farber and Sherry, *Beyond All Reason*, 135–6.

84 Lasch, *Revolt of the Elites*, 20.

85 Marx's eleventh thesis on Feuerbach is generally seen as the origin of this notion. See Karl Marx, "Theses on Feuerbach," 13.

86 Massey, "Book Review," 1280.

87 Canadian Bar Association, Working Group on Racial Equality in the Canadian Legal Profession, *Report: Racial Equality in the Canadian Legal Profession* (Ottawa, 1999) enthusiastically embraces Critical Race Theory. This report should be regarded as the companion to one prepared for the Canadian Bar Association by former Supreme Court justice Bertha Wilson: Canadian Bar Association,

Task Force on Gender Equality in the Legal Profession Report: *Touchstones for Change: Equality, Diversity and Accountability* (Ottawa, 1993). The two reports suffer from massive methodological deficiencies and are profoundly suspect.

88 Marx and Engels, "Critique of the Gotha Programme," 18.
89 *Red Action Bulletin*, vol. 4, no. 10 (April 2001). www.redaction.org/bulletins/editorials
90 See Alan Grove and Ross Lambertson, "Pawns of the Powerful: The Politics of Litigation in the Union Colliery Case."·
91 In commenting on this case, Michael Mandel issued a comforting homily which allowed him to express his opposition to racist laws (Michael Mandel, *The Charter of Rights and the Legalization of Politics in Canada*). Justice L'Heureux-Dubé qualified her endorsement of *Union Colliery*, stating that "It cannot really be said that equality rights won a resounding victory in this or any other like-minded decision": see her speech "Are we There Yet? Gender Equality in the Law of Canada" to the American Bar Association Annual Meeting, Toronto, 1 August 1998.
92 Michael Novak, "Defining Social Justice," 11.
93 This criticism was first made by Justice Gerard La Forest writing in dissent in *Reference re Remuneration of Judges of the Provincial Court of Prince Edward Island*.
94 *Canada (Combines Investigation Acts, Director of Investigation and Research) v. Southam*, S.C.R. at 155.
95 *Nova Scotia (A.G.) v. Canada (A.G.)*, [1951] S.C.R. at 34.
96 *Reference Re Manitoba Language Rights* at 753.
97 *Supreme Court Act*, R.S.C. 1985, c. S-19.
98 I was once described as a "left-wing charterphobe." See Richard Sigurdson, "Left-and Right-Wing Charterphobia in Canada: A Critique of the Critics," 95.
99 The most scathing criticism of a court ever written by a Canadian was Frank Scott's "Some Privy Counsel."
100 *Lochner v. New York*; *Schechter Poultry Corporation v. U.S.*; and *Panama Refining Company v. Ryan*. In all these decisions the U.S. Supreme Court was being both activist and creative. English judges have tended not to indulge themselves in activism and creativity, but, when they have done so, they have shown themselves to be as reactionary as their U.S. counterparts. Good examples are *Priestley v. Fowler* at 1050 and *Roberts v. Hopwood*.
101 *Plessy v. Ferguson*.

102 See Charles Taylor, *Six Journeys: A Canadian Pattern* and, by the same author, *Radical Tories: The Conservative Tradition in Canada*. One reason that I am partial to the analysis presented by Christopher Lasch is that he is the closest thing to a Red Tory which has been produced in the United States. It will be helpful to explain what I mean by Red Tory and why I believe myself to be one. The Red part means that I am a socialist. Thus, I do not support private ownership of the means of production and believe that economic and political power should be in the hands of ordinary people. My notion of socialism is class-based and aggressively rejects what passes for the left in Canada today, namely a grand coalition of victim groups. The Tory part means that socially, culturally, and intellectually I tend to be conservative. I believe that all citizens should be treated as legal and political equals. I strongly support the Rule of Law and believe in the virtues of honesty, integrity, and courage.

    Fealty to these notions puts me at odds with our judges and with most of our law teachers.

CHAPTER ONE

1 Since 1982 fewer than 25 per cent of Supreme Court decisions have dealt with the Charter (see, Peter Russell, "The Supreme Court and the Charter: Quantitative Trends – Continuities and Discontinuities," 64).

2 Hadley Arkes has asserted that as U.S. judges abandoned principle "they were left with little more than the intuitions that sprang from their own exquisite sensibilities" (Arkes, "Liberalism and the Law," 99).

3 See *Norberg* v. *Wynrib*. *Norberg* v. *Wynrib* was a nasty bit of litigation. The plaintiff, Laura Norberg, was a young woman. She had become addicted to pain killers which she obtained initially from her sister and, subsequently, through manipulating various physicians. The defendant was a physician in his seventies. Using different pretexts and subterfuges, the plaintiff was able to obtain prescriptions from the defendant for her drugs. She also continued to obtain drugs from other physicians. Eventually, the plaintiff began to exchange sexual favours for her drugs. The plaintiff then sued Dr Wynrib for damages for battery, sexual assault, and breach of fiduciary duty. Her claim was dismissed by the trial

court because the court believed that she had consented to the
sexual activity with Dr Wynrib. Because the plaintiff's behaviour
had been immoral, if not criminal, the trial court dismissed her
claim on the basis of the principle *ex turpi causa non oritur actio*
(which may be loosely translated as "a cause of action may not be
based on evil or immoral conduct"). The B.C. Court of Appeal
upheld the trial judge's decision. The plaintiff appealed further to
the Supreme Court which upheld her claim and awarded her both
aggravated and punitive damages.

The decisions in the Supreme Court are a compendium of orthodox notions about victimology and feminist theology. In this case,
existing legal doctrine was stretched and bent in order to allow the
plaintiff to recover.

Justices McLachlin and L'Heureux-Dubé delivered a common
judgment. They were not prepared to hold that the sexual relations
between the plaintiff and the defendant were non-consensual.
Finding no solace for the plaintiff in the existing law of torts and
contract, they decided to invent new principles. The new doctrine
involved something called "breach of fiduciary relationship." The
really neat thing about breach of fiduciary relationship is that,
even in a case where the plaintiff might not succeed under existing tort law, this will allow her to win. The two judges gave a feel-
good direction to this doctrine, noting that "This Court has an
honourable tradition of recognizing new claims of the disempow-
ered against the exploitive." They gave some encouragement to
feminist notions of victimology, observing that "Women, who can
be so easily exploited by physicians for sexual purposes, may find
themselves particularly vulnerable." All the judges who heard the
appeal seemed to agree that Laura Norberg had not gone to Dr
Wynrib for medical treatment, but primarily in order to get drugs.
Justices McLachlin and L'Heureux-Dubé concluded that Norberg's
claim could not be denied because of the *ex turpi causa* principle,
arguing that to do so would amount to "blaming the victim." They
actually said this. (*Norberg* v. *Wynrib*, S.C.R. at 275, 291, 279, 286.)

In finding that Dr Wynrib had breached his fiduciary duty
toward Norberg, all the judges adopted the reasoning of a 1991
document, *Final Report of the Task Force on Sexual Abuse of Patients*.
This committee was established by the Ontario College of Physicians and Surgeons and chaired by feminist lawyer Marilou
McPhedran. The report ordained that all sexual activity between

a medical practitioner and a patient amounted to sexual abuse and recommended "zero tolerance" of it.

In the result, the two judges awarded Norberg $75,000, including $25,000 in punitive damages.

The Supreme Court's decision is replete with feminist theology about sexual relations between men and women. The idea of a woman voluntarily consenting to sexual relations with a man is questioned. Furthermore, in the passages dealing with damages, the Court strongly suggests that sexual relations between men and women are, by their nature, a zero-sum game.

4 *M. (K) v. M. (H)*. In this case, a twenty-eight-year-old woman brought an action against her father based on his having committed incest with her when she was between the ages of ten and sixteen. A trial judge dismissed the action on the ground that the claim was time-barred because it had not been initiated within the period specified in the Ontario Limitations Act (R.S.O. 1980, c. 240). The Ontario Court of Appeal upheld the trial judge's decision and the plaintiff appealed to the Supreme Court. LEAF (the Women's Legal Education and Action Fund) intervened to support the appellant.

The appellant's claim was largely based on the psychological and emotional injuries she claimed to have suffered as a result of her father's abuse. It was argued that only after attending a self-help group and receiving counselling did the plaintiff become aware that her psychological and emotional difficulties resulted from the incest. It was also argued that the limitation period should not have begun to run until such time as the plaintiff had become aware of the full extent of the injuries flowing from the incest.

Justice LaForest sought to justify the Court's disregard of the Limitations Act by stating that observing the statute might mean that "victims would be required to report incidents before they were psychologically prepared for the consequences of that reporting" (*M. (K) v. M. (H)*, S.C.R. at 31). The judge gave no hint of how he had come to learn this. As will be noted in chapter 6, Justice La Forest has often acted in a highly principled fashion.

The judges were also prepared to uphold the plaintiff's claim on the basis that it was an action for breach of fiduciary duty and, thus, by its nature, not subject to limitations legislation.

As often happens, the judges paid a great deal of attention to material written by feminist academics, material which Justice

L'Heureux-Dubé referred to as "scientific literature" (*M. (K) v. M. (H)*, S.C.R. at 47).

5 *Stewart* v. *Pettie*. The facts in *Stewart* v. *Pettie* were improbable, so improbable that they resemble a problem concocted for a law school torts exam. The plaintiff had become a quadriplegic when her brother, Stuart Pettie, crashed the car he was driving her in. One of the defendants, Mayfield, owned a dinner theatre in Edmonton in which the brother had been drinking prior to the accident. The Supreme Court was prepared to find a legal nexus between the commercial establishment and the plaintiff, thereby accepting that the dinner theatre could be held liable in respect of her injuries. While the Court did decide that a "duty of care did exist between the dinner theatre establishment, Mayfield, and the plaintiff," it stopped short of holding that this defendant had breached the "standard" of care expected of it. In the Supreme Court, Justice Major decided that Mayfield "had no obligation to take any positive steps to ensure that Stuart Pettie (the driver who actually caused the accident) did not drive." In the result, the plaintiff was able to recover compensation from her brother, but not from Mayfield. (*Stewart* v. *Pettie*, S.C.R. at 148.)

6 Kostal, "Casenote," 173, 174, 176.

7 *Cooper* v. *Hobart*, at 561. The decision in *Cooper* v. *Hobart* stems largely from judicial self-interest. The defendant, the Registrar of Mortgage Brokers, was performing a quasi-judicial function. A decision that the plaintiff could recover in negligence from the Registrar might have opened the way for negligence actions against judges.

8 Counsel for CARAL was Elizabeth Symes, the same Elizabeth Symes who challenged the constitutionality of the Income Tax Act on the grounds that it prevented her from deducting her nanny's salary from Symes's $200,000 income. There is more information about Symes in chapter 7.

9 *Dobson (Litigation Guardian of)* v. *Dobson*, S.C.R. at 769.

10 Ibid., at 799.

11 *Winnipeg Child and Family Services (Northwest Area)* v. *G. (D.F.)*, S.C.R. at 959.

12 Arnold, "Reflections."

13 *Inland Revenue Commissioners* v. *Duke of Westminster*.

14 Arnold, "Reflections," 3, 9.

15 Hart, *Concept of Law*; Fuller, *Morality of Law*.

16 Fuller, *Morality of Law,* 209, 211.

17 *Sharpe* v. *Wakefield,* at 179.

18 Supreme Court of Canada, *Performance Report for the Period Ending March 31, 2001,* 3.

19 Harvey, "Rule of Law," 494.

20 Christopher Manfredi has provided a useful and helpful chart of LEAF interventions in hearings before the Court. (See Manfredi, "Judicial Power and the Charter," 120).

21 *Edmonton Journal* v. *Alberta (A.G.),* S.C.R. at 1355.

22 Wilson, "Decision-Making in the Supreme Court," 245.

23 See *R.* v. *Marshall* [1999] 3 S.C.R. 456; and *Delgamuukw* v. *British Columbia.* There is a fundamental contradiction in the arguments of the aboriginal litigants in these cases. The litigants sought to present themselves as members of autonomous, self-governing nations. But, by the very act of arguing before a Canadian court, they were accepting the authority of the Canadian state. In order to claim rights under the Constitution of Canada, one must accept that one is subject to that constitution and, therefore, to the Canadian state. Thus the act of making these arguments contradicts the arguments themselves. Marshall was a Micmac Indian who had fished for eels off the coast of Nova Scotia. His way of fishing was in breach of applicable federal fishing regulations: he had fished without a licence, he was using illegal nets, he was fishing during a closed season, and he had sold eels without a licence. Marshall argued that because of treaties of 1760–61 between the Micmacs and the Crown he was not subject to the federal regulations. The judges of the Court turned themselves, not for the first time, into amateur historians and, on this basis, acquitted Marshall. Much of the Court's decision is taken up with a lengthy digression into the history of relations between the Micmacs and the Crown. A major confrontation developed in the summer of 2000 between native fishers and federal officials, possibly as a result of the *R.* v. *Marshall* decision. (See Deborah Nobes and Kevin Cox, "N.B. Natives Told to Halt Fishery Today.") *Delgamuukw* involved a claim that section 35(1) of the Constitution Act, 1982 affirmed certain rights in land and was, in addition, a basis for the recognition of aboriginal self-government. Chief Justice Lamer effectively established his own amateurishness at history, genealogy, linguistics, anthropology, and archeology as the result was not convincing. The chief justice recognized that the admission of oral history as

evidence probably contradicted the hearsay rule, but he was none-theless prepared to accept such evidence – which he variously described as "songs" and "legends" – as the basis for recognizing an aboriginal title to land.

24 See Luiza Chwialkowska, "P.M. Set to Overhaul Native Policy."

25 *Winnipeg Child and Family Services* v. *K.L.W.*, S.C.R. at 574.

26 *R.* v. *Sharpe.*

27 *Winnipeg Child and Family Services* v. *K.L.W.*, S.C.R. at 570, 577.

28 Ibid., at 536.

29 Children's Aid Societies regularly behave as if they are completely above the law: see Christie Blatchford, "A Thin Line between Abuse and Discipline." L'Heureux-Dubé's judgment in *K.L.W.* parallels her dissent in *Trinity Western University* v. *British Columbia College of Teachers* (discussed in more detail in chapter 5). The lesson to be drawn from both decisions is that, if a state agency claims to be seeking objectives with which L'Heureux-Dubé agrees, the agency is not to be constrained by either the law or the Constitution.

30 *Winnipeg Child and Family Services* v. *K.L.W.*, at 551.

31 Ian Brodie, "Interest Group Litigation and the Embedded State."

32 Ibid.

33 See *Mahe* v. *Alberta.*

34 See *Vriend* v. *Alberta.* A very different constitution is the 1996 Constitution of South Africa. This Constitution, in several places, expressly imposes obligations on the state. South Africa's Constitu-tion creates a right to education (s.29), a right to housing (s.26), and rights to health care, food, water, and social security (s.27). These rights, by their nature, could only be implemented through positive judicial review.

35 See chapter 7 below.

36 See Willick v. *Willick.* She observed in this case that "the judi-ciary's long-recognised function as a policy finder compels it to consider social authority [sic] even when the parties do not, them-selves, present relevant evidence on relevant questions of social policy," and that "this court has ... recognized the usefulness of social science research and judicial notice of social context in debunking myths and exposing stereotypes and assumptions which desensitize the law to the realities of those affected by it." These can only be interpreted as the words of a judge who believes herself to be omniscient.

37 L'Heureux-Dubé, "Re-examining the Doctrine of Judicial Notice in the Family Law Context," 558.

38 Ibid., 568.

39 See chapter 7, below.

40 The fact that L'Heureux-Dubé was following a personal agenda was made clear in a ceremony held in June 2002 to mark her departure from the Court. At this ceremony, Chief Justice McLachlin observed of L'Heureux-Dubé that, "She developed an abiding passion for social justice" In the same speech, the chief justice tried to downplay L'Heureux-Dubé's appearance of being a feminist activist. She defined *feminist* as "a person who advocates for [sic] the rights of women, based on the theory of the equality of the sexes" (Sue Bailey, "Supreme Court Pays Tribute to Colourful, Contentious Judge"). This is a strikingly benign definition of *feminist* and is identical to Christina Hoff Sommers's notion of "equity," as opposed to "gender," feminists (Sommers, *Who Stole Feminism?* 22–3).

41 L'Heureux-Dubé, "Re-examining the Doctrine," 577.

42 Williams, "Grasping a Thorny Baton," 182.

43 Ibid., 225.

44 Ibid., 227.

45 These figures come from Bill C-12, 2001, clause 1(a) and 1(b).

46 *Reference re Secession of Québec.*

47 *R. v. Marshall,* [1999] 3 S.C.R. 456.

48 These matters are more fully discussed in chapter 8, below.

49 It has recently become fashionable to criticize the very notion of judicial impartiality: see Richard Devlin and Dianne Pothier, "Redressing the Imbalances: Rethinking the Judicial Role after *R. v. R.D.S.*" The authors decry the notion of judicial neutrality. A helpful distinction, I believe, is that between "uninterested" and "disinterested." If the courts are to be called upon to address the major issues of the day, the judges can hardly be expected to be "uninterested," but they should be required to be "disinterested" as between the litigants actually before the court.

50 See *S. v. Masasanye; S. v. Baleka;* and *Gumede v. Minister of Law and Order.*

51 Chwialkowska, "Revamped Bench Big on Unanimity."

CHAPTER TWO

1 *Canada Elections Act,* S.C. 1960, c. 39, s. 14.

2 C.B. Macpherson's *The Real World of Democracy* is a superb introduction to this subject.

3 Peter McCormick, *Supreme at Last: The Evolution of the Supreme Court of Canada*, 172–3. This disappointing book is largely an apology for the Court. It does not address issues of principle, but confines itself to the minutiae of institutional decision-making. Another disappointing book about the Supreme Court is James G. Snell and Frederick Vaughan, *The Supreme Court of Canada: History of the Institution.*

4 These matters are discussed in detail in Royal Commission on Electoral Reform and Party Financing, *Report*. The scriptural character of the Charter is underlined in this report, which calls the Charter "now the foremost constitutional document in the country" and makes the extraordinarily anti-democratic recommendation that only those political parties whose party constitutions promote "values and practices consistent with the 'spirit and intent' of the Charter" be allowed to contest elections (vol. 1, 246).

5 Dickson, "Role and Function of Judges," 140.

6 *Supreme Court Act*, R.S.C. 1985, c. S-26, s. 9(2).

7 In one of her many public speeches, Justice L'Heureux-Dubé boasted that "the courts are taking the lead in changing society's attitudes to same-sex partnerships" ("Opening Remarks to the Panel Discussion: Same-Sex Partnerships in Canada," [speech delivered at the *Conference on the Legal Recognition of Same-Sex Partnerships*, London, UK, 1 July 1999]). In a democracy, judges should not "take the lead" in changing society's attitudes.

8 *Schachter* v. *Canada*, S.C.R. at 695.

9 See Dale Gibson, "Founding Fathers-in-Law: Judicial Amendment of the Canadian Constitution."

10 *Tetreault-Gadoury* v. *Canada (Employment and Immigration Commission)*, S.C.R. at 43.

11 Black, "I Dreamt of Canada."

12 Martin, "Dismantling the State."

13 It is noteworthy that the Supreme Court's earliest Charter decisions were largely affirmations of freedom of commerce. See *Canada (Combines Investigation Acts, Director of Investigation and Research)* v. *Southam*; and *R.* v. *Big M Drug Mart*. The latter case arose because a drugstore chain in Alberta did not like the fact that a 1906 federal statute called the Lord's Day Act prevented it from opening on Sundays. The decision is an early manifestation of the Court's predilection for playing fast and loose with the constitutional text. The Supreme Court managed to torture the guarantee

of "freedom of religion" in section 2 of the Charter into a disestab-
lishment clause, and in so doing struck down a fetter on commercial freedom. For many years, the mass media in Canada have
been dominated by a small number of large corporations. In
Southam, a newspaper in the Southam chain was challenging an
entry and search of its premises pursuant to the Combines Investigation Act, a statute ostensibly designed to control monopolies and
oligopolies. In 1976, the Supreme Court had decided a case called
R. v. K.C. Irving Ltd. The result of this decision was that any utility
there might have been in the Combines Investigation Act as a
means of controlling media conglomerates was dissolved. *Southam*
was another step in the same direction of protecting newspaper
chains against state interference.

14 *Constitution Act* 1867, s. 91.
15 Marx and Engels, *The German Ideology*, 64.
16 Lasch, *Revolt of the Elites*, 180.
17 Martin, "Review."
18 Greene, Bar, et al., *Final Appeal*, 10, 200.
19 Ibid., 15, 211.
20 Greene, *Charter of Rights*, 62. Greene's work is, again, best seen as a
statement of the orthodoxy, in that he appears to believe the whole
point of a democratic political system is to uphold human rights.
21 Lasch, *Revolt of the Elites*, 20.
22 See F.L. Morton, "Rulings for the Many by the Few." The enlightened appear to believe that majority rule is a bad and dangerous
thing. Hence, there is a widespread fascination with alternatives to
majority rule like proportional representation. See Andrew Coyne,
"Majority Rules, Even If It's a Minority." In December 2001, the
Law Commission of Canada, a bastion of orthodoxy, invited
"scholars" to submit proposals for research into the "values"
which should be represented in our electoral system. The Commission stated that it wished to "encourage dialogue on alternatives to
the current voting system" (Law Commission of Canada,
"Renewing Canadian Democracy," 2002: http//www.lcc.gc.ca).

The first fruits of the Law Commission's ruminations about
democracy are ominous and disturbing. The title the Commission
gave to its project is presumptuous and a bit unnerving: *Renewing
Canadian Democracy.* This title suggests that Canadian democracy is,
in some way or other, fundamentally flawed. As part of this
project, some background papers were prepared. Of particular

interest is the Commission's series of papers "Citizen Engagement in Voting System Reform," and specifically Law Commission of Canada/Fair Vote Canada, "Phase One: Lessons from Around the World" (Ottawa, 2002), as well as Law Commission of Canada, "Votes, Victories and Values" (Ottawa, 2002). Two methodological choices made by the Commission are cause for concern. First, the main consultant engaged by the Commission was a York University political scientist and, second, the Commission decided to "partner" with (as it would probably have put it) an interest group, Fair Vote Canada. What, in the view of the Commission, is wrong with Canada's electoral system? Why, in other words, does it need "renewing"? The answer is that the wrong people get elected. According to "Votes, Victories and Values," our electoral system is flawed because not enough women and members of minority groups get elected. The problem, I surmise, is that since the unenlightened get to vote in elections, they turn, in their unenlightened way, to white men. The papers prepared by the Commission leave the impression that they were written by a struggling Grade Ten student: incomprehensible jargon, grammatical errors, and unsubstantiated assertions abound. "Votes, Victories and Values" makes reference to "most democratic nations" without providing a clue as to what is being talked about. The notion of "one person, one vote" is dismissed with disdain. The problem with "one person, one vote," of course, is that the vote of an unenlightened citizen is given the same weight as the vote of an enlightened citizen. Rather than renewal, I fear that the result of the Law Commission's project may be the *end* of Canadian democracy.

23 Greene notes that legislators may have been shirking their responsibilities in correcting human rights abuses (Greene, *Charter of Rights*, 210). The problem with legislators of course, is that the unenlightened get to vote for them. The mantra of those who favour the new, dominant judicial role is "Politicians bad, judges good." See Kirk Makin, "Has Democracy Been Dulled?" and "We Are Not Gunslingers."

24 Quoted in F.L. Morton and Rainer Knopff, *Charter Revolution and the Court Party*, 150.

25 Mandel, "Rule of Law," 280. The process which Mandel describes has seen the Charter invested with magical properties. Osgoode Hall law professor Alan Hutchinson was quoted as saying, "What has the *Charter* done for the homeless or the dispossessed?" in

Kirk Makin, "Rights Gone Wrong?" Implicit in Hutchinson's assertion is a belief that the Charter could have *done* something for the
homeless and the dispossessed, but did not. Hutchinson's anthro-
pomorphic assertion appears to bespeak a belief that a collection of
legal abstractions, like the Charter, might actually be capable of
doing things.

A recent editorial in the *Law Times* suggested that the Charter
has made Canada a better country: "Canada, its Constitution and
Charter of Rights afford us a life much better than most countries"
(*Law Times*, 8 April 2002).

26 Martin, "Ideology and Judging," 801.

27 It would be inaccurate to describe this clique as a class. Classes are
defined primarily by their relation to the means of production. The
current ruling clique is largely parasitic and, thus, having no relation to the means of production, cannot be described as a class.
(See E.P. Thompson, *The Making of the English Working Class*, 9–15).

28 For critical comment, see Claire Hoy, "The Hill." The report is
Canadian Human Rights Act Review Panel, *Report: Promoting
Equality; a new Vision*. This document is a lengthy and sanctimonious statement of many elements of the orthodoxy, especially the
notion that all "discrimination," by its very nature, is bad. The
authors of the report did not seem to understand that a person
who is incapable of "discrimination" is incapable of thought or
action. We have lost sight of the fact that, while discrimination
amongst human beings on certain bases is unacceptable, all discrimination is not. The authors dwell at length on a central tenet of
the orthodoxy – the belief that anything undesirable that happens
to an individual must be the result of "discrimination." The panel
was made up of a former Supreme Court judge and two university professors. I must enquire whether it occurred to this august
collection of personages that the fact that the majority of Canadians
are neither Supreme Court judges nor university professors must
be the result of "discrimination."

29 Mandel, *The Charter of Rights and the Legalisation of Politics in Canada*.

30 Tocqueville, *Democracy in America*, vol. 1, 290. Scarcely any political question arises in the United States that is not resolved, sooner
or later, into a judicial question.

31 Strayer, "Life under the Canadian Charter," 352.

32 McCormick, *Supreme at Last*, 173. It must be evident that
McCormick would cite Greene with approval.

33 Ian Buruma wrote, "Identity is a bloody business ... is what gets the blood boiling, what makes people do unspeakable things to their neighbours" (Buruma, "The Blood Lust of Identity").

34 See *Andrews* v. *Law Society of British Columbia*.

35 A full discussion of the destructive effects which these tendencies have had on the legal system and legal education in the U.S. can be found in Daniel A. Farber and Suzanna Sherry, *Beyond All Reason: The Radical Assault on Truth in American Law*.

36 See *Reference Re Workers Compensation Act 1983 (Nfld.)*. Morton and Knopff assert that the Court has adopted an "open-door policy" on intervenors (Morton and Knopff, *Charter Revolution*, 55).

37 See *Canadian Council of Churches* v. *Canada (Minister of Employment and Immigration)*.

38 *Canada (Minister of Justice)* v. *Borowski* [1981].

39 A fascinating discussion of these cases can be found in F.L. Morton, *Morgentaler v. Borowski: Abortion, the Charter and the Courts*.

40 Morton and Knopff, *Charter Revolution*.

41 James B. Kelly, "The *Charter*," 654.

42 Glendon, *Rights Talk*. Glendon also argued that "rights talk" has been a major factor in creating the vicious and acrimonious atmosphere which surrounds the debate over abortion in North America. Conducted largely in the rhetoric of rights, public discourse about abortion has created a situation in which opponents regularly hurl abuse at each other, and sometimes murder each other.

43 Lasch, *Revolt of the Elites*, 10.

44 *Reference Re Alberta Legislation*.

45 Ibid., at 133.

46 *Irwin Toy Ltd.* v. *Québec (A.G.)*, S.C.R. at 976.

47 Coyne, "Some Freedom for Some Speech."

48 *R.* v. *Sharpe*, S.C.R. at 22–4.

49 The foolish nature of these concepts can be gleaned from Rosemary J. Coombe, "The Properties of Culture and the Politics of Possessing Identity: Native Claims in the Cultural Appropriation Controversy."

50 *R.* v. *Keegstra*, S.C.R. at 728.

51 See Terry Heinrichs, "Censorship as Free Speech: Free Expression Values and the Logic of Silencing." A recent and disappointing monograph by University of Windsor law professor Richard Moon echoes the Supreme Court's lack of enthusiasm for free expression.

Moon's uncritical analysis suggests that he agrees with the Court. In his *The Constitutional Protection of Freedom of Expression*, Moon took an approach to expression which recognized its "social character" and "its potential for harm." The problem was that "Expression can cause fear, it can harass, and it can undermine self-esteem" (4).

52 Anderson, *Judging Bertha Wilson*, 136.

53 See *RJR-MacDonald v. Canada (A.G.)*.

54 The Court stated that it is difficult to imagine a guaranteed right more important to a democratic society than freedom of expression. Indeed a democracy cannot exist without the freedom to express new ideas and to put forward opinions about the functioning of public institutions (*Libman v. Québec (A.G.)*, S.C.R. at 590).

The specific issue before the Court in this case was the constitutionality of a $600 statutory ceiling on spending during referendum campaigns by third parties, which is to say, persons or organizations not part of the two official sides of a campaign. Manfredi elaborated an observation about the decision being one of "judicial micro-management" by stating, "Once the court accepted the proposition that the *Charter* permits limits on independent expenditures, there was no legal or constitutional principle against which to evaluate the specific amount of the expenditure ceiling" (Manfredi, *Judicial Power and the Charter*, 151).

55 Ibid., 151. For further comment, see C. Feasby, "The Emerging Egalitarian Model." Feasby appears to believe that unconstrained freedom of expression should be accorded lesser protection than "fairness."

56 R.S.C. 1985, c. C-46.

57 Guly, "Photo Labs Vigilant about Child Porn."

58 Bill C-329, *An Act to Amend the Criminal Code*, 3d Sess., 30th Parl., 1977.

59 House of Commons, Standing Committee, *Report on Pornography.*

60 Bill C-54, *An Act to Amend the Criminal Code and Other Acts in Consequence Thereof*, 2d Sess., 33d Parl., 1987.

61 S.C. 1993, c. 46.

62 *R. v. Sharpe*, D.L.R. at 16–59.

63 Ibid., at 42, 43, 39, 51.

64 The chief justice's discussion of freedom of expression is found at 22–4.

65 *Irwin Toy v. Québec (A.G.) and R.J.R. MacDonald Inc. v. Canada (A.G.)*.

66 *R. v. Keegstra* (1990).

67 *R. v. Butler.*

68 Hogg, *Constitutional Law of Canada,* 965.

69 Emerson, *System of Freedom of Expression.*

70 This question is discussed in Richard Moon, *The Constitutional Protection of Expression,* 8–24.

71 *Irwin Toy v. Québec (A.G.),* S.C.R. at 976.

72 *R. v. Sharpe,* D.L.R., at 22–4.

73 The "harm" principle has a long lineage in Canadian jurisprudence on expression. See *R. v. Boucher; R. v. Keegstra* (1990); and *R. v. Butler.*

74 *R. v. Sharpe,* D.L.R., at 39.

75 Ibid., at 48.

76 Ibid., at 60–104.

77 To be fair to Justice L'Heureux-Dubé, I should note that her judgments were probably drafted in French and then translated into English. This process could explain why many of her judgments are difficult to follow.

78 *R. v. Sharpe,* D.L.R., at 66.

79 Ibid., at 70–3.

80 Ibid., at 73, 74, 81.

81 Ibid., at 79.

82 See *R. v. Ewanchuk; R. v. O'Connor; R. v. Mills; Symes v. Canada;* and *Thibaudeau v. Canada.* In one public speech, she suggested that equality rights should take precedence over fundamental rights: L'Heureux-Dubé, "Are We There Yet?"

83 Benzie, "Child Pornography Ruling 'Loopholes.'"

84 Landsberg, "Porn Law Loopholes."

85 Dueck, "Road Not Taken."

86 Bill C-15, *An Act to Amend the Criminal Code and to Amend Other Acts,* 1st Sess., 37th Parl., 2001.

87 Anne McLellan, "Letter to the Editor."

88 See Dave Brown, "Bill 117 Guts Men's Rights."

89 Phillip, "The Paedophile Bogeyman."

90 Brazao and Shephard, "Teacher Arrested on Child Porn Charges."

91 See Robert Martin, *Media Law,* 79–106.

92 *R. v. Sharpe,* D.L.R., at 49.

93 *R. v. Zundel.*

94 *R.J.R.-MacDonald Inc. v. Canada (A.G.).*

95 *Little Sister's Book and Art Emporium v. Canada.*

96 *R. v. Turpin,* at 1333.

97 *Andrews* v. *Law Society of British Columbia.* The text of the Charter itself clearly distinguishes between citizens and non-citizens in section 3.

98 *Singh* v. *Canada (Minister of Employment and Immigration).* One result of *Singh* is a refugee system which is, today, financially and administratively out of control. See Margaret Wente, "How the Refugee System Got Undermined."

99 See Brian Lee Crowley, *The Road to Equity: Gender, Ethnicity and Language.* See also Loney, *Pursuit of Division*, 10.

100 *R.* v. *Marshall.* See also *Delgamuukw* v. *British Columbia.* These cases are discussed in detail in chapter 1.

101 *R.* v. *Morgentaler*, [1988] S.C.R. at 164.

102 See Martin, "Lament for British North America," 3.

103 There is a substantial body of pseudo-history in which our past has been reinvented to make it correspond to the ideological demands of the practitioners of identity politics. As examples, see Margaret Conrad and Alvin Finkel, with Veronica Strong-Boag, *History of the Canadian Peoples*; and Canadian Bar Association, Working Group on Racial Equality in the Canadian Legal Profession, *Report: Racial Equality in the Canadian Legal Profession*, 3. See also, Constance Backhouse's *Petticoats and Prejudice: Women and Law in Nineteenth Century Canada* and *Colour-Coded: A Legal History of Racism in Canada.* An observation made about Nazi historiography applies fully to this pseudo-history: "history becomes nothing but a tool of the present, with no integrity whatsoever of its own" (Ecksteins, *Rites of Spring*, 313). Loney regards much of what passes for historical writing in Canada today as unabashed lying (Loney, *Pursuit of Division*, 22–49, 78–106, 288–325).

104 *Dagenais* v. *Canadian Broadcasting Corp.*, D.L.R., at 76.

105 Lipset *Continental Divide*, 225. A detailed analysis of the role of the *Charter* in Americanizing our legal system is found in Donald V. Macdougall, "Canadian Legal Identity and American Influences."

106 In the 1960s, American law teachers enthusiastically supported a project called SAILER – Staffing African Institutes of Legal Education and Research. The point of SAILER was to place American instructors in law faculties in Africa. See L.C.B. Gower, *Independent Africa: The Challenge to the Legal Profession*, 141.

107 See James Gardner, *Legal Imperialism: American Lawyers and Foreign Aid in Latin America.*

108 Ibid., 6.

109 Ibid., 12.

110 Morton and Knopff, *Charter Revolution*, 134–5.

111 Black was a significant member of the Canadian Human Rights Act Review Panel which reported in 2000.

112 Kyer and Bickenbach, "Fiercest Debate." This point is conceded indirectly in Consultative Group on Research and Education in Law, *Law and Learning: Report to the Social Sciences and Humanities Research Council of Canada*, 64.

113 *Vriend* v. *Alberta*, S.C.R. at 564. In this decision the Court asserted that it interfered with the work of the legislature only to protect "democratic values" (ibid., at 566).

114 Ibid., at 567.

115 Ibid., at 564.

116 Ibid., at 565–6.

117 *Reference re s. 94(2) B.C. Motor Vehicle Act*, S.C.R. at 497. Apologists for the court have been equally willing to rewrite history to support their point of view. See Clayton Ruby, "Conservatives Decry Liberal 'Bias' in Judges, but What They Really Want Is Bias in Their Favour." Ian Greene made his own contribution to the rewriting of Canadian history, arguing that "judges have reluctantly accepted the policy-making role that was … thrust upon them by politicians" (Greene, *Charter of Rights*, 220). Nothing could be further from the truth.

118 See Luiza Chwialkowska, "High Court's Rulings Curb Provincial Laws."

119 Manfredi, *Judicial Power and the Charter*, 199.

120 *Operation Dismantle* v. *The Queen*.

121 The sad story is recounted in Michael Mandel, "The Rule of Law and the Legalisation of Politics in Canada."

122 *R.* v. *Askov*, at 1240.

123 "S.C.C. Justices Were 'shocked' by Fallout from *Askov*, Cory J.," *The Lawyers' Weekly*, 26 July 1991.

124 R.S.C. 1985, c. A-1, s. 2(1).

125 The executive director of the Court Challenges Program recently asserted that secrecy is essential to its operation (Bakogeorge, "Secret, but Important Program").

CHAPTER THREE

1 The classic statement can be found in W.R. Lederman, "Independence of the Judiciary," 109. See also Bora Laskin, "Judicial Integrity and the Supreme Court of Canada."

2 See the discussion in Robert Martin, "An Open Legal System."

3 See W.R. Lederman, "Independence of the Judiciary." Material which is supplied to prospective judicial appointees by the Department of Justice includes this admonition:

> The judge ... should avoid expressing personal opinions on major social issues which might lead to an apprehension of bias when such issues come to be adjudicated by the courts. (Commissioner for Federal Judicial Affairs, "Considerations which Apply to an Application for Judicial Appointment.")

4 Ibid.

5 Martin, "Open Legal System."

6 Bindman, "Sopinka, Robins Lock Horns over Right of Judges to Speak." This debate took place at the Canadian Institute for Advanced Legal Studies held at Cambridge University in the UK in 1991.

7 Supreme Court of Canada, *Performance Report for the Period Ending March 31, 2001*, 7.

  The influence of the Supreme Court is beginning to extend beyond Canada's borders. In 1998 the Constitutional Court of South Africa had to decide whether the "right to life," which was guaranteed to everyone in section (11) of that country's constitution, extended to a foetus. In deciding that it did not, the South African court relied heavily on Supreme Court of Canada decisions (*Christian Lawyers Association of South Africa and Others v. Minister of Health and Others*). The South African Court of Appeal followed a number of Supreme Court of Canada decisions in *National Media Ltd. and Others v. Bogoshi*. The Ghanaian Supreme Court followed certain Supreme Court of Canada decisions in *Republic v. Tommy Thompson Books*.

8 Wilson, "Will Women Judges Really Make a Difference?" A volume of Wilson's speeches is available at the Supreme Court.

9 Justice L'Heureux-Dubé's speeches are also available from the Court. See Robert Martin, "Judges Should Cease and Desist from Bashable Behaviour."

10 Canadian Bar Association, Task Force, *Touchstones*.

11 There is a certain dismal coherence in the orthodoxy. If one combines the emphasis on the social construction of reality with the attachment to solipsistic ways of thinking, one can reach the mindless result suggested by Martin Loney: "There must ... be many

young people in Saskatchewan whose personal experience might lead them to believe the world is flat" (Loney, *Pursuit of Division*, 316).

12 Canadian Bar Association, Task Force, *Touchstones*, 4.

13 *R.* v. *Morgentaler* [1988], S.C.R. at 171.

14 Gilligan, *In a Different Voice: Psychological Theory and Women's Development*.

15 Wilson's opinions, once again, were borrowed from Carol Gilligan. As might be expected, Christina Hoff Sommers has been critical of Gilligan. Sommers spoke of the "want of empirical evidence" in Gilligan's book and asserted that "independent research tends to *disconfirm* Gilligan's thesis that there is a substantive difference in the moral psychology of men and women" (Sommers, *Who Stole Feminism?* 152). For other critical views of Gilligan's work, see Christina Hoff Sommers, "The Fonda Effect," and Andy Lamey, "Take Care, Such Ethics Can Backfire."

Gilligan's ideas became very popular with feminist legal academics and led to some strikingly muddled thinking in the law schools about "women's ways of learning." It does seem to me that Justice Wilson's invention of the "contextual approach" to the interpretation of the *Charter* must have been inspired by her reading of Gilligan.

16 *R.* v. *R.D.S.*, S.C.R. at 506. In this case, the trial judge, in court, expressed her own prejudices concerning the issues raised in a case being tried before her, but the Supreme Court found nothing improper in her behaviour. As an argument in favour of the idea of judges as delegates, see Errol P. Mendes, "Promoting Heterogeneity of the Judicial Mind: Minority and Gender Representation in the Canadian Judiciary," s. 91. This theory of judicial apartheid would make the operation of our judicial system impossible – only female judges could judge female litigants and only minority judges could judge minority litigants and so on. For some reason, LEAF intervened in the *R.D.S.* appeal and, of course, ended up on the winning side.

17 *R.* v. *R.D.S.*, S.C.R. at 505, 501.

18 Devlin and Pothier, "Addressing the Imbalances," 3. Both Devlin and Pothier teach at the Dalhousie Law School.

19 Ibid., at 14, 19, 21, 33.

20 As is true of many Canadian legal academics, Devlin's stock in trade appears to be ideology masquerading as scholarship. See his

"Towards an/Other Legal Education: Some Critical and Tentative Proposals to Confront the Racism of Modern Legal Education."

21 L'Heureux-Dubé, "Re-examining the Doctrine," 575. A near incomprehensible argument in favour of judicial apartheid and solipsistic ways of thinking is Jennifer Nedelsky's "Embodied Diversity and the Challenges to Law." The author was rhapsodic in her praise of Carol Gilligan. A thoughtful, coherent and lawyerlike analysis of these issues is to be found in David M. Paciocco, "The Promise of R.D.S.: Interpreting the Law of Judicial Notice and Apprehension of Bias."

22 Southin, [Letter to the Editor]. See also *The Lawyers Weekly,* 21 July 1995.

23 Canadian Bar Association, Task Force, *Touchstones*, 23–46, 155–76.

24 Feldthusen, "Gender Wars," 92. This article is shot through with analytical and methodological deficiencies which, in an undergraduate term paper, would have led to a failing grade. The author consistently makes assertions like "many male law professors" (68), "most Canadian law schools" (69), "Mostly, male law professors" (71), "Most men" (73), "Most of my male colleagues" (76), and "most male law professors" (78). He is able to assert, "I have seen women colleagues intimidated physically by male colleagues" without providing any supporting evidence beyond his own say-so (79). As would probably be expected, Feldthusen treats Carol Gilligan's *In a Different Voice* as if it were divine revelation (74–6).

25 Canadian Bar Association, Task Force, *Touchstones*, 33.

26 Ibid., 162.

27 Ibid., 25.

28 Ibid., 13.

29 United Church of Canada, *Record of Proceedings*, 523.

30 Ibid., 503.

31 The decision is discussed at length in F.L. Morton, *Morgentaler v. Borowski: Abortion, the Charter and the Courts.*

32 Hovius, "Morgentaler Decision," 152.

33 The cases are *Symes* v. *Canada; R.* v. *Butler;* and *R.* v. *Seaboyer.*

34 Majury, "Strategizing in Equality," 186.

35 L'Heureux-Dubé, "Search for Equality."

36 Majury, "Equality and Discrimination."

37 L'Heureux-Dubé, "Search for Equality."

38 See *R.* v. *Ewanchuk.*

39 See *R. v. Ewanchuk*, S.C.R. at 372.
40 Greenspan, "Judges Have No Right to Be Bullies."
41 "Defence Lawyer Criticizes Radical Feminist Ruling," *Toronto Star*, 26 February 1999.
42 "Judging the Judges," *Ottawa Citizen*, 3 March 1999.
43 *Debates of the Senate* (4 March 1999) at 2707.
44 "Judge Reiterates Belief That Teen Wasn't Assaulted," *National Post*, 27 February 1999.
45 MacCharles, "Marleau Defends L'Heureux-Dubé."
46 R.S.C. 1985, c. J-1, ss. 59–69.
47 Morton and Knopff, *Charter Revolution*, 128.
48 See *R. v. Lippé*, S.C.R. at 133.
49 "Stop Singling Out Judges for Criticism: L'Heureux-Dubé," *National Post*, 22 August 2000.
50 Makin, "Media Blasted for Savage Attacks on Top Court Judge."
51 *Canada (Minister of Citizenship and Immigration) v. Tobiass*.
52 *R. v. Lippé*, S.C.R. at 139.
53 Amiel, "Feminists, Fascists and Other Radicals."
54 Schmitz, "Chief Justice Says Pressure Will Not Sway Court."
55 Schmitz, "Bastarache Explains Dissents."
56 Schmitz, "S.C.C. Wrong Forum."
57 "Mr. Justice Bastarache Is Wrong, Says Law Professor," *Globe and Mail*, 17 January 2001.
58 Schmitz, "Bastarache's Candid Comments."
59 Tibbetts, "Chief Justice Seeks Help."
60 Tibbetts, "Lamer Attacks Alliance 'Yelping.'"
61 Kirk Makin, "Crisis in Legal Aid Dire, Arbour Warns."

CHAPTER FOUR

1 R.S.C. 1985, c. S-19.
2 Ibid., s. 5.
3 Ibid., s. 6.
4 Conventions are discussed in *Reference Re Resolution to Amend the Constitution*.
5 John Sopinka and Ian Binnie were both appointed to the Court directly from private practice.
6 Dickson, "Role and Function of Judges," 140.
7 Canadian Bar Association, Committee on the Appointment of Judges in Canada, *Report*.

8 In the 1960s, Justice Leo Landreville of the then Supreme Court of Ontario came perilously close to being removed. See, William Kaplan, *Bad Judgment: The Case of Mr. Justice Leo Landreville*.

9 Martin, "Ideology and Judging."

10 This chapter was drafted while Claire L'Heureux-Dubé was still a judge of the Court.

11 For an adoring account of Arbour's work with war crimes tribunals, see Carol Off, *The Lion, the Fox and the Eagle: A Story of Generals and Justice in Yugoslavia and Rwanda*, 261–366. If one believes, as I do, that modesty and circumspection are desirable qualities in a judge, this book makes clear that Arbour is not overburdened with either. For a discussion of the substantial naïveté underlying the belief in the efficacy of international tribunals as a means of protecting humanity against barbarism, see Robert D. Kaplan, *The Coming Anarchy: Shattering the Dreams of the Post Cold War*.

12 Morton and Knopff, *Charter Revolution*, 112.

13 R.S.C. 1985, c. J-1.

14 *Debates of the Senate* (28 October 1996) at 2989.

15 S.C. 1996, c. 30.

16 Carol Off did mention this incident in passing, but did not seem to grasp that Arbour's behaviour was questionable or that Parliament's action was unprecedented (Off, "Lion, Fox, and Eagle," 288–290).

17 Ibid.

18 Lamer actually boasted of his lobbying in a television interview. See speech of Senator Anne Cools, *Debates of the Senate* (25 March 1999).

19 *Reference re Remuneration of Judges of the Provincial Court of Prince Edward Island*.

20 *Debates of the Senate* (22 September 1993) at 1915.

21 McGregor "A Family Law of Their Own."

22 Blatchford, "Heikamp Visits Judge."

CHAPTER FIVE

1 *Operation Dismantle v. The Queen*.

2 The saga is recounted in F.L. Morton, *Morgentaler v. Borowski: Abortion, the Charter and the Courts*.

3 *R. v. Morgentaler* (1975).

4 *Criminal Code*, s. 686(4)(b)(ii).

5 *R.* v. *Morgentaler*, [1988].

6 This procedure happened several times at Foothills Hospital in Calgary in 1999 and was called "genetic termination." See Marni Ko, "What Really Goes On at Foothills Hospital?" This information became public through the actions of nurses who objected to being forced to take part in such procedures. The Calgary Regional Health Authority sought and received an injunction to prevent further publication of this information. See Richard Cairney, "Leak of Abortion Information Creates Turmoil at Foothills." See also, Mark Cooper, "Abortions Probed."

7 *R.* v. *Morgentaler*, [1993].

8 *Winnipeg Child and Family Services (Northwest Area)* v. *G. (D.F.)*. See also *Dobson (Litigation Guardian of)* v. *Dobson*. Both cases are discussed in chapter 1.

9 *Rodriguez* v. *British Columbia (A.G.)*.

10 Ibid., S.C.R. at 530–80, 616–37.

11 In 1994 the Ontario government sought, and was granted, an injunction against picketing at abortion clinics. See *Ontario (A.G.)* v. *Dieleman*.

12 In 1994 an American journalist, Ellen Goodman, wrote: "Americans are at the same point in the debate over suicide, assisted suicide, and the right to die and euthanasia, that we were at in abortion in the early 1970's. We're at the beginning" (quoted in Hunter, *Three Faces of the Law*, 60).

13 See M.J. Sobran, "Abortion: The Class Religion," 28.

14 Lugosi, "Law of the Sacred Cow." See also Ian Hunter, "Humpty Dumpty's Take on Free Speech."

15 The judgment of the trial judge may be the most idiotic ever rendered in Canada. *R.* v. *Latimer* (Sask.Q.B).

16 *R.* v. *Latimer* (2001).

17 Bourrie, "Parliament Must Decide on Compassionate Sentencing."

18 *R.* v. *Goltz*.

19 *R.* v. *Latimer* [2001], S.C.R. at 37–9.

20 Manfredi, *Judicial Power and the Charter*, 156.

21 Blatchford, "Deaf Bombard Hospitals with Rights Grievances." Two Charter enthusiasts have argued that delays in the provision of medical services may amount to violations of Charter rights. See Stanley H. Hartt and Patrick J. Monahan, "Waiting Lists Are Unconstitutional."

22 One of the more tedious aspects of life in Canada today is being subjected to relentless homosexual propaganda (Kingston, "Two Dads, Two Mums, Too Much Fuss"). Nowadays, it seems that the love which once dared not speak its name seldom shuts up. A school board in Surrey, British Columbia, prohibited the use in kindergarten and Grade One classrooms of books focusing on homosexual parents. The teacher involved, James Chamberlain, challenged the school board's ruling and the matter ended up before the Supreme Court. As if to dispel any illusions that she might have approached the matter in an unbiased fashion, Justice L'Heureux-Dubé asked Chamberlain's lawyer, "What you're basically saying is that it's ok for children to learn about human rights at any age?" (ibid.). I must enquire whether there can be anyone over the age of six who has any doubt as to how the Court will resolve this matter.

23 *Trinity Western University* v. *British Columbia College of Teachers*, at 774–5.

24 Ibid., at 819 ff.

25 L'Heureux-Dubé did state that she found her "colleagues' emphasis on the need for positive proof of discriminatory conduct sadly ironic" (ibid., at 847).

26 Ibid., at 848.

27 Svend Robinson is an MP from British Columbia. He is openly homosexual. He wrote that a university lecturer once said something which caused his (Robinson's) feelings to be hurt. Because his feelings were hurt once, Robinson argued that universities should have speech codes which limit what may be said in classrooms. See Svend Robinson, "The Collision of Rights."

28 See chapter 3.

29 Troy, "Defined by Conduct."

30 Ibid.

CHAPTER SIX

1 Hogg, *Constitutional Law of Canada*, 3.

2 Ibid., 15.

3 *Operation Dismantle* v. *The Queen*.

4 *New Brunswick Broadcasting* v. *Nova Scotia (Speaker of the House of Assembly)*, S.C.R. at 377.

5 *Reference re Remuneration of Judges of the Provincial Court of Prince Edward Island*, S.C.R. at 64.
6 Ibid., at 69.
7 Ibid., at 71.
8 Ibid., at 179.
9 Ibid., at 183.
10 Ibid., at 184.
11 *Reference re Secession of Quebec*, S.C.R. at 263.
12 Ibid., at 248.
13 *Lalonde v. Ontario (Health Services Restructuring Commission)* (1999) (Ont. Div. Ct.).
14 See the discussion in chapter 10.
15 *Reference re s. 94(2) B.C. Motor Vehicle Act*, S.C.R. at 503.
16 *Operation Dismantle v. The Queen*.
17 *R. v. Morgentaler* [1988].
18 *Rodriguez v. British Columbia (A.G.)*.
19 *Andrews v. Law Society of British Columbia*, S.C.R. at 152.
20 *Corbiere v. Canada (Minister of Indian and Northern Affairs)*, S.C.R. at 249–50.

CHAPTER SEVEN

1 A great deal of information about LEAF can be found in Morton and Knopff, *Charter Revolution*, 98, 125–8. For further information on LEAF, see Manfredi, *Judicial Power and the Charter*, 113–20.
2 Smith, "Love Is Strange."
3 Ibid.
4 Ibid.
5 See her book *Only Words*.
6 Smith, "Love Is Strange."
7 Ibid.
8 MacKinnon, *Only Words*, 1.
9 Dworkin, "Women and Pornography."
10 Ronald Dworkin, letter to the author, 3 December 1993.
11 Greenfield, "Amazing Influence."
12 Martin, "Bill C-49."
13 Ibid.
14 A detailed analysis can be found in Julian Roberts and Renate M. Mohr, eds, *Confronting Sexual Assault: A Decade of Legal and Social Change*.

15 *An Act to amend the Criminal Code in Relation to Sexual Offences and Other Offences Against the Person*, S.C. 1980–81–82–83, c. 125.

16 For a semi-official general survey, see Department of Justice, *New Sexual Assault Offences*.

17 Ibid., 23.

18 Ibid., 13. See also Department of Justice, Research Section, *Overview*, 11–13.

19 Department of Justice, Research Section, *Overview*, 17, 61.

20 Ibid., 63–4.

21 Department of Justice, *Sentencing Patterns in Cases of Sexual Assault*.

22 Clark and Lewis, *Rape*, 167–8. Logically, of course, this paragraph argues against the very existence of a separate offence of sexual assault, since on the authors' view of things, common assault should suffice.

23 MacKinnon, *Feminism, Marxism, Method and the State: An Agenda for Theory*, 530–3.

24 MacKinnon, *Feminism Unmodified*, 218. One reviewer said of *Feminism Unmodified* that MacKinnon's logic "depends on slogans, false premises, half-information, sinister innuendo and ad hoc reasoning" and her arguments "sink into sweeping, indiscriminate accusations that are never substantiated" (Maureen Mullarkey, "Hard Cop, Soft Cop," *The Nation*, 30 May 1987, 720).

25 MacKinnon, *Feminism Unmodified*, 6.

26 Littleton, "Feminist Jurisprudence," 777.

27 Tyler, "U.S. Feminist Applauds Canada's Rape-Law Plan." An admiring, to put it mildly, journalistic portrait of MacKinnon is F. Strebeigh, "Defining Law on the Feminist Frontier."

28 MacKinnon, *Feminism, Marxism, Method and the State: Toward Feminist Jurisprudence*, 653–5.

29 Campbell, "Letter to the Editor."

30 "An Assault on the Law, Not to Say Common Sense" *Toronto Globe and Mail*, 19 May 1992.

31 LEAF, "Women's Groups Meet with Justice Minister" (1992) 4:4 *Leaf Lines* 4.

32 Landolt, "Letter to the Editor."

33 Campbell, "Letter to the Editor."

34 Given Sheila McIntyre's important role in the story of Bill C-49, it is useful to gain some insight into her thought. I quote from an article by McIntyre: "Anti-feminism, however, has not readily been seen as a form of sexual harassment even though its expression

and damaging effects have much in common with predatory and environmental harassment. This may be because we tend to conceptualise anti-feminism primarily as ideological hostility to a political perspective without registering that it does personal and professional harm to individual women as women in a context of institutional gender inequality. (McIntyre, *Bulletin*).

35 Vienneau, "Proposed Rape Law's Message."

36 York, "Lawyers Oppose Proposed Rape Law." See also D. Vienneau, "Beware Mixing Drink, Sex, Top Defence Lawyer Warns."

37 "An Assault on the Law, Not to Say Common Sense," *Toronto Globe and Mail*, 19 May 1992.

38 Ibid.

39 Ibid.

40 Schmitz, "Criminal Lawyers Fear Concept in New Sex Assault Bill."

41 York, "Sexual Assault Legislation Attacked."

42 Don Stuart, letter to Kim Campbell, 25 May 1992. Stuart had difficulty obtaining permission to address his concerns to Parliament. He was finally able to speak to a legislative committee on 2 June 1992; see Canada, "House of Commons Legislative Committee on Bill C-49 Criminal Code (Amdt. – Sexual Assault)," 3d Sess., 34th Parl., 1991–92.

43 Ruby, "Fifth Column."

44 See Department of Justice, *New Sexual Assault Offences: Emerging Legal Issues*; and Department of Justice, *Overview*.

45 *R. v. Ewanchuk*, S.C.R. at 336.

46 *R. v. Seaboyer*, S.C.R. at 583.

47 Ibid., at 585.

48 This decision is discussed more fully in chapter 3.

49 Pearlman, "Through Jewish Lesbian Eyes," 317.

50 This is one of the major theses advanced in Christina Hoff Sommers, *Who Stole Feminism?* Sommers noted that the most inaccurate feminist writing addressed eating disorders. See also, Donna La Framboise, "Anorexia Researcher Delivers the Usual Spin."

51 See Canadian Panel on Violence Against Women, *Final Report: Changing the Landscape: Ending Violence – Achieving Equality*.

52 Ibid., part one, 3.

53 Ibid., part five, 89.

54 Ibid., 23

55 See chapter 3.

56 John Fekete, in *Moral Panic*, presented a detailed critical analysis of the Can Pan report, identifying its many methodological failings. He noted that the report was adorned with a sampling of horror stories ("I was 18 months old when my father and two grandfathers started abusing me"; and, "I was married to Satan at the age of seven and was raped after the ceremony") (Fekete, *Moral Panic*, 101).

57 Canadian Panel on Violence against Women, *Final Report*, part one, 3.

58 Ibid., part one, 7.

59 Brown, "Men Challenge 'Bible' of Violence Against Women."

60 Small, "Hadley 'Snapped' from Stress, MD Says."

61 Landsberg, "Pair Try to Explain Away Hadley Murder."

62 Canadian Panel on Violence against Women, *Final Report*, part one, 8. It would be wrong to suggest that the panel's report is the only, or even the most, misleading statement about the nature, scope, and extent of violence against women in Canada. See the useful article by Brian Lee Crowley, 'Sex, Lies and Violence." John Fekete gives a detailed dissection of the panel's report in his *Moral Panic*, 98–169.

63 While discussing fraudulent and misleading social science research, one must not forget a report written in 1993 by two Carleton University sociologists on "date abuse" in Canada. Like the members of the Canadian Panel on Violence against Women, the authors of this report, Walter DeKeseredy and Katherine Kelly, cooked their definition so that almost anything amounted to "abuse." The authors administered a questionnaire to 3,142 female students at Canadian colleges and universities. As I interpret the questionnaire, respondents were asked, in effect, "Did you ever go out on a date with a guy who did something that pissed you off?" The astounding thing about this survey is not that 81% of respondents answered "Yes," but that 19% answered "No." The report did not appear initially in an academic journal; it was published by the Family Violence Prevention Division of the Department of National Health and Welfare, which paid the authors $236,000. See James Deacon, Hal Quinn, et al, "What is 'Abuse'? A Striking Survey Provokes a Heated Reaction." See also Walter S. DeKeseredy and Katherine Kelly, "Woman Abuse in University and College, Dating Relationships: The Contribution of the Ideology of Familial Patriarchy" for a somewhat restrained version of the report.

64 *Vriend* v. *Alberta*, S.C.R. at 565.
65 Bass and Davis, *Courage to Heal.*
66 Here are four sample guidelines:

1. The therapist/counsellor is willing to help the woman client to explore alternative life options in addition to the culturally defined gender role.
2. The therapist/counsellor realizes that women do not bear the total responsibility for the success of marriage and for childrearing.
3. The therapist/counsellor recognizes the existence of social bias against women, and explores with the client the possibility that her problems may be based in society's definition of women's role rather than entirely within herself.
4. While respecting the right of the therapist/counsellor to determine the appropriate therapeutic strategy for a client, he or she is sensitive to and avoids the use of theoretical concepts that serve to reinforce the female stereotype of dependency or passivity, or to limit the woman's personal development.

67 See Elizabeth F. Loftus and Melvin J. Guyer, "Who Abused Jane Doe? The Hazards of the Single Case History: Part 1," 24.
68 Mersky, "Ethical Issues," 327–8.
69 L'Heureux-Dubé, "Applying Women's International Human Rights in Canada," (speech to *United Nations Platform for Action Committee,* Winnipeg, Manitoba, 26 March 1999).
70 *M. (K.)* v. *M. (H.).* In this decision, which is discussed in more detail in chapter 1, the Court did not seem concerned that the plaintiff, who had been the victim of incest committed by her father, had not been aware of the extent of the psychological injury she had suffered from the incest until this was suggested to her by a therapist. In 1996, the B.C. Supreme Court came close to recognizing therapists. The court held that communications to a therapist were "privileged" in the context of a defamation action. The Court also referred to the "professional duty" of a therapist: *C. (L.G.)* v. *C. (V.M.).*
71 *R.* v. *A.G.*, C.C.C. at 41–3.
72 Ibid., S.C.R. at 443.
73 Ibid.

74 *R. v. O'Connor*, S.C.R. at 500.

75 *R. v. Mills*, S.C.R. at 689.

76 Ibid., at 724.

77 Ibid., at 727.

78 Ibid., at 687. A news item aired on the CTV news of 21 January 2002 demonstrated that some sexual assault "therapists" consciously make illegible notes of interviews with clients and that some rape crisis centres keep no records. If either of these things were done in order to prevent material becoming evidence in a judicial proceeding, it would amount to the offence of obstructing justice in section 139 of the Criminal Code.

79 Tyler, "Rights of Accused Eroded." The Supreme Court went further in the direction of removing the state from sexual assault prosecutions in a 1995 decision where the trial judge had made an order, under section 486(3) of the Criminal Code, banning publication of the complainant's identity. The Court held that the trial judge could not rescind the banning order without the complainant's request (*R. v. Adams*).

80 *Southam Inc. and the Queen (No. 1), Re*, at 119.

81 *Nova Scotia (A.G.) v. MacIntyre*, S.C.R. at 185.

82 *Canadian Broadcasting Corp. v. New Brunswick (A.G.)*, S.C.R. at 495, 499.

83 *Canadian Newspapers Co. v. Canada (A.G.)*, S.C.R. at 132.

84 *Canadian Broadcasting Corp. v. New Brunswick (A.G.)*, S.C.R. at 505, 484.

85 Ibid., at 521.

86 Bourrie, "Judge Flip-flops on Publication Ban."

87 Tu and Petrunie, "Alleged Rape Victim."

88 *R. v. Regan*, C.C.C. at 146.

89 Janet L. Hiebert has commented on these issues in a compelling and convincing fashion. See her "Wrestling with Rights: Judges, Parliament and the Making of Social Policy."

90 "Donald Marshall, Guy Paul Morin, Donald Marshall and Gerald Regan," *Globe and Mail*, 15 February 2002.

91 Jonas, "Regan a Victim of Matriarchal Justice."

92 Hunter, "Even Nasty Men Deserve a Fair Trial."

93 Ehrenreich, "Maid to Order," 59.

94 Rosa Luxemburg saw this with her accustomed clarity. She said, "Aside from the few who have jobs or professions, the women of

the bourgeoisie do not take part in social production. They are nothing but co-consumers of the surplus value their men extort from the proletariat" (Dick Howard, ed., *Selected Political Writings of Rosa Luxemburg*, 219).

95 It now appears to be impermissible to say "nanny." The correct term is *child-care worker*.

96 *Symes* v. *Canada*.

97 Morton and Knopff, *Charter Revolution*, 97.

98 *Symes* v. *Canada*, S.C.R. at 790, 798, 801.

99 Ibid., at 807.

100 *Thibaudeau* v. *Canada*, S.C.R. at 627.

101 Ibid., at 667, 656, 657, 659.

102 *Income Tax Act*, S.C. 1998, c. 19.

103 A meticulous reconstruction of what happened can be found in David M. Paciocco, *Getting Away with Murder: The Canadian Criminal Justice System*, 297–306. Paciocco is a former Crown prosecutor, an experienced criminal defence counsel, and a professor in the Faculty of Law of the University of Ottawa.

104 Ibid., 306.

105 *R.* v. *Lavallée*.

106 Sommers, *Who Stole Feminism?* 189–92. In a recent article in which she argued that judges should expand the notion of judicial notice to give themselves even greater discretion to accept "social framework facts," Justice L'Heureux-Dubé made extensive and enthusiastic reference to material written by Lenore Walker. See Claire L'Heureux-Dubé, "Re-examining the Doctrine of Judicial Notice in the Family Law Context."

107 Paciocco, *Getting Away with Murder*, 308, 309.

108 The idea that someone could shoot another person who was sleeping and then raise the defence of "self-defence" is ludicrous.

109 Wente, "How to Get Away with Murder (for Women Only)."

110 Commission of Inquiry, *Report of a Judicial Inquiry.*

111 Ibid., 4.

112 Ibid., 54, 24.

113 *Hryciuk* v. *Ontario (Lieutenant Governor)* (Ont. Div. Ct.).

114 *Hryciuk* v. *Ontario (Lieutenant Governor)* (Ont. C.A.).

115 Blackwell, "Council Clears Judge."

116 *Kreklewetz* v. *Scopel*.

117 See "In the Name of the Father," *National Post*, 24 June 2002.

118 Gibbons, "Lay Off Men, Lessing Tells Feminists."

CHAPTER EIGHT

1 *Reference Re Residential Tenancies Act (Ont.).*
2 These are discussed extensively in Geoffrey Marshall, *Constitutional Theory,* 97–103.
3 R.S.C. 1985, c. W-2.
4 See *Re Grey.*
5 *Fraser* v. *Public Service Staff Relations Board,* S.C.R. at 469.
6 See *Harris* v. *Minister of the Interior; Minister of the Interior* v. *Harris;* and *Collins* v. *Minister of the Interior.* These cases are discussed further in chapter 10.
7 See note 1 above.
8 See *Liyanage* v. *R.; Bribery Commissioner* v. *Ranasinghe; Ibralebbe* v. *R.;* and *Kariapper* v. *Wijesinha.*
9 *Constitution of Sri Lanka,* s. 5(a).
10 *Cooper* v. *Canadian Human Rights Commission; Bell* v. *C.H.R.C.* at 871, quoting Dickson, C.J.C. in *Fraser* v. *Public Service Staff Relations Board,* S.C.R. at 470.
11 L'Heureux-Dubé, "Re-examining the Doctrine," 574.
12 *Operation Dismantle* v. *The Queen.* Having decided in this case that there could be no political questions doctrine, the Court appeared in *Reference Re Canada Assistance Plan* to accept just such a doctrine.
13 *Reference Re Workers Compensation Act 1983 (Nfld.).* Morton and Knopff have asserted that the Court has adopted an "open door" policy on intervenors and now accepts 90 per cent of applications (Morton and Knopff, *Charter Revolution,* 55).
14 The Court Challenges Program, reinstated in 1994, may provide up to $120,000 for litigants bringing test cases involving language rights and equality rights. LEAF has been the single most substantial beneficiary of the program. See Ian Brodie, "Interest Group Litigation and the Embedded State."
15 *Canadian Council of Churches* v. *Canada (Minister of Employment and Immigration).*
16 The Constitution of Ireland, in article 26, establishes a reference procedure. See J.M. Kelly, *The Irish Constitution,* 213–14.
17 This case is discussed in more detail in chapter 7.
18 Tyler, "U.S. Feminist Applauds Canada's Rape-Law Plan." MacKinnon's ideas have infected female law professors in Canada to a significant degree. See Gayle MacDonald and Karen Gallagher, "The Myth of Consenting Adults."

19 See L'Heureux-Dubé, "Re-examining the Doctrine."

20 Crump, "Law Clerks," 238.

21 Makin, "Today's Judge Chats On-line."

22 In her book about Justice Wilson, Ellen Anderson referred to clerks drafting judgments (Anderson, "Judging Bertha Wilson," 328).

23 Sossin, "Sounds of Silence."

24 Calamai, "Dickson Court's First Year."

25 Jimenez, "Perspective."

26 This is apparent from the annual surveys of law schools conducted by *Canadian Lawyer*. See *Canadian Lawyer* for January 1997 and January 1998.

27 In *Reference Re Workers' Compensation Act 1983 (Nfld.)* Justice Sopinka stated, "This criteria is ..." The Court generally prefers complicated and convoluted ways of saying things. The word denoting a connection between two things, people, or ideas is *relation*. This simple word has largely been replaced by "relationship." Not content with *relationship*, the Court has come to prefer "inter-relationship," which means the same as *relation*, but has several more syllables. The adjective to describe something which is of or relating to society is *social*. The judges have come to prefer the non-word "societal." Awkward constructions are regularly used, such as describing a law as "violative of the Charter," rather than "violating the Charter" (*Weber v. Ontario Hydro*). In giving judgment in *R. v. Butler*, Justice Sopinka did, indeed, use "inter-relationship." Bob Blackburn's *Words Fail Us: Good English and Other Lost Causes* is an eloquent exposition of the erosion of English in Canada. Neither *woman* nor *women* is an adjective, despite the fact that both words are regularly misused in this fashion. The best-known illustration of this error is, undoubtedly, Bertha Wilson, "Will Women Judges Really Make a Difference?"

28 Chialkowska, "Law Professors May Have Tried to Influence Court."

29 George Grant said of the judges, "The more the judges quote philosophy or religious tradition, the less they give the sense they understand what they are dealing with" (Christian and Grant, eds, *George Grant Reader*, 150).

30 Justice L'Heureux-Dubé has defended the Court's judgment writing practices and argued that judges are "educators" as well as "decision-makers" (L'Heureux-Dubé, "Length and Plurality"). See

also *Lavigne* v. *Ontario Public Service Employees Union*. It is almost impossible to determine what the Court decided in this case.

31 Abel, "Book review."

32 Analogous grounds are not spelled out in the Charter text, but have been added to section 15 at the whim of the judges. See *Andrews* v. *Law Society of British Columbia*.

33 Constitution Act 1982, Part V.

34 See note 32 above.

CHAPTER NINE

1 Mandel, *Charter of Rights and Legalization of Politics*. Another law professor, Yves-Marie Morisette, a professor and former dean at the McGill Law Faculty, has spoken out. See his "Canada as a Postmodern Kritarchy: Why Should Judges Make Political Decisions?"

2 Roach, *Supreme Court on Trial*.

3 Ibid., 79.

4 James MacPherson, "Canadian Constitutional Law," 240.

5 Gibson, "Founding Fathers-in-Law," 284.

6 Hutchison, "Judges Can't Avoid Making Political Choices."

7 See Carol Gilligan, *In a Different Voice: Psychological Theory and Women's Development*.

8 Lessard, "Equality and Access," 49.

9 Ibid., 35.

10 See Joyce Appleby, Lynn Hunt, and Margaret Jacobs, *Telling the Truth about History*, and Gertrude Himmelfarb, "Where Have all the Footnotes Gone?"

11 Gotlieb, "And You Thought It Was about Cheating." On another occasion, Dean Daniels spoke of "our dream of ensuring that Canada has one of the world's great law schools" (Daniels, "Price of Excellence"). See also Jonathon Gatehouse, "Embattled Prof. Meets with Law School Official"; and David Gambrill, "Are Market Pressures Forcing Students to Lie?"

12 R.J. Daniels, Dean, Faculty of Law, U. of T., letter to the author, 10 May 2001. I received this letter because I am a graduate of the U. of T. Faculty of Law.

13 Ibid.

14 Ibid.

15 Gambrill, "17 U. of T. Students Get One-Year Suspension."

16 Ruby, "Setting the Record Straight."

17 Gambrill, "Law School Should Probe Hiring Practices: Réaume."

18 Ibid. I use "sic" because these are students who have graduated, not graduate students.

19 Schmidt, "U. Of T. Law School Looks at Raising Tuition." Both the chancellor of the University of Toronto and a substantial number of Law Faculty graduates have denounced the plan to raise tuition fees (Sarah Schmidt, "Jackman Fuels Dispute over Law Tuition").

20 Daniels, "Price of Excellence."

21 Schmidt "U. of T. Law School Looks at Raising Tuition."

22 Tyler, "Dean Won't Appeal Marks Ruling."

23 Janisch and Phillips, "Rule of Law at U. of T."

24 Hogg, "Letter to the Editor."

25 McMahon, "Making the Grade," *Canadian Lawyer*, January 2002, 39.

26 Backhouse, *Petticoats and Prejudice*, 1, 2.

27 Backhouse, "Response to Cossman, Kline and Pearlman," 352. For a convincing elaboration of the ways the orthodoxy has intimidated Canadian academics into conformity, see Robert Fulford, "From Delusions to Destruction."

28 Marx and Engels, *The German Ideology*, 65.

29 Tibbets, "Top Court Excludes Critics from Anniversary 'Love-in.'"

30 Beatty, *Talking Heads and the Supremes*.

31 "Editorial," *Globe and Mail*, 3 February 2001.

32 Russell, "Standing Up for Notwithstanding."

33 James MacPherson, "Canadian Constitutional Law," 220.

34 Dickson, "Role and Function of Judges."

35 Hunt, "Living Dangerously on the Deconstructive Edge." This article is a tedious and lengthy review of Allan Hutchinson, *Dwelling on the Threshold*.

36 Hunt, "Living Dangerously on the Deconstructive Edge," 887.

37 One commentator has identified "activism and irrationalism against reason and contract" as crucial to fascism. See Eugen Weber, *Varieties of Fascism*, 7.

CHAPTER TEN

1 Ardrey, *African Genesis*, 35.

2 In January 2002 Chief Justice McLachlin gave a speech to the Ontario Bar Association. Her speech was delivered in Toronto on the 17th and was titled "Reaction and Pro-action: Bringing Family

Law Advocacy into the 21st Century." The words the chief justice used in her speech underscored the perception that the Supreme Court is our predominant policy-making institution. She stated that the "task 'of we in the justice system' ... is to solve peoples' problems." She concluded that, "It is our task to ensure that family law continues to meet both the needs and expectations of our changing society." The entire speech was reminiscent of what a prime minister launching an election campaign might say.

3 McCormick, *Supreme at Last*, 2.

4 Yves-Marie Morissette stated, "We see a pronounced devolution of power from legislatures to courts" (Morissette, "Canada as a Post Modern Kritarchy," 148).

5 McCormick, *Supreme at Last*, 171–2. See, generally, Robert H. Bork, *Coercing Virtue: The Worldwide Rule of Judges*.

6 *Debates of The Senate* (25 March 1999) at 2989.

7 David Beatty is a law professor at the University of Toronto. In July 2002, he took to the pages of the *Globe and Mail* to chide a *Globe* columnist for having the effrontery to criticize judges for their having usurped a dominant policy-making role. With exquisite condescension he asserted that, "ours is a system of government under law, including the *Charter*" (Beatty, "Unfair to Judges").

8 Quoted in Morton and Knopff, *Charter Revolution*, 16.

9 Ibid.

10 The cases are discussed in Robert Martin, "Judges and the Charter."

11 Bickel, *Least Dangerous Branch*, 75.

12 In *West Coast Hotel Company* v. *Parrish* the Supreme Court backed off its attack on the New Deal.

13 *Harris* v. *Minister of the Interior*.

14 *Minister of the Interior* v. *Harris*.

15 *Collins* v. *Minister of the Interior*.

16 Griswold, "The Coloured Vote Case in South Africa," 1374.

17 Paul Bobier, "Politicians Don't Always Support Rights and Freedoms" is a particularly unconvincing and ungrammatical statement of this point of view.

18 Government of Canada, *The Constitution and You*, i, 9, 13.

19 This point is made very convincingly by Allan Bloom in his *The Closing of the American Mind*.

20 McGregor, "I.C.C. Needed."

21 Michael Mandel, "The I.C.C. as Political Instrument" provides a skeptical, if not entirely rational, perspective on an international court.

22 Hobsbawn, "War and Peace."

CHAPTER ELEVEN

1 Lenin, *Selected Works*, 123.

2 Martin, "Criticising the Judges."

3 The depth of feminist hostility toward our legal system is made clear in Joan Brookman, *Gender in the Legal Profession: Fitting or Breaking the Mould* (sic). See also Sheelagh O'Donovan-Polten, *The Scales of Success*. This last book purports to track the careers of a number of successful lawyers, both male and female. In a striking illustration of the degree to which an apartheid mentality has become part of orthodox thought, the author carefully introduces each of her subjects by identifying his or her ethnic background.

4 *Canada (A.G.)* v. *Lavell; Murdoch* v. *Murdoch; Bliss* v. *Canada (A.G.)*.

5 Fox-Genovese, "From Separate Spheres," 239, 245, 246. Fox-Genovese's astute observation offers a convincing explanation for the unfocused nihilism of feminists. It also explains why the approach of feminists to the legal system has been one of all-out war.

6 *Bliss* v. *Canada (A.G.)*, S.C.R. at 190–1.

7 Lynn McDonald, "The Supreme Court of Canada," 45–54.

8 Kome, *Taking of Twenty-Eight*. This lobbying could be seen as the origin of both the politicization of the Constitution and the constitutionalization of politics.

9 Eksteins, *Rites of Spring*, 317.

10 Way, "Bill C-49," 328.

11 See Jeffrey Asher, "Lynched by the Sisterhood."

12 Broadbeck, "Parents 'Livid.'"

13 McIntyre, letter, 3.

14 This discussion of *Butler* is taken from the Court's decision in *Little Sister's Book and Art Emporium* v. *Canada (Minister of Justice)*.

15 *Little Sister's Book and Art Emporium* v. *Canada (Minister of Justice)*, D.L.R. at 218–20.

16 Ibid., at 220.

17 Ibid.

18 Ibid., at 221–2.

19 Ibid., at 222–3.

20 Doidge, "Feminist Cleavage."

21 See her *Only Words*.

22 Quoted in Doidge, "Feminist Cleavage." This observation was also quoted in Ronald Dworkin, "Women and Pornography."

23 Quoted by John Leo, "A for Effort. Or for Showing Up," *U.S. News and World Report*, 5 December 1994, 5. This bit of deranged musical appreciation is also quoted in Sommers, 28. The observation about Newton is quoted in Gertrude Himmelfarb, "A Sentimental Priesthood."

24 Sommers, "Who Stole Feminism?," 76–8.

25 Kenneth Minogue provides an incisive analysis in "How Civilizations Fall."

26 The cost of operating the Supreme court in 1999–2000 was just under $20 million. See Supreme Court of Canada, *Estimates, Performance Report for the Period Ending 31 March 2000*. The money which Parliament votes for the Supreme Court is administered by the Department of Justice, which answers to Parliament for the operations of the Court.

27 In 2000–01 the total on travel for the Supreme Court was $290,492.00. See Anne Roland, Registrar of the Supreme Court, letter to Michele Alton, Reference Librarian, Library of Parliament, 4 June 2001 (letter in my possession).

28 James O'Reilly, Executive Legal Officer, Supreme court of Canada, letter to the author, 20 June 2001.

29 The CCP now costs Canadians $2.75 million per year. See Ian Brodie, "Interest Group Litigation and the Embedded State," 14. See also Peter Bakogeorge, "A secret, but Important Program."

30 Morton and Knopff, *Charter Revolution*, 95–9.

31 As Martin Loney has noted, the advocates of identity politics are largely funded by the state. He has also noted that NAC has been strikingly unsuccessful in raising money from its members (Loney, *Pursuit of Division*, 3–5, 19).

32 See Howard Leeson, "Section 33, the Notwithstanding Clause: A Paper Tiger?" for a detailed discussion of section 33.

33 This observation was suggested by Barbara Amiel, "Feminists, Fascists and Other Radicals."

34 In May 2002, it was announced that L'Heureux-Dubé would leave the Court on 1 July 2002. On the same day this fact was made public, L'Heureux-Dubé gave an interview in which she reflected on her time with the Supreme Court. Her remarks were consistent

with her time on the Court. She portrayed herself as a victim, complaining of "discrimination" by male judges. She described those who had criticized her or disagreed with her as "misogynists" and enemies of the independence of the judiciary. She also denied that she had an "agenda" (Makin, "Supreme Court Judge Announces Retirement"). A lawyer who was a cheerleader for L'Heureux-Dubé boasted that the South African Constitutional Court had adopted her "framework for analyzing equality and discrimination" and continued, "the South African court had its pick of the world's best minds – and it picked her approach" (ibid.). (In *National Coalition for Gay and Lesbian Equality* v. *Minister of Home Affairs*, South Africa's Constitutional Court adopted "reading in" as a means of recognizing same-sex unions).

35 Her great judgments are in *Winnipeg Child and Family Services* v. *K.L.W.* and *R.* v. *Sharpe*.

36 Hogg, *Constitutional Law of Canada*, 3d ed., 205. Hogg noted further that "the practice of alternation, which had been followed since 1944, was departed from in 1984, when Dickson, C.J. was appointed to succeed Laskin, C.J. The practice was resumed when Lamer, C.J. was appointed to succeed Dickson, C.J." (ibid.).

37 Abella, "The Future after Twenty Years under the Charter."

38 Copy of the letter in the possession of the author.

Table of Cases

Bibliography

Abel, Albert. Review of *In the Last Resort* by Paul Weiler. Toronto: Carswell, 1974. (1974) 24 *University of Toronto Law Journal* 318.

Abella, Rosalie. "The Future after Twenty Years under the Charter." Speech to the *Association for Canadian Studies*, Ottawa, 20 April 2002.

Amiel, Barbara. "Feminists, Fascists and Other Radicals." *National Post*, 6 March, 1999.

Anderson, Ellen. *Judging Bertha Wilson: Law as Large as Life*. Toronto: The Osgoode Society, 2001.

Appleby, Joyce, Lynn Hunt, and Margaret Jacobs. *Telling the Truth about History*. New York: Norton, 1994.

Ardrey, Robert. *African Genesis: A Personal Investigation into the Animal Origins and Nature of Man*. New York: Dell Publishing, 1961.

Arkes, Hadley. "Liberalism and the Law." In *The Betrayal of Liberalism*, ed. Hilton Kramer and Roger Kimball. Chicago: Ivan R. Dee, 1999.

Arnold, Brian. "Reflections on the Relationship Between Statutory Interpretation and Tax Avoidance." (2001) 49 *Canadian Tax Journal* 1.

Asher, Jeffrey. "Lynched by the Sisterhood." *Ottawa Citizen*, 6 October 2001.

Backhouse, Constance. *Colour-Coded: A Legal History of Racism in Canada*. Toronto: The Osgoode Society, 1999.

– *Petticoats and Prejudice: Women and Law in Nineteenth Century Canada*. Toronto: The Osgoode Society, 1991.

– "Response to Cossman, Kline and Pearlman." (1992) 5 *Canadian Journal of Women and the Law* 351.

Bailey, Sue. "Supreme Court Pays Tribute to Colourful, Contentious Judge." *National Post*, 11 June 2002.

Bakogeorge, Peter. "A Secret, but Important Program." *Law Times*, 6 May 2002.

Bass, Ellen and Laura Davis. *The Courage to Heal: A Guide for Women Survivors of Child Sexual Abuse.* Toronto: Harper Collins, 1994.

Bayefsky, Anne F. *Canada's Constitution Act 1982 & Amendments: A Documentary History.* 2 vols. Toronto: McGraw-Hill Ryerson, 1989.

Beatty, David. *Talking Heads and the Supremes: The Canadian Production of Judicial Review.* Toronto: Carswell, 1990.

– "Unfair to Judges." *Globe and Mail,* 31 July 2002.

Benda, Julien. *Treason of the Intellectuals (La Trahison des clercs).* Trans. Richard Aldington. New York: Norton, 1969.

Benzie, Robert. "Child Pornography Ruling: 'Loopholes.'" *National Post,* 27 January 2001.

Bickel, Alexander M. *The Least Dangerous Branch: The Supreme Court at the Bar of Politics,* 2nd ed. New Haven, CT: Yale University Press, 1986.

Bindman, Stephen. "Sopinka, Robins Lock Horns over Right of Judges to Speak." *Lawyers Weekly,* 26 July 1991.

Bissoondath, Neil. *Selling Illusions: The Cult of Multiculturalism in Canada.* Harmondsworth: Penguin, 1994.

Black, C. "I Dreamt of Canada." *National Post,* 16 November 2001.

Blackburn, Bob. *Words Fail Us: Good English and Other Lost Causes.* Toronto: McLelland and Stewart, 1993.

Blackwell, Tom. "Council Clears Judge for Writing Letter about Abuse." *National Post,* 11 May 2002.

Blatchford, Christie. "Deaf Bombard Hospitals with Rights Grievances." *National Post,* 27 June 2001.

– "Heikamp Visits Judge Who Ended Her Criminal Trial." *National Post,* 14 July 2001.

– "A Thin Line between Abuse and Discipline." *National Post,* 4 July 2002.

Bloom, Allan. *The Closing of the American Mind.* New York: Simon and Schuster, 1987.

Bobier, Paul. "Politicians Don't Always Support Rights and Freedoms." *Law Times,* 12 March 2001.

Bork, Robert H. *Coercing Virtue: The Worldwide Rule of Judges.* Toronto: Vintage Canada, 2002.

Bourrie, Mark. "Judge Flip-flops on Publication Ban." *Law Times,* 27 November, 2000.

– "Parliament Must Decide on Compassionate Sentencing." *Law Times,* 22 January 2001.

Boyle, Christine. "The Role of the Judiciary in the Work of Madame Justice Wilson." (1992) 15 *Dalhousie Law Journal* 241.

Bradbury, Malcolm. *Mensonge.* Harmondsworth: Penguin, 1987.

Brazao, Dale and Michelle Shephard. "Teacher Arrested on Child Porn Charges." *Toronto Star*, 24 March 2001.

Broadbeck, Tom. "Parents 'Livid' after Students Taught to Masturbate with Fruits, Vegetables." *Winnipeg Sun*, 5 June 2001.

Brodie, Ian. "Interest Group Litigation and the Embedded State." (2001) 34 *Canadian Journal of Political Science* 1.

Brookman, Joan. *Gender in the Legal Profession: Fitting or Breaking the Mould*. Vancouver: University of British Columbia Press, 2001.

Brown, Dave. "Bill 117 Guts Men's Rights." *Ottawa Citizen*, 20 December 2000.

– "Burying Ghosts of a Violent Past." *Ottawa Citizen*, 5 December 2001.

– "'I Learned It's a System that Doesn't Listen.'" *Ottawa Citizen*, 6 December 2001.

– "Men Challenge 'Bible' of Violence Against Women." *Ottawa Citizen*, 4 December 2001.

– "Provincial Ridicule, at Your Own Expense." *Ottawa Citizen*, 18 April 2001.

– "Turning Domestic Violence into a Religion." *Ottawa Citizen*, 7 December 2001.

Brownmiller, Susan. *Against Our Will: Men, Women and Rape*. New York: Simon & Schuster, 1975.

Buruma, Ian. "The Blood Lust of Identity." *The New York Review of Books*, 11 April 2002.

Cabral, Amilcar. *Revolution in Guinea: An African People's Struggle*. London: Stage 1, 1969.

Cairney, Richard. "Leak of Abortion Information Creates Turmoil at Foothills." (1999) 161 *Canadian Medical Association Journal* 424.

Calamai, P. "The Dickson Court's First Year." *Ottawa Citizen*, 4 August, 1986.

Campbell, Kim. "Letter to the Editor." *Lawyers Weekly*, 29 May 1992.

Canadian Bar Association. Committee on the Appointment of Judges in Canada. *Report*. Ottawa: Canadian Bar Foundation, 1985.

Canadian Bar Association. Task Force on Gender Equality in the Legal Profession (chaired by Bertha Wilson). *Touchstones for Change: Equality, Diversity and Accountability*. Ottawa: Canadian Bar Association, 1993.

Canadian Bar Association. Working Group on Racial Equality in the Canadian Legal Profession. *Report: Racial Equality in the Canadian Legal Profession*. Ottawa: Canadian Bar Association, 1999.

Canadian Human Rights Act Review Panel. *Report: Promoting Equality; a New Vision*. Ottawa: Department of Justice, 2000.

Canadian Lawyer. "Law School Survey, 1997." (1997) 21:1 *Canadian Lawyer* 17.

– "Law School Survey, 1998." (1998) 22:1 *Canadian Lawyer* 22.

– "Report Card on Canadian Law Schools, 2002." (2002) 26:1 *Canadian Lawyer* 36.

Canadian Panel on Violence Against Women. *Final Report: Changing the Landscape: Ending Violence – Achieving Equality.* Ottawa: Supply and Services Canada, 1993.

Christian, William and Sheila Grant, eds. *The George Grant Reader.* Toronto: University of Toronto Press, 1998.

Chwialkowska, Luiza. "High Court's Rulings Curb Provincial Laws." *National Post*, 13 April 2002.

– "Law Professors May Have Tried to Influence Court." *National Post*, 25 September 2000.

– "P.M. Set to Overhaul Native Policy." *National Post*, 8 December 2001.

Clark, Lorenne and Debra Lewis. *Rape: The Price of Coercive Sexuality.* Toronto: Women's Press, 1977.

Commission of Inquiry re: His Honour Judge W. P. Hryciuk, a Judge of the Ontario Court (Provincial Division) *Report of a Judicial Inquiry re Judge W. P. Hryciuk.* Toronto: Ontario Ministry of the Attorney General, 1993.

Commissioner for Federal Judicial Affairs. Department of Justice. "Considerations which Apply to an Application for Judicial Appointment." Ottawa, 2002.

Conference on the Legal Recognition of Same-Sex Partnerships, London, U.K., 1 July 1999. "Opening Remarks to the Panel Discussion: Same-Sex Partnerships in Canada."

Conrad, Margaret and Alvin Finkel, with Veronica Strong-Boag. *History of the Canadian Peoples.* 2 vols. Mississauga, Ont.: Copp Clark, Pittman, 1993.

Consultative Group on Research and Education in Law. *Law and Learning: Report to the Social Sciences and Humanities Research Council of Canada.* Ottawa: Social Sciences and Humanities Research Council of Canada, 1983.

Coombe, Rosemary J. "The Properties of Culture and the Politics of Possessing Identity: Native Claims in the Cultural Appropriation Controversy." (1993) 6 *Canadian Journal of Law and Jurisprudence* 249.

Cooper, Mark "Abortions Probed." *Calgary Sun*, 6 May 1999.

Cossman, B., Shannon Bell, and Becki Ross. *Bad Attitude/s on Trial: Pornography, Feminism, and the Butler Decision.* Toronto: University of Toronto Press, 1997.

Coyne, Andrew. "Majority Rules, Even If It's a Minority." *National Post*, 13 August 2001.

– "Some Freedom for Some Speech." *National Post*, 18 December 2000.

Crowley, Brian Lee. *The Road to Equity: Gender, Ethnicity and Language*. Toronto: Stoddart Publishing, 1994.

– "Sex, Lies and Violence." (1994) 3 *Inroads* 123.

Crump, D. "Law Clerks: Their Roles and Relationships with their Judges." (1985–86) 69 *Judicature* 236.

Daniels, Ronald J. "The Price of Excellence." *National Post*, 17 December 2001.

Davenport, T.R.H. *South Africa: A Modern History*. 4th ed. Toronto: University of Toronto Press, 1991.

Dawson, T. Brettel. "Social Context Education: a Retrospective and a Prospectus." (2000) 13:2 *National Judicial Institute Bulletin* 3.

Deacon, James, Hal Quinn, et al, "What Is 'Abuse'? A Striking Survey Provokes a Heated Reaction." *Maclean's*, 22 February 1993.

DeKeseredy, Walter S. and Katherine Kelly. "Woman Abuse in University and College, Dating Relationships: The Contribution of the Ideology of Familial Patriarchy." (1993) 4:2 *Journal of Human Justice* 25.

Department of Justice. *The New Sexual Assault Offences: Emerging Legal Issues*. Sexual Assault Legislation in Canada: An Evaluation, Report No. 2, by G. Ruebsaat. Ottawa: Supply and Services Canada, 1985.

– *Sentencing Patterns in Cases of Sexual Assault*. Sexual Assault Legislation in Canada: An Evaluation, Report No. 3, by J.V. Roberts. Ottawa: Supply and Services Canada, 1990.

Department of Justice, Research Section. *Overview*. Sexual Assault Legislation in Canada: An Evaluation, Report No. 5. Ottawa: Supply and Services Canada, 1990.

"The Democratic Intellect, Papers Presented at a Symposium to Honour the Contribution of Madame Justice Bertha Wilson, Dalhousie Law School, October 5, 1991 & The Horace E. Read Memorial Lecture Delivered on October 4, 1991, by The Right Honourable Brian Dickson, P.C., C.C., Former Chief Justice of Canada." (1992) 15 *Dalhousie Law Journal* 1.

Devlin, Richard. "Towards an/Other Legal Education: Some Critical and Tentative Proposals to Confront the Racism of Modern Legal Education." (1989) 38 *University of New Brunswick Law Journal* 89.

Devlin, Richard and Dianne Pothier. "Redressing the Imbalances: Rethinking the Judicial Role after *R. v. R.D.S.*" (1999–2000) 31 *Ottawa Law Review* 1.

Dickson, Brian. "The Role and Function of Judges." (1980) 14 *L.S.U.C. Gazette* 138.

Doidge, Norman. "Feminist Cleavage." *National Post*, 22 March 2000.

"Donald Marshall, Guy Paul Morin, and Gerald Regan." *Globe and Mail*, 15 February 2002.

Dueck, Lorna. "The Road Not Taken." *Globe and Mail*, 29 January 2001.

Dworkin, Ronald. "Women and Pornography." *New York Review of Books*, 22 October 1993.

Ehrenreich, Barbara. "Maid to Order: The Politics of Other Women's Work." *Harper's Magazine*, April 2000.

Eksteins, Modris. *Rites of Spring: The Great War and the Birth of the Modern Age*. Toronto: Lester and Orpen Dennys, 1989.

Elshtain, Jean Bethke. "The Bright Line: Liberalism and Religion." In *The Betrayal of Liberalism*, ed. Hilton Kramer and Roger Kimball. Chicago: Ivan R. Dee, 1999.

– *Democracy on Trial*. Concord, Ont.: House of Anansi Press, 1993.

Ely, J.H. *Democracy and Distrust: A Theory of Judicial Review*. Cambridge, Mass.: Harvard University Press, 1980.

Emberley, Peter C. *Zero Tolerance: Hot Button Politics in Canada's Universities*. Toronto: Penguin Books, 1996.

Emerson, Thomas I. *The System of Freedom of Expression*. New York: Random House, 1970.

Farber, Daniel A. and Suzanna Sherry. *Beyond All Reason: The Radical Assault on Truth in American Law*. New York: Oxford University Press, 1997.

Feasby, C. "The Emerging Egalitarian Model." (1999) 44 *McGill Law Journal* 5.

Fekete, John. *Moral Panic: Biopolitics Rising*. 2nd ed. Montreal: Robert Davies, 1994.

Feldthusen, Bruce. "The Gender Wars: Where the Boys Are." (1990) 4 *Canadian Journal of Women and the Law* 66.

Fletcher, Joseph E. and Paul Howe. "Canadian Attitudes toward the Charter and the Courts in Comparative Perspective." (2000) 6:3 *Choices*, 4.

Fox-Genovese, Elizabeth. "From Separate Spheres to Dangerous Streets: Postmodernist Feminism and the Problem of Order." (1993) 60 *Social Research* 235.

Fulford, Robert. "From Delusions to Destruction." *National Post*, 6 October 2001.

– "What's Wrong with Welsh on a Bet?" *National Post*, 4 September 2001.

Fuller, Lon. *The Morality of Law.* Rev. ed. New Haven: Yale University Press, 1969.

Fussell, Paul. *The Great War and Modern Memory.* New York, London: Oxford University Press, 1975.

Gambrill, David. "Are Market Pressures Forcing Students to Lie?" *Law Times,* 26 February 2001.

– "Law School Should Probe Hiring Practices: Réaume." *Law Times,* 25 June 2001.

– "17 U. of T. Students Get One-Year Suspension." *Law Times,* 14 May 2001.

Gardner, James. *Legal Imperialism: American Lawyers and Foreign Aid in Latin America,* Madison: University of Wisconsin Press, 1980.

Gatehouse, Jonathon. "Embattled Prof. Meets with Law School Official." *National Post,* 1 March 2001.

Gibbons, Fiachra. "Lay Off Men, Lessing Tells Feminists." *Guardian,* 14 August 2001.

Gibson, Dale. "Founding Fathers-in-Law: Judicial Amendment of the Canadian Constitution." (1992) 55 *Law and Contemporary Problems* 261.

Giese, Rachel. "Vancouver Feminists and Gender Politics." *Toronto Star,* 24 January 2002.

Gilligan, Carol. *In a Different Voice: Psychological Theory and Women's Development,* Cambridge, Mass.: Harvard University Press, 1982.

Glendon, Mary Ann. *Rights Talk: the Impoverishment of Political Discourse.* New York: The Free Press, 1991.

Gotlieb, Allan. "And You Thought It Was about Cheating: The Law School Scandal Is Being Blamed on Victimization, Elitism and Capitalism." *National Post,* 28 February 2001.

Government of Canada. *The Constitution and You.* Ottawa: Supply and Services Canada, 1982.

Gower, L.C.B. *Independent Africa: The Challenge to the Legal Profession.* Cambridge, Mass.: Harvard University Press, 1967.

Greene, Ian. *The Charter of Rights.* Toronto: Lorimer, 1989.

Greene, Ian, Carl Baar, et al. *Final Appeal: Decision-Making in Canadian Courts of Appeal.* Toronto: Lorimer, 1998.

Greenfield, Nathan. "Amazing Influence." *Ottawa Citizen,* 21 June 1995.

Greenspan, Edward L. "Judges Have No Right to Be Bullies." *National Post,* 2 March 1999.

Griswold, Erwin. "The Coloured Vote Case in South Africa." (1952) 65 *Harvard Law Review* 1361.

Grove, Alan and Ross Lambertson. "Pawns of the Powerful: The Politics of Litigation in the Union Colliery Case." (1994) 103 *B.C. Studies* 3.

Guly, Christopher. "Photo Labs Vigilant about Child Porn: Ottawa Father Charged after Taking Snapshots of Naked Son." *Ottawa Citizen*, 28 March 2000.

Hamilton, Alexander, James Madison and John Jay. *The Federalist*, ed. B.F. Wright. Cambridge, Mass.: Harvard University Press, 1966.

Hart, H.L.A. *The Concept of Law*. Oxford: Clarendon Press, 1961.

Hartt, Stanley H. and Patrick J. Monahan. "Waiting Lists Are Unconstitutional." *National Post*, 15 May 2002.

Harvey, W.B. "The Rule of Law in Historical Perspective." (1961) 59 *Michigan Law Review* 487.

Hein, Gregory. "Interest Group Litigation and Canadian Democracy." (2000) 6:2 *Choices* 3.

Heinrichs, Terry. "Censorship as Free Speech: Free Expression Values and the Logic of Silencing." (1998) 36 *Alberta Law Review* 835.

Henry, William A., III. *In Defense of Elitism*. New York: Anchor Books, 1994.

Hiebert, Janet L. "Wrestling with Rights: Judges, Parliament and the Making of Social Policy." (1999) 5:3 *Choices* 27.

Himmelfarb, Gertrude. *On Looking Into the Abyss: Untimely Thoughts on Culture and Society*. New York: Knopf, 1995.

– *One Nation, Two Cultures*. New York: Vintage Books, 2001.

– "A Sentimental Priesthood." *Times Literary Supplement*, 11 November 1994.

– "Where Have All the Footnotes Gone?" In *On Looking Into the Abyss: Untimely Thoughts on Culture and Society*. New York: Knopf, 1995.

Hobsbawn, Eric. "War and Peace." *Guardian*, 22 February 2002.

Hogg, Peter W. *Constitutional Law of Canada*. 3d ed. Toronto: Carswell, 1992.

– *Constitutional Law of Canada*, 4th ed. Toronto: Carswell, 1997.

– "Letter to the Editor." *Globe and Mail*, 14 February 2002.

House of Commons. Standing Committee on Justice and Legal Affairs. *Report on Pornography*. Minutes of Proceedings and Evidence, 3d Sess., 30th Parl., no. 18. Ottawa: Queen's Printer, 1978.

Hovius, B. "The Morgentaler Decision: Parliament's Options." (1988) 3 *Canadian Family Law Quarterly* 137.

Howard, Dick, ed. *Selected Political Writings of Rosa Luxemburg*. New York: Monthly Review Press, 1971.

Hoy, Claire. "The Hill." *Law Times*, 10 July 2000.

Hunt, Alan. "Living Dangerously on the Deconstructive Edge." (1988) 26 *Osgoode Hall Law Journal* 867.

Hunter, Ian. "Even Nasty Men Deserve a Fair Trial." *Globe and Mail*, 27 February 2002.

– "Humpty Dumpty's Take on Free Speech." *National Post*, 14 May 2001.

– *Three Faces of the Law.* Mississauga, Ont.: Work Research Foundation, 1996.

Hutchinson, Allan. *Dwelling on the Threshold.* Toronto: Carswell, 1988.

– "Judges Can't Avoid Making Political Choices." *Globe and Mail*, 17 January 2001.

International Bar Association. *Report of Zimbabwe Mission, 2001.* London: International Bar Association, 2001.

International Legal Center. Committee on Legal Education in the Developing Countries. *Legal Education in a Changing World; Report.* New York: International Legal Center, 1975.

Janisch, Hudson and Jim Phillips. "The Rule of Law at U. of T." *Law Times*, 11 February 2002.

Jimenez, Maria. "Perspective." *National Post*, 24 March 1999.

Jonas, George. "Regan a Victim of Matriarchal Justice." *National Post*, 18 February 2002.

Kaplan, Robert D. *The Coming Anarchy: Shattering the Dreams of the Post Cold War.* New York: Random House, 2000.

Kaplan, William. *Bad Judgment: The Case of Mr. Justice Leo Landreville.* Toronto: University of Toronto Press, 1996.

Kelly, James B. "The Charter of Rights and Freedoms and the Rebalancing of Liberal Constitutionalism in Canada, 1982 – 1997." (1999) 37 *Osgoode Hall Law Journal* 626.

Kelly, J. M. *The Irish Constitution*, 3rd ed., by Gerard Hogan and Gerry Whyte. Dublin: Butterworths, 1994.

Kenney, Gerard I. *Arctic Smoke and Mirrors.* Prescott, Ontario: Voyager Publishing, 1994.

Kingston, Anne. "Two Dads, Two Mums, Too Much Fuss." *National Post*, 3 July 2002.

Knopff, R. and F.L. Morton. *The Supreme Court As the Vanguard of the Intelligentsia.* Calgary: University of Calgary, Research Unit for Socio-Legal Studies, 1992.

Ko, Marni. "What Really Goes On at Foothills Hospital?" *Calgary Herald*, 11 August 1999.

Kome, Penney. *The Taking of Twenty-Eight: Women Challenge the Constitution.* Toronto: Women's Educational Press, 1983.

Kostal, R.W. "Case-note, Liability for the Sale of Alcohol, Stewart v. Pettie." (1996) 75 *Canadian Bar Review* 169.

Kramer, Hilton and Roger Kimball, eds. *The Betrayal of Liberalism*. Chicago: Ivan R. Dee, 1999.

Kyer, C. Ian and Jerome E. Bickenbach. *The Fiercest Debate; Cecil A. Wright, The Benchers and Legal Education in Ontario, 1923–1977*. Toronto: The Osgoode Society, 1987.

La Framboise, Donna. "Anorexia Researcher Delivers the Usual Spin." *National Post*, 5 September 2001.

Lamey, Andy. "Take Care, Such Ethics Can Backfire." *National Post*, 3 July 2002.

Landolt, C.G. "Letter to the Editor." *Lawyers Weekly*, 20 March 1992.

Landsberg, Michele. "Pair Try to Explain Away Hadley Murder." *Toronto Star*, 13 January 2002.

– "Porn Law Loopholes an Affront to Children's Dignity." *Toronto Star*, 4 February 2001.

Lasch, Christopher. *The Revolt of the Elites and the Betrayal of Democracy*. New York: W.W. Norton, 1995.

– *The True and Only Heaven: Progress and its Critics*. New York, London: Norton, 1991.

Laskin, Bora. "Judicial Integrity and the Supreme Court of Canada." (1978) 12 *Law Society of Upper Canada Gazette* 116.

Law Commission of Canada. "Votes, Victories and Values: Probing the Issue of Electoral Reform in Canada." Ottawa: Law Commission of Canada, 2002. http://www.lcc.gc.ca

Law Commission of Canada/Fair Vote Canada. "Phase One: Lessons from Around the World." Prepared by Denis Pilon for series Renewing Canadian Democracy: Citizen Engagement in Voting System Reform. Ottawa: Law Commission of Canada/Fair Vote Canada, 2002. http://www.lcc.gc.ca

LEAF. "Women's Groups Meet With Justice Minister." (1992) 4:4 *Leaf Lines* 4.

Lederman, W.R. "Independence of the Judiciary." *Continuing Canadian Constitutional Dilemmas*. Toronto: Butterworths, 1981.

Leeson, Howard. "Section 33, the Notwithstanding Clause: A Paper Tiger?" (2000) 6:4 *Choices* 3.

Lehman, David. *Signs of the Times: Deconstruction and the Fall of Paul de Man*. New York: Poseidon Press, 1991.

Lenin, V.I. *Selected Works in Three Volumes*. Vol. 1. Moscow: Foreign Languages Publishing House, 1960.

Lessard, Hester. "Equality and Access to Justice in the Work of Bertha Wilson." (1992) 15 *Dalhousie Law Journal*, 35.

L'Heureux-Dubé, Claire. "Are We There Yet? Gender Equality in the Law of Canada," Keynote Address to the American Bar Association Annual Meeting, Toronto, 1 August 1998.

– "The Length and Plurality of Supreme Court of Canada Decisions." (1990) 28 *Alberta Law Review* 581.

– "Re-examining the Doctrine of Judicial Notice in the Family Law Context." (1994) 26 *Ottawa Law Review* 551.

– "The Search for Equality: A Human Rights Issue." Domestic Partnership Conference, Queen's University, Kingston, Ontario, 21–23 October 1999.

Lipset, Seymour Martin. *Continental Divide: The Values and Institutions of the U.S. and Canada*, New York: Routledge, 1990.

Littleton, C.A. "Feminist Jurisprudence: The Difference Method Makes." (1989) 41 Stanford Law Review 751.

Loewenstein, Karl. "Reflections on the Value of Constitutions in Our Revolutionary Age." In *Comparative Politics*, ed. Harry Eckstein and David Apter. New York: The Free Press, 1963.

Loftus, Elizabeth F. and Melvin J. Guyer. "Who Abused Jane Doe? The Hazards of the Single Case History: Part 1." (2002) May/June *Skeptical Inquirer* 24.

Loney, Martin. *The Pursuit of Division: Race, Gender and Preferential Hiring in Canada*. Montreal: McGill-Queen's University Press, 1998.

Lugosi, Charles. "The Law of the Sacred Cow: Sacrificing the First Amendment to Defend Abortion on Demand." (2001) 79 *Denver University Law Review* 1.

MacCharles, Tonda. "Marleau Defends L'Heureux-Dubé." *Toronto Star*, 9 March 1999.

MacDonald, Gayle and Karen Gallagher. "The Myth of Consenting Adults: The New Sexual Assault Provisions." (1993) 42 *University of New Brunswick Law Journal* 373.

Macdougall, Donald V. "Canadian Legal Identity and American Influences." (1991) 15 *Legal Studies Forum* 15.

MacKinnon, Catharine. "Feminism, Marxism, Method and the State: An Agenda for Theory." (1982) 7 *Signs* 515.

– "Feminism, Marxism, Method and the State: Toward Feminist Jurisprudence." (1983) 8 *Signs* 635.

– *Feminism Unmodified: Discourses on Law and Life*. Cambridge, Mass.: Harvard University Press, 1987.

– *Only Words*. Cambridge, Mass.: Harvard University Press, 1993.

Macklem, P., R.C.B. Risk, et al. *Canadian Constitutional Law*. Toronto: Emond Montgomery, 1994.

Macpherson, C.B. *The Real World of Democracy.* Oxford: Clarendon Press, 1966.

MacPherson, James. "Canadian Constitutional Law and Madame Justice Bertha Wilson – Patriot, Visionary and Heretic." (1992) 15 *Dalhousie Law Journal* 217.

Majury, Diana. "Equality and Discrimination According to the Supreme Court of Canada." (1991) 4 *Canadian Journal of Women and the Law* 407.

– "Strategizing in Equality." (1987) 3 *Wisconsin Women's Law Journal* 69.

Makin, Kirk. "Crisis in Legal Aid Dire, Arbour Warns." *Globe and Mail*, 2 March 2002.

– "Has Democracy Been Dulled?" *Globe and Mail*, 10 April 2002.

– "Media Blasted for Savage Attacks on Top Court Judge." *Globe and Mail*, 15 August 2001.

– "Rights Gone Wrong?" *Globe and Mail*, 6 April 2002.

– "Supreme Court Judge Announces Retirement." *Globe and Mail*, 2 May 2002.

– "Today's Judge Chats On-line." *Globe and Mail*, 13 December 2000.

– "We Are Not Gunslingers." *Globe and Mail*, 9 April 2002.

Malcolm, Ian. "Letter." (1997) 6 *Inroads* 5.

Mallick, Heather. "Read My Lips. Not Even Stupidity Excuses Bush's 'Pakis' Slur." *Globe and Mail*, 12 January 2002.

Mandel, Michael. *The Charter of Rights and the Legalization of Politics in Canada.* Rev. ed. Toronto: Thompson Educational Publishing, 1994.

– "The I.C.C. as Political Instrument." *Law Times*, 28 January 2002.

– "The Rule of Law and the Legalisation of Politics in Canada." (1985) 13 *International Journal of the Sociology of Law* 273.

Manfredi, Christopher P. *Judicial Power and the Charter: Canada and the Paradox of Liberal Constitutionalism*, 2nd ed. Don Mills, Ont.: Oxford University Press, 2000.

Marshall, Geoffrey. *Constitutional Theory.* Oxford: Clarendon Press, 1971.

Martin, Robert. "Bill C-49: A Victory for Interest Group Politics." (1993) 42 *University of New Brunswick Law Journal* 357.

– "Criticising the Judges." (1982) 28 *McGill Law Journal* 1.

– "Dismantling the State." (1997) 1 *National History* 106.

– "Ideology and Judging in the Supreme Court of Canada." (1988) 26 *Osgoode Hall Law Journal* 797.

– "The Judges and the Charter." (1984) 2 *Socialist Studies* 66.

– "Judges Should Cease and Desist from Bashable Behaviour." *Law Times*, 30 November 1998.

– "A Lament for British North America." In *Rethinking the Constitution: Perspectives on Canadian Constitutional Reform, Interpretation and Theory,* ed. Anthony A. Peacock. Toronto: Oxford University Press, 1996.

– *Media Law.* Toronto: Irwin Law, 1997.

– "An Open Legal System." (1985) 21 *University of Western Ontario Law Review* 169.

– "Review" of Ian Greene's *The Charter of Rights* (Toronto: Lorimer, 1989). (1992) 23:3 *Interchange* 327.

– "Social Conservatism and Economic Radicalism: An Agenda for a Revived Canadian Left." (1996) 5 *Inroads* 160.

Marx, Karl. "Theses on Feuerbach." In *Selected Works in Three Volumes,* by Karl Marx and Frederick Engels. Vol. 1. Moscow: Progress Publishers, 1969.

Marx, Karl and F. Engels. "Critique of the Gotha Programme." In *Selected Works in Three Volumes.* Vol. 3. Moscow: Progress Publishers, 1970.

– *The German Ideology.* New York: International Publishers, 1970.

Massey, Calvin R. "Book Review: Law's Inferno." (1988) 39 *Hastings Law Journal* 1269.

Matsuda, Mari J. "Public Response to Racist Speech: Considering the Victim's Story." (1989) 87 *Michigan Law Review* 2320.

McCormick, Peter. *Supreme at Last: the Evolution of the Supreme Court of Canada.* Toronto: Lorimer, 2000.

McDonald, Lynn. "The Supreme Court of Canada and the Equality Guarantee in the Charter." (1984) 2 *Socialist Studies* 45.

McGregor, Glen. "A Family Law of Their Own." *Ottawa Citizen,* 12 September 1998.

McGregor, Ron. "I.C.C. Needed to Fill Holes of Ad Hoc Tribunals." *Law Times,* 28 January 2002.

McIntyre, Sheila. Letter in Canadian Association of University Teachers, *Bulletin,* "Status of Women Supplement," March 1989.

McLachlin, Beverley. "Reaction and Pro-action: Bringing Family Law Advocacy Into the 21st Century." Speech to the Ontario Bar Association, Toronto, 17 January, 2002.

McLellan, Anne. "Letter to the Editor." *Toronto Star,* 31 March 2001.

McMahon, Kirsten. "Making the Grade." (2002) 26:1 *Canadian Lawyer* 36.

Mendes, Errol P. "Promoting Heterogeneity of the Judicial Mind: Minority and Gender Representation in the Canadian Judiciary." In *Appointing Judges: Philosophy, Politics and Practice.* Toronto: Ontario Law Reform Commission, 1991.

Merskey, Harold. "Ethical Issues in the Search for Repressed Memories." (1996) 50 *American Journal of Psychotherapy* 323.

Mill, J.S. *On Liberty*. Chicago: Henry Regnery Company, 1947.

Minogue, Kenneth. "How Civilizations Fall." (2001) 19:8 *New Criterion* 4.

Moon, Richard. *The Constitutional Protection of Freedom of Expression*. Toronto: University of Toronto Press, 2000.

– "*R. v. Butler*: the Limits of the Supreme Court's Feminist Re-interpretation of Section 163." (1993) 25 *Ottawa Law Review* 361.

Morisette, Yves-Marie. "Canada as a Post-modern Kritarchy: Why Should Judges Make Political Decisions?" (1994) 3 *Inroads* 144.

Morton, F.L. *Morgentaler v. Borowski: Abortion, the Charter and the Courts*. Toronto: McClelland and Stewart, 1992.

– "Rulings for the Many by the Few." *National Post*, 2 September 2000.

Morton, F.L. and Rainer Knopff. *The Charter Revolution and the Court Party*. Peterborough, Ont.: Broadview Press, 2000.

Mossman, Mary Jane. "The 'Family' in the Work of Madame Justice Wilson." (1992) 15 *Dalhousie Law Journal* 115.

"Mr. Justice Bastarache is Wrong, Says Law Professor." *Globe and Mail*, 17 January, 2001.

Mullarkey, Maureen. "Hard Cop, Soft Cop." *The Nation*, 30 May 1987.

National Judicial Institute. "Social Context Education: A Retrospective and Prospectus." (2000) 13:2 *Bulletin*.

National Judicial Institute, Social Context Education Project. *Principles of Operation*, May 2001.

Nedelsky, Jennifer. "Embodied Diversity and the Challenges to Law." (1997) 42 *McGill Law Journal* 91.

Nobes, Deborah and Kevin Cox. "N.B. Natives Told to Halt Fishery Today." *Globe and Mail*, 22 September 2000.

Novak, Michael. "Defining Social Justice." (2000) 108 *First Things* 11.

O'Donovan-Polten, Sheelagh. *The Scales of Success*. Toronto: University of Toronto Press, 2001.

Off, Carol. *The Lion, the Fox and the Eagle: A Story of Generals and Justice in Yugoslavia and Rwanda*. Toronto: Random House, 2000.

Ontario College of Physicians and Surgeons, Task Force on Sexual Abuse of Patients. *Final Report*. Toronto: College of Physicians and Surgeons of Ontario, 1991.

Paciocco, David M. *Getting Away with Murder: The Canadian Criminal Justice System*. Toronto: Irwin Law, 1999.

– "The Promise of R.D.S.: Interpreting the Law of Judicial Notice and Apprehension of Bias." (1998) 3 *Canadian Criminal Law Review* 319.

Pearlman, Lynne. "Through Jewish Lesbian Eyes: Rethinking Clara Brett Martin." (1992) 5 *Canadian Journal of Women and the Law* 317.

Phillip, Melanie. "The Paedophile Bogeyman and the Paranoid Parents." *Sunday Times*, 18 March 2001.

Randall, Peter, ed. *Anatomy of Apartheid*. The Study Project on Christianity in Apartheid Society, Occasional Publication No. I. Johannesburg: Study Project on Christianity in Apartheid Society, 1970.

Renke, Wayne N. "Should Victims Participate in Sentencing?" (1996) 17:1 *Policy Options* 13.

Roach, Kent. "For a Victim Rights Model of Criminal Justice." (1996) 17:1 *Policy Options* 17.

– *The Supreme Court on Trial: Judicial Activism or Democratic Dialogue*. Toronto: Irwin Law, 2001.

Roberts, Julian and Renate M. Mohr, eds. *Confronting Sexual Assault: A Decade of Legal and Social Change*. Toronto: University of Toronto Press, 1994.

Robinson, Svend. "The Collision of Rights." (1995) 44 *University of New Brunswick Law Journal* 61.

Royal Commission on Aboriginal Peoples. *Report*. Vol. 2. Ottawa: The Commission, 1996.

Royal Commission on Electoral Reform and Party Financing. *Report*. Ottawa: Supply and Services Canada, 1991.

Royal Commission on the Status of Women in Canada. *Report*. Ottawa: Information Canada, 1970.

Ruby, Clayton. "Conservatives Decry Liberal 'Bias' in Judges, but What They Really Want Is Bias in Their Favour." *Globe and Mail*, 14 December, 2000.

– "Fifth Column." *Globe and Mail*, 19 May 1992.

– "Setting the Record Straight." *Globe and Mail*, 22 May 2001.

Russell, Peter. "Standing up for Notwithstanding." (1991) 29 *Alberta Law Review* 293.

– "The Supreme Court and the Charter: Quantitative Trends – Continuities and Discontinuities." (1998) 6 *Canada Watch* 61.

Ryan, William. *Blaming the Victim*. Rev. ed. New York: Vintage Books, 1976.

Schmidt, Sarah. "Jackman Fuels Dispute Over Law Tuition." *National Post*, 2 July 2002.

– "U. of T. Law School Looks at Raising Tuition to $25,000." *National Post*, 12 December 2001.

Schmitz, Christin. "Bastarache Explains Dissents in One-third of S.C.C. Decisions." *Lawyers Weekly*, 19 January 2001.

- "Bastarache's Candid Comments Bring Both High Praise and Condemnation." *Lawyers Weekly*, 2 February 2001.
- "Chief Justice Says Pressure Will Not Sway Court." Southam News Service, 2 January 2001.
- "Criminal Lawyers Fear Concept in New Sex Assault Bill." *Lawyers Weekly*, 17 January 1992.
- "S.C.C. Wrong Forum for Native Land Claims: Bastarache." *Lawyers Weekly*, 19 January 2001.
- "Top Judge Views Social Context Training as Threat." *Lawyers Weekly*, 5 April 1996.

"S.C.C. Justices Were 'Shocked' by Fallout from *Askov*, Cory J." *Lawyers Weekly*, 26 July 1991.

Scott, Frank. "Some Privy Counsel." (1950) 28 *Canadian Bar Review* 780.

Senate. Debates of the Senate, 22 September 1993; 28 October 1996; 4 March 1999; 25 March 1999. Ottawa, 1993–1999.

Senate. Standing Senate Committee on National Finance. *Second Report*, 37th Parl., 1st sess., 22 March 2001. Ottawa: Senate of Canada, 2001.

Sigurdson, Richard. "Left- and Right-Wing Charterphobia in Canada: A Critique of the Critics." (1993) 7 *International Journal of Canadian Studies* 95.

Small, Peter. "Hadley 'Snapped' from Stress, MD says." *Toronto Star*, 9 January 2002.

Smith, Dinitia. "Love is Strange." *New York*, 22 March, 1993.

Snell, James G. and Frederick Vaughan. *The Supreme Court of Canada: History of the Institution*. Toronto: Osgoode Society, 1985.

Sobran, M. J. "Abortion: the Class Religion." *National Review*, 23 January 1976.

Sommers, Christian Hoff. "The Fonda Effect." *On the Issues*, May 2001.
- *Who Stole Feminism? How Women Have Betrayed Women*. New York: Simon and Schuster, 1994.

Sossin, Lorne. "The Sounds of Silence: Law Clerks, Policy-Making and the Supreme Court of Canada." (1996) 30 *British Columbia Law Review* 279.

Southin, Mary. "Letter to the Editor." *Vancouver Sun*, 24 August 1993.

Special Committee on Pornography and Prostitution. *Pornography and Prostitution in Canada: Report* (The Fraser Report). Vol. 1. Ottawa: Supply and Services Canada, 1985.

Stange, Mary Zeiss. "The Political Intolerance of Academic Feminism." *The Chronicle of Higher Education*, 21 June 2002.

Steyn, Mark. "Pacifists' Ill-breeding Scorns Actual People." *National Post*, 4 October 2001.

Strayer, Barry L. "Life under the Canadian *Charter*: Adjusting the Balance between Legislatures and Courts." (1988) *Public Law* 347.

Strebeigh, F. "Definining Law on the Feminist Frontier." *The New York Times Magazine,* 6 October 1991.

"Struggles of Anthony Lewis." *The New Criterion,* January, 2002.

Supreme Court of Canada. *Performance Report for the Period Ending March 31, 2001.* Ottawa: Treasury Board, 2001.

Supreme Court of Canada. *Estimates, Performance Report for the Period Ending 31 March 2000.* Ottawa: Treasury Board , 2000.

Taylor, Charles. *Radical Tories: The Conservative Tradition in Canada.* Toronto: House of Anansi Press, 1982.

– *Six Journeys: A Canadian Pattern.* Toronto: House of Anansi Press, 1977.

Thompson, E.P. *The Making of the English Working Class.* Harmondsworth: Penguin, 1968.

Tibbetts, Janice. "Chief Justice Seeks Help to Limit Equality Rights." *National Post,* 7 April 2001.

– "Lamer Attacks Alliance 'Yelping'." *National Post,* 14 April 2001.

– "Top Court Excludes Critics from Anniversary 'Love-in.'" *Ottawa Citizen,* 28 September 2000.

Tocqueville, Alexis de. *Democracy in America.* Vol. 1. New York: Knopf, 1945.

Troy, J. E. "Defined by Conduct." *National Post,* 13 November 2000.

Tu, Thanh Ha and Josipa Petrunie. "Alleged Rape Victim Won't Have to Testify at Second Trial." *Globe and Mail,* 28 June 2001.

Tyler, Tracey. "Dean Won't Appeal Marks Ruling." *Toronto Star,* 17 January 2002.

– "Rights of Accused Eroded: Lawyers." *Toronto Star,* 7 April 2001.

– "U.S. Feminist Applauds Canada's Rape-Law Plan." *Toronto Star,* 17 February 1992.

United Church of Canada, 28th General Council, August 15–August 24, 1980, Halifax, N.S. *Record of Proceedings.* Toronto, 1980.

Vienneau, D. "Beware Mixing Drink, Sex, Top Defence Lawyer Warns." *Toronto Star,* 13 December 1991.

– "Proposed Rape Law's Message: No Means No." *Toronto Star,* 21 November 1991.

Way, Rosemary Cairns. "Bill C-49 and the Politics of Constitutionalized Fault." (1993) 42 *University of New Brunswick Law Journal* 325.

Weber, Eugen. *Varieties of Fascism.* New York: Van Nostrand, 1964.

Weeks, Linton. "You're the Dr." *Washington Post,* 18 March 2002.

Wente, Margaret. "Food, Sex and Racism, But What about the History Lessons?" *Globe and Mail,* 29 November 2001.

– "Global Warming: A Heretic's View." *Globe and Mail*, 23 May 2002.
– "How the Refugee System got Undermined." *Globe and Mail*, 3 November 2001.
– "How to Get Away with Murder (for Women Only)." *Globe and Mail*, 10 March 2000.
Will, George F. "Feminism Hijacked." *Washington Post*, 19 May 2002.
Williams, J.R. "Grasping a Thorny Baton... A Trial Judge Looks at Judicial Notice and Courts' Acquisition of Social Science." (1996) 4 *Canadian Family Law Quarterly* 179.
Wilson, Bertha. "Decision-Making in the Supreme Court." (1986) 36 *University of Toronto Law Journal* 227.
– "Will Women Judges Really Make a Difference?" (1990) 28 *Osgoode Hall Law Journal* 507.
Windschuttle, Keith. *The Killing of History: How Literary Critics and Social Theorists are Murdering our Past*. San Francisco: Encounter Books, 1996.
York, G. "Lawyers Oppose Proposed Rape Law." *Globe and Mail*, 15 May 1992.
– "Sexual Assault Legislation Attacked." *Globe and Mail*, 20 May 1992.

Index

DATE DUE